## Praise for Hunter S. Thompson

"Thompson should be recognized for contributing some of the clearest, most bracing, and fearless analysis of the possibilities and failures of American democracy in the past century."

—*Chicago Tribune*

"Thompson's voice still jumps right off the page, as wild, vital, and gonzo as ever."

—*The Washington Post*

"[R]ollickingly funny throughout, Thompson's latest proves that the father of gonzo journalism is alive and well."

—*Publishers Weekly*

"Thompson gives another side to every story, another wall to cast your view of reality against. In doing so, he adds something often lacking or poorly executed in modern journalism. He makes it fun."

—*South Bend Tribune*

"Thompson's wicked humor, mixed with characteristic hubris, offers leaps of insight that it seems only he could unleash. He writes what others would fear to think, let alone lay down in such an unbridled manner."

—Denver *Rocky Mountain News*

"Hunter Thompson is the most creatively crazy and vulnerable of the New Journalists. His ideas are brilliant and honorable and valuable— the literary equivalent of Cubism: all rules are broken."

—Kurt Vonnegut, Jr.

"His hallucinated vision strikes one as having been, after all, the sanest."

—Nelson Algren

"He amuses; he frightens; he flirts with doom. His achievement is substantial."

—Garry Wills

"There are only two adjectives writers care about anymore—'brilliant' and 'outrageous'—and Hunter Thompson has a freehold on both of them."

—Tom Wolfe

"What we have here is vintage Hunter S. Thompson, a literary orgy of wicked irreverence."

—*The Boston Globe*

"Thompson is a spirited, witty, observant, and original writer."

—*The New York Times*

"Obscene, horrid, repellent . . . driving, urgent, candid, searing . . . a fascinating, compelling book!"

—*New York Post*

"No one can ever match Thompson in the vitriol department, and virtually nobody escapes his wrath."

—*The Flint Journal*

"While Tom Wolfe mastered the technique of being a fly on the wall, Thompson mastered the art of being a fly in the ointment. He made himself a part of every story, made no apologies for it, and thus produced far more honest reporting than any crusading member of the Fourth Estate. . . . Thompson isn't afraid to take the hard medicine, nor is he bashful about dishing it out. . . . He is still king of beasts, and his apocalyptic prophecies seldom miss their target."

—*Tulsa World*

# Kingdom of Fear

**Loathsome Secrets of a Star-Crossed Child in the Final Days of the American Century**

## Hunter S. Thompson

Simon & Schuster Paperbacks
New York   London   Toronto   Sydney

The author gratefully acknowledges permission from the following sources
to reprint matierial in their control:
Page 56: "Guilt by Association at Heart of Auman Case" by Karen Abbott, from the *Rocky Mountain News*, April 29, 2002; page 92: "The Battle of Aspen" from *Rolling Stone #67*, October 1, 1970; Page 112: Lyrics for "Take a Walk on the Wild Side" by Lou Reed © lou Reed/EMI, All Rights Reserved; Page 117: "Dr. Hunter S. Thompson and the Last Battle of Aspen" by Loren Jenkins, from *SMART* magazine, Jan/Feb 1990; Page 194: Lyrics for "American Pie" by Don McLean © Songs of Universal/ BMI, All Rights Reserved; Page 242: "Knock, Knock—Who's There" by Edward T. Cross, from the *Aspen Times Daily*, June 18, 1990; Page 245: "D.A. Snags Thompson in Sex Case" by David Matthews-Price, from the *Aspen Times Daily*; Page 251: "Gonzo's Last Stand?" from *The Village Voice*, May 15, 1990; Page 253: "D.A. May File Case Against Aspen Writer" by Eve O'Brien, from *The Denver Post*, March 14, 1990; Page 258: "Thompson Bound Over For Trial" by David Matthews-Price, from the *Aspen Times Daily*; Page 262: "Thompson Rejects Plea Bargain; Takes Delivery of Convertible" by David Matthews-Price, from the *Aspen Times Daily*; Page 266: "The Sinister Sex and Drugs Case of Hunter S. Thompson" by Richard Stratton, from *High Times* magazine; Page 292: Lyrics for "One Time One Night" written by David Hidalgo and Louis Perez © 1988 DAVINCE MUSIC (BMI/NO K.O. MUSIC (BMI)/Administered by Bug. All Rights Reserved.

SIMON & SCHUSTER PAPERBACKS
Rockefeller Center
1230 Avenue of the Americas
New York, NY 10020

First Simon & Schuster paperback edition 2003

SIMON & SCHUSTER PAPERBACKS and colophon are
registered trademarks of Simon & Schuster, Inc.

For information about special discounts for bulk purchases,
please contact Simon & Schuster Special Sales:
1-800-456-6798 or business@simonandschuster.com.

DESIGNED BY LAUREN SIMONETTI

Manufactured in the United States of America

30  29  28  27  26  25  24  23  22

The Library of Congress has cataloged the hardcover edition as follows:
Thompson, Hunter S.
Kingdom of fear : loathsome secrets of a star-crossed child in the final days of
the American century / Hunter S. Thompson.
p.   cm.
1. Thompson, Hunter S.  2. Journalists—United States—Biography.  I. Title.
PN4874.T444 A3   2003
070.92—dc21   [B]   2002191228

ISBN-13: 978-0-684-87323-7
ISBN-10:     0-684-87323-0
ISBN-13: 978-0-684-87324-4 (Pbk)
ISBN-10:     0-684-87324-9 (Pbk)

To Anita

*Weave a circle round him thrice,*
*And close your eyes with holy dread,*
*For he on honey-dew hath fed,*
*And drunk the milk of Paradise.*

—Samuel Taylor Coleridge

# Contents

# Foreword by Timothy Ferris

If, as Paul Valéry put it, "the true poet is the one who inspires," Hunter Thompson is a true poet. His writing has inspired countless imitators (all of whom fail hideously, of course; nobody writes like Hunter) while opening glittering veins of savage wit and searing indignation to journalists sensible enough to benefit from his example without trying to copy his style. His notoriously vivid lifestyle—chronicled in his own works and, more fragmentarily, by scores of others who managed to hang on for part of the ride—has inspired plenty of imitators, too, although most have prudently avoided flying too close to that particular dark star. Most everybody who knows anything about Hunter is fascinated by him, and the concatenation of his work and his persona has made him a figure of uncommon fame. Five biographies of him have been published, two Hollywood feature films have been made from his books, and his name turns up on half a million Internet web pages—more than William Burroughs, Allen Ginsberg, Jack Kerouac, Norman Mailer, and Tom Wolfe combined.

But, given that he is also the onstage protagonist of most of his works, the question arises as to who is primarily responsible for all this inspiration and intrigue: Hunter the writer, or Hunter the written-about? This turns out to be a timely issue, insomuch as *Kingdom of Fear* constitutes a memoir, and as such represents an author's confrontation with himself. The answers are not easy to come by—especially since *Kingdom of Fear*, like Einstein's *Autobiographical Notes*, quickly veers from reflections on who the author is to demonstrations of what he does. Nor, once arrived at, do they give us anything like the whole picture. Every man is many men—Whitman was stating the facts when he said that he contained multitudes—and no simple scheme of an artist as creator versus the same artist as subject can produce more than a flash photo of reality. Still, an examination of the relationship between Hunter the writer and his first-person protagonist may cast at least a thin beam of torchlight into the cavernous darkness of his abundant creativity.

Hunter's writing is, first of all, extremely funny; he ranks among the finest American humorists of all time. It is also, like all real humor, essentially serious. At its center resides a howling vortex of outrage and pain, which Hunter has managed to transmute into works of lasting value. These works have the additional virtue of being factually reliable, so long as he intends them to be. Hunter is a meticulous reporter who wasn't joking when he told an audience at The Strand in Redondo Beach, "I am the most accurate journalist you'll ever read." Over the thirty years that we've been friends he has corrected my grammar and word usage more often, and more accurately, than I have corrected his—and not just because he is customarily armed with, say, the .454 Magnum pistol with which he shot up one of his many IBM Selectric typewriters. ("That gun really is too much, unless you want to destroy a Buick at two hundred yards," he recalled, musing over the Selectric-shooting episode. "The bullet went through the typewriter at such a speed that it just pierced it, like a *ray* of some kind. You could hardly see where it hit. So I went and got a 12-gauge Magnum shotgun and some .00 buckshot. That produced a very different shot pattern.") He is capable of sea-anchoring an otherwise sheets-to-the-wind drinking fiesta with studious ponderings about matters ranging from whether to credit a rumor, at the 1972 Democratic National Convention, that George McGovern was about to offer the second spot on his ticket to United Auto Workers President Leonard Woodcock (Hunter decided that he didn't trust it, and as usual was proved right) to browsing thesaurus entries for the word *force*. ("They include *violence, vehemence, might, rigor, impetuosity, severity, fierceness, ferocity, outrage, eruption, convulsion, violent passion*. . . . It's scary; kind of a word picture of *me*.")

But then, with little more than a barely perceptible signal, his works slip anchor and venture into a kind of hyperspace, where the facts shrink to a pinpoint like a cosmonaut's view of the receding Earth, and the goal shifts from factual literalness to a quest for deeper truth. Few readers can infallibly detect these points of departure, so many have raised the recurring question: How much of Hunter's accounts of his own escapades—the fast cars, furious motorcycles, big-bore firearms and powerful explosives, the beautiful women and mind-warping drugs, the frightening misadventures and reckless flirtations with imminent disaster that have made "fear and loathing" part of the language—are exaggerated?

Not nearly enough for comfort.

Hunter is a lifelong student of fear—and a teacher of it, too. He titled a song that he wrote recently with Warren Zevon "You're a Whole Different Person When You're Scared," and he doesn't feel that he knows you properly until he knows *that* person. On various occasions he has lunged at me with an evil-looking horse syringe; brandished loaded shotguns, stun guns, and cans of Mace; and taken me on high-speed rides to remote murder sites in the dead of night—and I doubt that he finds my reaction to such travails particularly interesting, since I have always calmly trusted him with my life. Those whom such treatment transforms into someone more apt to arouse Hunter's infared sensors of viperous curiosity are in for an interesting evening.

At the same time, this howling violence freak, habitually loaded with potent intoxicants and a skull full of Beethoven-grade egomania, is studious and thoughtful, courtly and caring, curiously peace loving in his way, and unwaveringly generous. When he and I were young and broke, and I was fired from the last job I've ever held, the first thing he did was offer to send me four hundred dollars—which, although he didn't know I knew it, was all the money he had left in the bank at the time. His fundamental decency helps explain how he has managed to survive his many excesses, as does the fact that he's blessed with extraordinary reflexes. I once saw him accidentally knock a drink off a table with the back of his hand while reaching for a ringing phone and then catch it, unspilled, with the same hand on the way down. When we onlookers expressed astonishment at this feat, he said, "Yes, well, when we're applauding my aptitude at making rescues, we should keep in mind who causes most of the accidents in the first place." I've never met anyone who really knew Hunter who didn't love him.

So what we have here is a thrilling if frightening man of action, as spectacular and unpredictable as a bolt of lightning, being observed by an owl-like, oracular author who, although he shares his skin, is as perpetually surprised and bemused by his behavior as the rest of us are. In *Kingdom of Fear,* the interactions of this curious couple informs adventures like Hunter's predawn excursion to his old friend Jack Nicholson's house, his Jeep loaded with "all kinds of jokes and gimcracks" intended to gladden the hearts of Nicholson's children: "In addition to the bleeding elk heart, there was a massive outdoor amplifier, a tape recording of a pig being eaten alive by bears, a 1,000,000-watt spotlight, and a 9-mm Smith & Wesson semiautomatic pistol with teakwood handles and a box of high-powered ammunition. There was also a 40-million-candlepower parachute flare that would light up the valley for 40 miles for 40 seconds that would seem to anyone lucky enough to be awake at the time like the first blinding flash of a midrange nuclear device that might signal the end of the world." When the detonation of these devices from a precipice overlooking the Nicholson household fails to produce the anticipated joyful welcome, Hunter feels, disconcertingly, that he is "being snubbed."

"I was beginning to have mixed feelings about this visit," he confesses, while preparing to leave the bleeding elk heart on Nicholson's doorstep, but he soon cheers up, wondering, "Why am I drifting into negativity?"

Which, if you drain off the color and turn down the volume, is pretty much the human condition. We do things without knowing why, wonder at the consequences, and know neither where we came from nor where we are going. Robert Frost wrote that we dance round in a ring and suppose, but the secret sits in the center and knows. Hunter dances, all right, but rather than suppose, never ceases striving to know. His aim, as Joseph Conrad put it in his preface to *The Nigger of the Narcissus,* a work that mightily impressed a young Hunter ("That was something to roll around in my craw and compare myself to; it set a high standard") is "by the power of the written word to make you hear, to make you feel . . . to make you see," to bring us "encouragement, consolation, fear, charm—all you demand—and, perhaps, also that glimpse of truth for which you have forgotten to ask."

And that, in part, is why we love him.

# Memo from the Sports Desk

I was watching the Denver–Oakland football game on TV last night when it was interrupted by a "BREAKING NEWS" bulletin from the FBI about unknown terrorists who were planning to destroy major targets all over the United States, perhaps within 24 hours. The FBI had learned this from trustworthy sources, the unseen voice explained. The American people were advised to be totally vigilant & ready to be evacuated at any moment. . . . Any person who talks suspiciously or looks dangerous should be reported to your local police or law enforcement agencies immediately! We were into *Condition Red*.

"Shit! Not again!" cried my lawyer. "I have to fly to Boston tomorrow. What the fuck is going on in this country?"

"Never ask that question," I warned her, "unless you already know the answer."

"I do," she said. "We are fucked, utterly fucked."

. . .

*The Author's Note—if it exists at all—is invariably the worst and lamest part of any book, my own included. That is because it is necessarily the last and most blind-dumb desperate "final touch" that gets heaped into a book just before it goes to the printer—and the whole book, along with the two years of feverish work and anguish, is doomed to failure and ruin if the author won't produce the note in time for publication.*

*Make no mistake about it. These 4 pointless pages of low-rent gibberish are by far the most important part of the book, they say Nothing else matters.*

*And so, with that baleful wisdom in mind, let us get on with the
wretched task of lashing this "author's note" together, for good or ill. I am
not really in much of a mood to deal with it, no more than I am eager to
take a course in how to write commercial advertising copy for my own
good, at this time.*

*I savagely rejected that swill 40 years ago because I hated it and I hated
the people who tried to make me do it. But so what, eh? We are somehow
back to square one. . . . Is this a great country, or what?*

. . .

The safe answer to that question is "Yes, and thank you for asking."
Any other answer will get your name on the waiting list for accommo-
dations at Guantánamo Bay.

How's that for a great country, dude? It's all yours now, and good
luck in jail. Cuba is a beautiful island, perhaps the most beautiful I've
ever seen. They don't call it *The Pearl of the Antilles* for nothing. The
white sand beaches are spectacular, and every soft Caribbean breeze
that you feel in the midnight air will speak to you of love and joy and
atavistic romance.

Indeed, the future looks good for Cuba, especially with the *dollar-
economy* that will come when the entire island is converted to a spa-
cious concentration camp for the U.S.A., which is already happening.
Little did President Theodore Roosevelt know, when he effectively
annexed Cuba in 1906, that he had seized for his country what would
later become the largest and most permanent prison colony in the history of the world.

Good old Teddy. Everything he touched was doomed to be beautiful. The man could do no wrong.

. . .

Meanwhile, back at the ranch, the Raiders were whipping the shit out
of the heavily favored Broncos, who were wallowing in their own Condition Red. Their top-ranked Defense had gone all to pieces, and now
they were being humiliated.

"George Bush is far greater than Roosevelt," said my lawyer. "I wish
we could be with him now."

"You fool," I snorted. "If Teddy Roosevelt were alive today, he would be so ashamed of this country that he would slit his own wrists."

"So what? I still have to get to Boston tomorrow," she muttered. "Will any planes be flying?"

Just then the football game was interrupted again—this time by a paid commercial about the terrors of smoking marijuana. "Jesus Christ," she said. "Now they say that if I smoke this joint, I'll be guilty of murdering a federal judge—Hell, that's a capital crime, the death penalty."

"You're right," I replied. "And if you even *offer* the filthy little thing to *me,* I will be guilty under the law of *conspiring* to murder a federal judge."

"Well, I guess we will have to stop smoking this stuff," she said mournfully, as she handed the joint to me. "What else can I smoke to relax after a losing day in court?"

"Nothing," I said. "Especially not Xanax: The Governor of Florida just sentenced his own daughter to jail for trying to buy Xanax."

And so much for drug talk, eh? Even talking about drugs can get you locked up these days. The times have changed drastically, but not for the better.

. . .

I like this book, and I especially like the title, which pretty well sums up the foul nature of life in the U.S.A. in these first few bloody years of the post-American century. Only a fool or a whore would call it anything else.

It would be easy to say that we owe it all to the Bush family from Texas, but that would be too simplistic. They are only errand boys for the vengeful, bloodthirsty cartel of raving Jesus-freaks and super-rich money mongers who have ruled this country for at least the last 20 years, and arguably for the past 200. They take orders well, and they don't ask too many questions.

The real power in America is held by a fast-emerging new Oligarchy of pimps and preachers who see no need for Democracy or fairness or even trees, except maybe the ones in their own yards, and they don't mind admitting it. They worship money and power and death. Their ideal solution to all the nation's problems would be another 100 Year War.

Coming of age in a fascist police state will not be a barrel of fun for anybody, much less for people like me, who are not inclined to suffer Nazis gladly and feel only contempt for the cowardly flag-suckers who would gladly give up their outdated freedom to *live* for the mess of pottage they have been conned into believing will be freedom from fear.

Ho ho ho. Let's not get carried away here. Freedom was yesterday in this country. Its value has been discounted. The only freedom we truly crave today is freedom from Dumbness. Nothing else matters.

. . .

My life has been the polar opposite of safe, but I am proud of it and so is my son, and that is good enough for me. I would do it all over again without changing the beat, although I have never recommended it to others. That would be cruel and irresponsible and wrong, I think, and I am none of those things.

Whoops, that's it, folks. We are out of time. Sorry. Mahalo.

*HST*

P.S. "The difference between the *almost*-right word & the *right* word is . . . the difference between the lightning bug and the lightning."

—*Mark Twain*

(Lynn Goldsmith)

# PART ONE

# When the Going Gets Weird, the Weird Turn Pro

*There are no jokes. Truth is the funniest joke of all.*
—Muhammad Ali

## The Mailbox: Louisville, Summer of 1946

My parents were decent people, and I was raised, like my friends, to believe that Police were our friends and protectors—the Badge was a symbol of extremely high authority, perhaps the highest of all. Nobody ever asked *why*. It was one of those unnatural questions that are better left alone. If you had to ask *that*, you were sure as hell Guilty of *something* and probably should have been put behind bars a long time ago. It was a no-win situation.

My first face-to-face confrontation with the FBI occurred when I was nine years old. Two grim-looking Agents came to our house and terrified my parents by saying that I was a "prime suspect" in the case of a Federal Mailbox being turned over in the path of a speeding bus. It was a Federal Offense, they said, and carried a five-year prison sentence.

"Oh no!" wailed my mother. "Not in prison! That's insane! He's only a child. How could he have known?"

"The warning is clearly printed on the Mailbox," said the agent in the gray suit. "He's old enough to read."

"Not necessarily," my father said sharply. "How do you know he's not blind, or a moron?"

"Are you a moron, son?" the agent asked me. "Are you blind? Were you just *pretending* to read that newspaper when we came in?" He pointed to the *Louisville Courier-Journal* on the couch.

"That was only the sports section," I told him. "I can't read the other stuff."

"See?" said my father. "I told you he was a moron."

"Ignorance of the law is no excuse," the brown-suit agent replied. "Tampering with the U.S. Mail is a Federal offense punishable under Federal law. That Mailbox was badly damaged."

Mailboxes were huge, back then. They were heavy green vaults that stood like Roman mile markers at corners on the neighborhood bus routes and were rarely, if ever, moved. I was barely tall enough to reach the Mail-drop slot, much less big enough to turn the bastard over and into the path of a bus. It was clearly impossible that I could have committed this crime without help, and that was what they wanted: names and addresses, along with a total confession. They already knew I was guilty, they said, because other culprits had squealed on me. My parents hung their heads, and I saw my mother weeping.

I had done it, of course, and I had done it with plenty of help. It was carefully plotted and planned, a deliberate ambush that we set up and executed with the fiendish skill that smart nine-year-old boys are capable of when they have too much time on their hands and a lust for revenge on a rude and stupid bus driver who got a kick out of closing his doors and pulling away just as we staggered to the top of the hill and begged him to let us climb on. . . . He was new on the job, probably a brain-damaged substitute, filling in for our regular driver, who was friendly and kind and always willing to wait a few seconds for children rushing to school. Every kid in the neighborhood agreed that this new swine of a driver was a sadist who deserved to be punished, and the Hawks A.C. were the ones to do it. We saw it more as a duty than a prank. It was a brazen Insult to the honor of the whole neighborhood.

We would need ropes and pulleys and certainly no witnesses to do the job properly. We had to tilt the iron monster so far over that it was perfectly balanced to fall instantly, just as the fool zoomed into the bus stop at his usual arrogant speed. All that kept the box more or less upright was my grip on a long "invisible" string that we had carefully stretched all the way from the corner and across about 50 feet of grass lawn to where we crouched out of sight in some bushes.

The rig worked perfectly. The bastard was right on schedule and going too fast to stop when he saw the thing falling in front of him. . . . The collision made a horrible noise, like a bomb going off or a freight train exploding in Germany. That is how I remember it, at least. It was the worst noise I'd ever heard. People ran screaming out of their houses like chickens gone crazy with fear. They howled at one another as the driver stumbled out of his bus and collapsed in a heap on the grass. . . . The bus was empty of passengers, as usual at the far end of the line. The man was not injured, but he went into a foaming rage when he spotted us fleeing down the hill and into a nearby alley. He knew in a flash who had done it, and so did most of the neighbors.

"Why deny it, Hunter?" said one of the FBI agents. "We know *exactly* what happened up there on that corner on Saturday. Your buddies already confessed, son. They *squealed* on you. We know you did it, so don't lie to us now and make things worse for yourself. A nice kid like you shouldn't have to go to Federal prison." He smiled again and winked at my father, who responded with a snarl: "Tell the Truth, damn it! Don't lie to these men. They have *witnesses*!" The FBI agents nodded grimly at each other and moved as if to take me into custody.

It was a magic moment in my life, a defining instant for me or any other nine-year-old boy growing up in the 1940s after World War II— and I clearly recall thinking: *Well, this is it. These are G-Men.* . . .

WHACK! Like a flash of nearby lightning that lights up the sky for three or four terrifying split seconds before you hear the thunder—a matter of *zepto-seconds* in real time—but when you are a nine-year-old boy with two (2) full-grown FBI agents about to seize you and clap you in Federal prison, a few quiet zepto-seconds can seem like the rest of your life. . . . And that's how it felt to me that day, and in grim retrospect, I was right. They had me, dead to rights. I was Guilty. Why deny it? Confess Now, and throw myself on their mercy, or—

What? What if I *didn't* confess? That was the question. And I was a curious boy, so I decided, as it were, to roll the dice and ask *them* a question.

"Who?" I said. "What witnesses?"

It was not a hell of a lot to ask, under those circumstances—and I really did want to know exactly who among my best friends and blood brothers in the dreaded Hawks A.C. had cracked under pressure and betrayed me to these thugs, these pompous brutes and toadies with badges & plastic cards in their wallets that said they worked for J. Edgar Hoover and that they had the Right, and even the duty, to put me in jail, because they'd heard a "Rumor in the neighborhood" that some of my boys had gone belly up and rolled on me. *What?* No. Impossible.

Or not *likely,* anyway. Hell, Nobody squealed on the Hawks A.C., or not on its President, anyway. Not on Me. So I asked again: "Witnesses? What Witnesses?"

. . .

And that was all it took, as I recall. We observed a moment of silence, as my old friend Edward Bennett Williams would say. Nobody spoke—especially not me—and when my father finally broke the eerie silence, there was *doubt* in his voice. "I think my son has a point, officer. Just exactly who *have* you talked to? I was about to ask that myself."

"Not Duke!" I shouted. "He went to Lexington with his father! And not *Ching*! And not *Jay*!—"

"Shut up," said my father. "Be quiet and let *me* handle this, you fool."

*And that's what happened,* folks. We never saw those FBI agents again. Never. And I learned a powerful lesson: Never believe the first thing an FBI agent tells you about anything—especially not if he seems to believe you are guilty of a crime. Maybe he has no evidence. Maybe he's bluffing. Maybe you are innocent. Maybe. The Law can be hazy on these things. . . . But it is definitely worth a roll.

In any case, nobody was arrested for that alleged incident. The FBI agents went away, the U.S. Mailbox was put back up on its heavy iron legs, and we never saw that drunken swine of a substitute bus driver again.

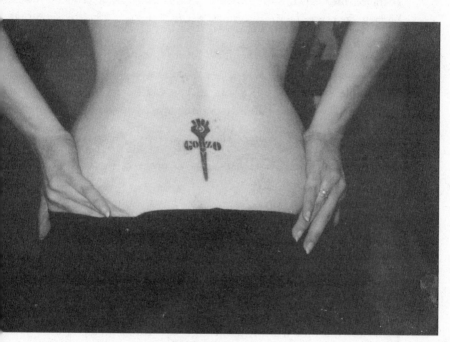

(HST archives)

# Would You Do It Again?

That story has no moral—at least not for smart people—but it taught me many useful things that shaped my life in many fateful ways. One of them was knowing the difference between Morality and Wisdom. Morality is temporary, Wisdom is permanent. . . . Ho ho. Take that one to bed with you tonight.

In the case of the fallen mailbox, for instance, I learned that the FBI was not *unbeatable,* and that is a very important lesson to learn at the age of nine in America. Without it, I would be an entirely different man today, a product of an utterly different environment. I would not be talking to you this way, or sitting alone at this goddamn typewriter at 4:23 A.M. with an empty drink beside me and an unlit cigarette in my mouth and a naked woman singing "Porgy & Bess" on TV across the room.

On one wall I see an eight-foot, two-handled logging saw with 200 big teeth and CONFESSIONS OF THE BEST PIECE OF ASS IN THE WORLD scrawled in gold letters across the long rusty saw blade. . . . At one end of it hangs a petrified elk's leg and a finely painted wooden bird from Russia that allegedly signifies peace, happiness & prosperity for all who walk under it.

That strange-looking bird has hung there for 15 extremely active years, no doubt for sentimental reasons, and this is the first time I have thought about adding up the score. Has this graven image from ancient Russian folk art been a *good* influence on my life? Or a bad one? Should I pass it on to my son and my grandson? Or should I take it out in the yard and execute it like a traitorous whore?

That is the Real question. Should the bird live and be worshiped for generations to come? Or should it die violently for bringing me bad luck?

The ramifications of that question are intimidating. Is it wise to add up the Score right now? What if I come out a Loser? Ye gods, let's be careful about this. Have we wandered into dangerous territory?

Indeed. At this point in my life I don't need a rush to judgment, whatever it is. Only a superstitious *native* would believe that kind of bullshit, anyway.

. . .

Suddenly I heard Anita screeching from the office, as if a fire had erupted somewhere on the other side of the house. Wonderful, I thought. I am a lucky man to get a break like this. Bring it on. Attack it *now*. I reached for a red 20-pound fire extinguisher near the door, thinking finally to have some real fun.

Ah, but it was not to be. Anita came rushing around the corner with a computer printout in her hands. "The President is threatening to seize the Saudi Arabian oil fields if they don't help us wipe out the Evil of Terrorism—seize them by military force." The look on her face was stricken, as if World War IV had just started. "This is insane!" she wailed. "We can't just go over there and invade Saudi Arabia."

I put my arm around her and flipped the dial to CNN, which was showing Defense Secretary Donald Rumsfeld waving his cast at the camera like a clenched fist as he denounced the rumor as "nonsense" and once again threatened to "track down and eliminate" these "irresponsible leaks" to the press from somewhere in the bowels of the Pentagon. He wanted to Punish somebody immediately. *Of Course* the United States would not declare war on a close Arab ally like the Saudis. That would be insane.

"Not necessarily," I said, "at least not until it turns into a disastrous botch and Bush gets burned at the stake in Washington. Sane is rich and powerful; Insane is wrong and poor and weak. The rich are Free, the poor are put in cages." *Res Ipsa Loquitur,* Amen, Mahalo. . . .

. . .

Okay, and so much for *that,* eh? No more of these crude hashish ravings. What if the bird says I am wrong and have been wrong all my life?

Certainly I would not be entirely comfortable sitting here by myself and preparing, once again, to make terminal judgments on the President of the United States of America on the brink of a formal war with a whole world of Muslims. . . . No. That would make me a traitor and a dangerous Security Risk, a Terrorist, a monster in the eyes of the Law.

Well, shucks. What can I say? We are coming to a big fork in the road for this country, another ominous polarization between right and wrong, another political mandate to decide *"Which side are you on?"* . . . Maybe a bumper sticker that asks ARE YOU SANE OR INSANE?

I have confronted that question on a daily basis all my life, as if it were just another form to fill out, and on most days I have checked off the SANE box—if only because I am not dead or in prison or miserable in my life.

. . .

There is no shortage of dangerous gibberish in the classrooms and courts of this nation. Weird myths and queer legends are coins of the realm in our culture, like passwords or keys to survival. Not even a monster with rabies would send his child off to school with a heart full of hate for Santa Claus or Jesus or the Tooth Fairy. That would not be fair to the child. He (or she) would be shunned & despised like a Leper by his classmates & even his teachers, and he will not come home with good report cards. He will soon turn to wearing black raincoats & making ominous jokes about Pipe Bombs.

Weird behavior is natural in smart children, just as curiosity is to a kitten. I was no stranger to it myself, as a youth growing up in Kentucky. I had a keen appetite for adventure, which soon led me into a maze of complex behavioral experiments that my parents found hard to explain. I was a popular boy, with acceptable grades & a vaguely promising future, but I was cursed with a dark sense of humor that made many adults afraid of me, for reasons they couldn't quite put their fingers on. . . .

But I was a juvenile delinquent. I was Billy the Kid of Louisville. I was a "criminal": I stole things, destroyed things, drank. That's all you have to do if you're a criminal. In the sixth grade I was voted head of the Safety Patrol—the kids who wear the badges and stop traffic during recesses and patrol. It was a very big position, and the principal hated that I was voted to it. She said, "This is horrible. We can't have Hunter doing anything. He's a Little Hitler." I wasn't sure what that meant, but I think it meant I had a natural sway over many students. And that I should probably be lobotomized for the good of the society.

I always figured I would live on the margins of society, part of a very small Outlaw segment. I have never been approved by any majority. Most people assume it's difficult to live this way, and they are right— they're still trying to lock me up all the time. I've been very careful about urging people who cannot live outside the law to throw off the traces and run amok. Some are not made for the Outlaw life.

The only things I've ever been arrested for, it turns out, are things I didn't do. All the "crimes" I really committed were things that were usually an accident. Every time they got me, I happened to be in the wrong place and too enthusiastic. It was just the general feeling that I shouldn't be allowed to get away with it.

. . .

It may be that every culture needs an Outlaw god of some kind, and maybe this time around I'm *it*. Who knows? I haven't studied it, but the idea just came to me in a flash as I read Peter Whitmer's article about me in the Jan/Feb 1984 *Saturday Review*.

I think of Lono, Robin Hood & Bacchus & the Greeks with their fat young boys & the Irish with their frantic drunken worship of doomed heroes. . . . Jesus, I'll bet that even the Swedes have some kind of Outlaw god.

But there is no mention of good Outlaws in the Holy Bible, I think—mainly because of The Church & all its spin-offs that believe in total punishment for all sinners. The Bible makes no exceptions for good-hearted social outlaws. They are all cast into the Lake of Fire. Punishment. Fuck those people.

## (PAUSE FOR INTERRUPTION)

Sorry, that was a call from *Newsweek* in New York, asking what I thought about the "shocking Mutombo–Van Horne trade" today, a major shift in the power balance of the NBA East that I was only vaguely aware of. It meant that the 76ers would be rid of that flashy albino pussy who always failed in the clutch. It made perfect sense to me, and that is why I picked up the telephone. . . . What the hell? I thought. People ask me these questions because they know I am a famous sportswriter.

"The trade is meaningless," I said. "It is like trading a used mattress for a $300 bill."

And that was that, apparently. The writer was suddenly called away from his desk and hung up on me. So what? I thought. I didn't want to talk to him anyway. I had serious work to do, and Anita was getting hungry. It was time for another road trip.

. . .

There are eight or nine truly exotic towns to visit in the great American West, but Thomasville, Colorado, is not one of them. Richard Nixon doomed the town when he reluctantly signed the Clean Air Act of 1970—which soon led to the forcible closing of both the town's gas stations because their 50-year-old underground storage tanks were rusted out and leaking rotten gasoline into the tumbling white waters of the Frying Pan River, a once-famous trout-fishing mecca.

It took us about five hours to climb the 30 steep miles up to Thomasville. I was driving my trusty Red Shark, a rebuilt 1973 454 Chevy Caprice with power windows and heated seats and a top speed of 135—although not on a winding uphill two-lane blacktop that rises 6,000 feet in 30 miles. That is serious climbing, from summer heat and peach trees up to chilly bleak timberline and then to the snowcapped peaks of the Continental Divide, where wild beasts roam and humans live in pain. This is the road that leads up to the dreaded Hagerman Pass.

But not yet. No, we are getting ahead of our story, and only a jackass would do that . . .

. . .

We were almost to Thomasville when I noticed a cluster of flashing police lights and a cop of some kind standing in the middle of the road waving a red flag. "Oh Jesus," I groaned. "What the fuck is this?" Anita was scrambling to get a half-gallon jug of Chivas Regal out of sight—which is not an easy thing to do in a huge red convertible with the top down and a beautiful half-naked girl leaning over the backseat. People will stare.

In any case, we soon learned that "the new plan, just in from Washington" is to keep weirdos, foreigners, and other dangerous bad apples *out* of all National Forests in the nation, lest they set fires and spread anthrax or anything else that swarthy terrorists are wont to do. . . . They are Evil, they are savage, and they *must* be arrested before they set fire to the whole goddamn country.

I have never had any special fear of Foreigners, myself, but I recognize a nationwide *nervous breakdown* when I see one. It is EMBARRASSING, for openers, AND IT SUCKS.

. . .

Most people are happy on Fridays, but not me—at least not yesterday, when I drove up the mountain to assess the fire-fighting & water-flow capacity of a bleak mountain community called Thomasville, on the map and right smack in the middle of a National Forest tinderbox that is already burning with monster firestorms that leap from hill to hill like summer lightning and kill everything they can reach.

. . .

Big Fire is a terrifying thing to deal with up close, and you never forget it—the panic, the heat, the deafening roar of the flames overhead. I feel queasy every time I think about it. . . . If freezing to death is the nicest way to die, then burning to death in a forest fire is no doubt the ugliest. Beware. Fire is like lightning; they will both kill you, but lightning doesn't hurt as much. It is a monumental WHACK with no warning at all, and hopefully that is it—gone, no more, and minimal mortuary charges.

*Surviving* a lightning strike is even worse than dying from it, according to people who have lived (returned from the dead, in fact) because 8,000,000,000 volts of electricity is an unacceptable trauma to tissue of the human body. It fries everything in its path and leaves every organ in the body, from blood vessels to brain cells and even the sexual system, charred like overcooked bacon for the rest of its delicate life.

My friend Tex got hit by lightning one gloomy afternoon in the parking lot of the Woody Creek Tavern. "It kicked the mortal shit out of me," he said later. "It blasted me fifty goddamn feet across the road and over a snow fence. I was out for forty minutes, and when I woke up I smelled like death."

I was there that day, and I thought a bomb had gone off right in front of me. I was unconscious for a while, but not for long. When I woke up I was being dragged toward a shiny sky-blue ambulance by two well-meaning medics from the Sheriff's Office. . . . I twisted out of their grasp and backed against an ice machine. "Okay, boys," I said calmly, "the Joke is over. Let's not get crazy about this. Give me some air, gentlemen," I croaked. "I feel a little jangled, but I know it will pass. Get your hands off me, you pigfucker."

No doubt it *sounded* rude to casual onlookers, but in truth it was not. I was just kidding with them. They know me.

. . .

Friday afternoons are usually loose and happy in this valley, but today was different. I live in the mountains at an altitude of 8,000 feet, which is roughly a mile and a half high. That is "big air," as they say in the zoom-zoom business. It makes for large lungs and thin blood, along with dangerously expensive real estate. Life has always been a little spooky up here, but now as this vicious new century swarms over us like a fester of kudzu vines, life in these mountains is becoming living relentless hell.

The whole state of Colorado is on fire, according to *The New York Times,* and the nerdish Republican Governor is raving like a banshee about the death of Colorado as we know it before the summer is over.

That would be about 90 days, on most calendars—or right about September 11, 2002, only one horrible year after those stupid bastards blew up the WTC . . . We will actually be at war by then, and anybody who doesn't like it will be locked up in a military holding pen.

. . .

Weird things happen when you get whacked by serious lightning. Many years ago, nineteen (19) members of the Strange family in North Carolina were struck at the same instant when they all leaned against a chain-link fence at a July 4 fireworks display. They all survived, but none prospered. It was like some horrible merciless coincidence out of the Old Testament—or extremely bad karma, to millions of non-Christians, among whom I definitely count myself. I have abandoned all forms & sects of the practicing Christian Church.

I have seen thousands of priests and bishops and even the Pope himself transmogrified in front of our eyes into a worldwide network of thieves and perverts and sodomites who relentlessly penetrate children of all genders and call it holy penance for being born guilty in the eyes of the Church.

I have seen the Jews run amok in Palestine like bloodthirsty beasts with no shame, and six million brainless Baptists demanding the death penalty without any trial at all for pagans and foreigners and people like me who won't pray with them in those filthy little shacks they call churches. They are like a swarm of rats fleeing a swoop fire, and I want no part of them. Indeed, I have my own faith and my own gods to worship, and I have been doing it with a certain amount of distinction for ten thousand years, like some fine atomic clock with ever-lasting batteries.

Whoops! I have wandered off on some kind of vengeful tangent, here, and we don't really need it now, do we? So let us save that wisdom for later.

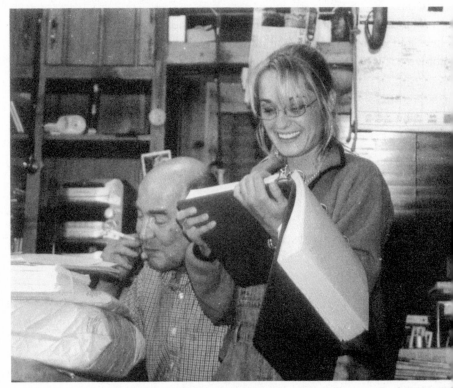

Anita reading *Kingdom of Fear* manuscript. *Res Ipsa Loquitur.* Owl Farm, 2(

(Jennifer Alise Stroup)

. . .

I was talking about driving up the mountain with Anita to survey the downside of a firestorm that seems certain to destroy about half of us before the summer is over. . . . The whole state of Colorado is officially *on fire,* according to the Governor and a few grifters in Washington who gave him 25 million dollars for Disaster Relief and Emergency Fire-fighting Equipment for an endless war against Fire.

It was Friday morning when the sheriff asked me to run up the hill and investigate. "You *must* go to Thomasville," he told me. "How are we going to evacuate them when the fires come? Go all the way up to the top and see how the river is running. Also check the Reservoir and tell me how deep it is. I fear we are running out of water in this valley."

Why not? I thought. We can take the red convertible and load up on gin at the Rainbow. Anything worth doing is worth doing Right.

. . .

It had been a few days since I first heard the weird story about "gangs of armed Jews roaming the neighborhood and beating the shit out of anybody who looked like an A-rab."

"Good god," I muttered. "Jews can't live at this altitude. There is something wrong with this story."

That is why we decided to go up to Thomasville in the *first* place. I wanted to check it out, and so did Anita . . . and so did the sheriff, as it turned out. The sheriff didn't need to deputize me, because I have been a certified Deputy Coroner of this county for twenty (20) years. . . . And, in Colorado, the County Coroner is the *only* public official with the legal power to *arrest the sheriff.*

That is the key to my oft-uttered wisdom in re: Politics is the art of controlling your environment. Indeed. Never forget it, or you will become a Victim of your environment. Rich nerds and lawyers will stomp all over you worse than any A-rab, and you will be like the eight ball on some country-club billiards table near Atlanta—*whack,* over and out. No more humor.

And so much for that, eh? Jews don't play pool anyway, and neither do A-rabs. They are *tribal* people, which means they are primitive thinkers. They feel a genetic imperative to kill each other, and it tends to get in their way. . . . Or maybe that brutal compulsion comes from the Holy Bible, which is definitely true. The Bible is *unforgiving*. There is not a scintilla of mercy or humor in the Holy Bible. None.

Think on it, Bubba. Point me to some laughs, or even a goddamn chuckle in that book.

People frequently ask me if I believe in God, as if it were some kind of final judgment or naked indicator of my pro or con value in this world. Ho ho. That is too stupid to even think about—like a WHITES ONLY sign on the pearly gates of Heaven.

But not really. Don't get me wrong, fellas. That is only a whooped-up "figure of speech," or maybe a failed metaphor. It is a term of Art, not a term of Law. If the freak who wrote the Book of Revelation had been busted and jailed for the horrible *threats* he made against the whole human race, he would have been executed on the spot by a Military Tribunal. So long, Johnny, we never really liked you anyway. Mahalo.

# The Witness

Not everybody understands the real meaning of being "brought within The System." It is legal language, the kind of talk you hear in the hallways at professional police conventions or pretrial hearings in musty urban courtrooms. As in, "The time has come, Judge, to drop the net on this loathsome criminal deviate and reel him into The System."

We are talking about The Criminal Justice System, here, and once you get brought into it, there will be a part of your brain that thinks about nothing else for the rest of your life. It will be as if a leech had attached itself to the small of your back forever. . . . Just ask Bill Clinton.

Some people call it Rehabilitation, but . . .

. . .

A cop killing is always big news—except when Police kill one of their own, in which case the death notice is rarely if ever made public. The Law Enforcement Fraternity is very tight when it comes to media embarrassment. There is a basic operating rule among Criminal Defense Lawyers that says: "Above all, the *lawyer* must not go to jail." It is not always an easy rule to observe, given that the lawyer is also an ordained Officer of the Court.

Be keenly aware of this fact when you get accused (on paper/formal charges are filed) of anything at all—*anything* from shoplifting to felony murder—that could/might/will result in your being Convicted and formally Punished *in any way* for any violation of *any* part of *any* Criminal Code. The law is not on your side when you become a defendant in a criminal courtroom. They *are* out to get you, and they *will,* if you are not alert.

"*He who goes to law takes a wolf by the ears.*" Robert Burton said that, and I am citing it as a very dangerous Reality in this war-torn world that we live in. This is 2002. The American Century was over in January of 2001. They were Punctual, as the Fascist mentality cannot survive without brute Punctuality. Never be *late,* for fear of being guilty of *Deviant Behavior,* and *brought within The System.* BANG! SLAM! BEND OVER. . . . *Seig heil!* Who is God? The Boss is God—and you're not. . . . Hey rube, you are Nothing! You are Guilty! You are lower than the shit of some filthy animal.

Yassuh, Boss. I'll do *anything,* just don't put me in Jail. I am guilty. I will do whatever you say.

Marilyn Chambers at 17
(HST archives)

. . .

It was a cold winter night when the Witness first came to my house. She was a very large woman, about 35 years old—dark hair, long legs, and tastefully enlarged breasts—who once worked in Southern California as a director of sex films. That is not a bad job to have in L.A., especially if you have a natural talent for it, and this woman did. I recognized it immediately.

I know the Sex Business. I was the Night Manager of the famous O'Farrell Theatre, in San Francisco, for two years, and I still have a keen eye for working girls. There is a certain lewd radiance about them that comes only from dancing naked in public for 2,000 nights. . . . Sex business people recognize one another immediately. They have ridden for the XXX brand, and the brand has ridden them.

It is not an unfriendly brand, nothing like a scar on the cheek, or a crude tattoo on top of a butt that says PROPERTY OF HELL'S ANGELS. That would not be appropriate for a stylish lap-dancing venue in Nashville or Toledo. The customers would be offended. Big tippers tend to be wary of a woman who has pulled the Hell's Angels train. The mark of the XXX business is an attitude more than a brand or a nasty tattoo.

The O'Farrell was once celebrated as "the Carnegie Hall of Public Sex in America." It was a nice place to work in those money-mad years of the Reagan Revolution. We had about 100 girls on the payroll, and many more on the waiting list. Naked women were a hot commodity in those days. It was the "Golden Era of pornography," according to chroniclers of that ilk, when sex movies were still shot with bright lights and reels of celluloid film.

*Deep Throat* and *Behind the Green Door* were still packing huge multisexual crowds into respectable theaters all over the country, Oral Sex was mainstream, and lush entertainment expenses were tax-deductible. Huge expense money was the oil that kept the national economy going, and sex was everywhere, 24 hours a day. Powder cocaine was the recreational drug of choice, but LSD-25 was still fashionable in upscale communes and coastal brokerage firms.

Those 20 sex-crazed years between the introduction of the birth control pill and the eruption of AIDS was a wild and orgiastic time in America, and I loved it.

Ah, but that was many years ago, or at least it seems that way. It was a good time to be young and reckless—when you could still take your date to a movie without having to worry about being hit on by strangers demanding blow jobs. That came in with the Democrats, who quickly discovered that getting busted in Washington for sodomy was a proven way to get re-elected in states like Arkansas and California. If Bill Clinton had not been term-limited by federal law, he would still be in the White House today and we would all be free from fear.

Or maybe not. There is another school of thought that says Clinton would have been assassinated if he'd been able to run for a third term. "The Texas Mafia would never have let it happen," my friend Curtis assured me. "He would have been jerked out like a bad tooth. . . ." Maybe you have to be from Texas to agree with talk like that, but I doubt it. Texas is not the only state full of wealthy freaks with sinister agendas. Some of them are friends of mine, in fact, and I have never doubted that just because they are nice people to have a few drinks with doesn't mean they won't do monstrous things. Cruelty and perversion are common jokes in the oil and orgy business.

Indeed, but we can save those stories for later, so let's get back to this woman I was trying to describe. Her name is Gail, but for vaguely legal reasons we will have to call her Jane. If I called her Gail we would have a lot of bitching from lawyers.

We will call her the Witness, which better suits her role in this drama. Some people called her the Victim, but not for long. That was a convenient legal fiction for the local D.A. and his (since-departed) gang of vengeful thugs. They are gone from this valley now, most of them fired or demoted into obscurity. The chief investigator in my case, the de facto boss of the gang, now works for the DEA in Europe. The Prosecutor, now known as Mr. Shiteyes, resigned soon after and is now a criminal lawyer in Aspen, where he is frequently seen on trial days with his arm around accused criminals wearing orange jumpsuits and handcuffs and jail haircuts, but he no longer works as a prosecutor. He "flipped," as they say in the cop shop. . . .

I didn't know the Witness personally, but she definitely knew me. She had been harassing me by mail for four or five months, telling me I didn't know how much FUN I was missing by not getting together with her immediately for a fascinating chat about her days in the Sex Business. We would have more FUN than a barrel of monkeys in heat, she hinted. Ho ho. She would even come out to Colorado in order to meet me on my own savage turf. She had already sent me a thick sheaf of lurid press clippings about her adventures as a wholesome college cheerleader who got into the Porno Movie business by accident and had been a big success. "I guess I was just lucky," she said demurely. "But once I saw how much talent I had, I never looked back. It's just amazing, isn't it."

It is important to understand that Jane had been extremely open with me, a complete stranger, about her background in the sex business. She was proud of it. Her record spoke for itself: nine successful XXX movies, including classics of abysmal lewdness like *Hot Lips, FleshSucker, Candy Goes to Hollywood, Eat Me While I'm Hot,* and a truly depraved saga about rape and degradation in a Japanese sex prison somewhere in the South Pacific called *Nazi Penetration,* starring Long John Holmes, one berserk Nazi, and five helpless white women with huge tits.

*Nazi Penetration* has long been one of my favorite films of the sex genre. It is a story of shipwreck, sadism, and absolutely hopeless female victims confined on a tiny tropical island with only a Nazi war criminal and two cruel Japanese nymphomaniacs to keep them company. The naked white girls are innocent prisoners of some long-forgotten war that is never mentioned in the movie except by way of the frayed and often bottomless military uniforms worn by the demented villains—who also carry spotless German Lugers and don't mind shooting them at escaped Sex Slaves who keep running away and fleeing into the jungle, only to be recaptured and relentlessly raped and tortured for their efforts. They are losers, and they will never be rescued—not even by the good-hearted Holmes, who also fucks them relentlessly.

I mention this epic of degenerate suffering only for reasons of historical context and Witness identification. If Jane had been a practicing Jehovah's Witness when I met her, my story might have a different ending, but she was not. She was just another one of those goofy, over-the-hump Porno Queens from the good old days who was looking around for some other line of work to get into, something where she could use her natural talents for harmless commercial sex without compromising her artistic integrity or her dubious social standing. I know them well, and I have a certain affection for most of them. They are girls who went to Hollywood when they were 17 years old, hoping to make the most of their whorish ambitions by becoming movie stars.

Very few succeeded, and many got sidetracked into the Sex Business, where work is always available. "My pussy is my ticket to ride," a stripper named Bambi once told me. "Men want to see my pussy and they want to see me fuck something scary. That's why they pay me, and that's why I do it."

Bambi was a lovely girl from a middle-class family in Sacramento, with an elegant body and a seductively morbid sense of humor. I liked her and used my influence to help her become a star at the O'Farrell, where she routinely made a thousand dollars a night. I was always tempted to fuck her, but I never did. I was deeply in love with my girlfriend Maria at the time. She was a sex star in her own right, and a jewel of a friend and a lover.

My Night Manager job put me in close contact with dozens of aggressively naked women every night, which never ceased to amaze me and kept me constantly high on sex. It was an overwhelming work environment, at times, but with Maria's help I soon became comfortable with it. Not everybody can handle being surrounded by lust, beauty, and clearly available nakedness at all times. It is like living in the Garden of Eden, with luscious apples hanging from every tree and the power to banish all snakes—which were Everywhere, writhing and cooing with a lust that bordered on madness.

Only a freak of passion could have resisted that kind of massive temptation, and on some nights I came close to caving in to it. "You are crazy as a goddamn loon not to fuck every one of these girls," Artie Mitchell told me. "They all love you and they all want to fuck you like animals. I've never seen anybody turn down so much guaranteed fine pussy. It makes me sick."

"So what?" I would say to him. "You are a sleazy whoremonger and you don't understand anything. Herb Caen told me you have syphilis."

"What?" he would scream. "You sick bastard! I'll kill Herb Caen if he ever prints that. Herb Caen sucks dicks!!"

Jim and Artie Mitchell were as bizarre a pair of brothers as ever lived. I loved them both, but the Sex Business had made them crazy. They made millions of dollars off of sex and smuggled guns to the IRA when they weren't fondling naked girls or entertaining corrupt cops and politicians. But they were not suave. Neither one of them had social ambitions, but they fought like wolves to protect their vice-ridden turf. They were deep into San Francisco politics, but they were always in desperate need of sound political advice.

That was my job. The Night Manager gig was only a cover for my real responsibility, which was to keep them out of Jail, which was not easy. The backstairs politics of San Francisco has always been a byzantine snake pit of treachery and overweening bribery-driven corruption so perverse as to stagger the best minds of any generation. All political power comes from the barrel of either guns, pussy, or opium pipes, and people seem to like it that way. The charm of the city is legendary to the point of worship all over the world, with the possible exception of Kabul, New Orleans, and Bangkok.

. . .

On that cold night in late February when the Witness came to my house, she was wearing a blue business suit that made her look a bit on the chubby side and high-heeled shoes that would have made her seem dangerously tall if my other guests had not been well over six feet and none too happy to see her. Her head was huge, far larger than mine, and her body was oddly muscular—more in the style of a female bodybuilder with an uncontrollable appetite for speed and lethal steroids who had spent too much time in sexually oriented weight rooms on the wrong side of Hollywood. She was clearly an athlete—a "big" girl, in a word—and she spoke with a wiggy confidence that made me nervous. My mother would have called her pushy, or perhaps even rude. But I am not so polite. To me, she looked sleazy. There was something corrupt about her, something foul and dishonest that would have put me instantly on my guard if I had cared enough to worry about it that night.

But I didn't. She meant nothing to me, at the time. We get all kinds of people in this house, from common thugs and deviates to stupid thieves with hearts full of hate and U.S. senators with amazing whores on their arms. Some arrive on private jets, and others drive stolen cars full of illegal drugs and weapons. It is an ugly mix, at times, but I have learned to live with it, if only because I am a professional journalist and a writer of books about life in the weird lane—which is "interesting" in the Chinese sense, but not necessarily uplifting.

It is not a criminal life, or a hurricane zoo of never-ending craziness. It may look that way, from a distance, but I consider it eminently sane, and most of my friends agree. *Sane* is a dangerous word. It implies a clear distinction, a sharp line between the Sane and the Insane that we all see clearly and accept as a truth of nature.

But it is not. No. The only real difference between the Sane and the Insane, in this world, is the Sane have the power to have the Insane locked up. That is the bottom line. CLANG! Go immediately to prison. You crazy bastard, you should have been locked up a long time ago. You are a dangerous freak—I am rich, and I want you castrated.

Whoops, did I say that? Yes, I did, but we need not dwell so long on it that it develops into a full-blown tangent on the horrors of being locked up and gibbed like a tomcat in a small wire box. We have enough grim things to worry about in this country as the 21st Century unfolds. We have Anthrax, we have smallpox, we have very real fears of being blasted into jelly in the privacy of our own homes by bombs from an unseen enemy, or by nerve gas sprayed into our drinking water, or even ripped apart with no warning by our neighbor's Rottweiler dogs. All these things have happened recently, and they will probably happen again.

We live in dangerous times. Our armies are powerful, and we spend billions of dollars a year on new prisons, yet our lives are still ruled by fear. We are like pygmies lost in a maze. We are not at War, we are having a nervous breakdown.

. . .

Right. And enough of that gibberish. We are champions, so let's get back to the story. We were talking about the Witness, the large and sleazy woman who came into my life like a sea snake full of poison and almost destroyed me.

There were two other people in my kitchen that night, and a girl who kept popping in and out. So let's say there were five people in the house, including the Witness. She was happy to be there, she said, because she had some questions to ask me.

"Not now," I said. "We're watching the basketball game." I said it sharply, more in the manner of a command than a gentle request from the host. Normally I don't speak in that tone to first-time visitors, but she was clearly not a woman who was going to pay attention to gentle requests. I was not rude to her, but I was definitely firm. That is a point I like to make immediately when a dingbat comes into my home and gets loud. That is unacceptable. We have Rules here: They are civilized rules, and oddly genteel in their way, yet some people find them disturbing in their eccentricity. Contradictions abound, as well as dangerous quirks that sometimes make people afraid—which is not a bad thing on some days: Fear is a healthy instinct, not a sign of weakness. It is a natural self-defense mechanism that is common to felines, wolves, hyenas, and most humans. Even fruit bats know fear, and I salute them for it. If you think the world is weird now, imagine how weird it would be if wild beasts had no fear.

That is how this woman tried to act when she came into my home on that fateful February night. She pranced around and wandered from room to room in a way that made me nervous. She was clearly a refugee from the sex business—a would-be *promoter* of Sexual Aids & first-class organ enlargement. . . . That was her *business plan,* in a nut, and nobody wanted to listen to it.

"Shut up!" Semmes screamed. "Can't you see that we are watching a goddamn basketball game?"

She ignored him and kept babbling. "What kind of Sex do you like?" she asked me. "Why won't you talk to me?"

I am not a Criminal, by trade, but over the years I have developed a distinctly criminal nervous system. Some people might call it paranoia, but I have lived long enough to know that there is no such thing as paranoia. Not in the 21st Century. No. Paranoia is just another word for ignorance.

# There Is No Such Thing as Paranoia

*There may be flies on you and me, but there are no flies on Jesus.*
—Hunter S. Thompson

## Strange Lusts and Terrifying Memories

My father had a tendency to hunch darkly over the radio when the news of the day was foul. We listened to the first wave of Pearl Harbor news together. I didn't understand it, but I knew it was bad because I saw him hunch up like a spider for two or three days in a row after it happened. "God damn those sneaky Japs," he would mutter from time to time. Then he would drink whiskey and hammer on the arm of the couch. Nobody else in our family wanted to be with him when he listened to the war news. They didn't mind the whiskey, but they came to associate the radio with feelings of anger and fear.

I was not like that. Listening to the radio and sipping whiskey with my father was the high point of my day, and I soon became addicted to those moments. They were never especially happy, but they were always exciting. There was a certain wildness to it, a queer adrenaline rush of guilt and mystery and vaguely secret joy that I still can't explain, but even at the curious age of four I knew it was a special taste that I shared only with my father. We didn't dwell on it, or feel a dark need to confess. Not at all. It was fun, and I still enjoy remembering those hours when we hunched together beside the radio with our whiskey and our war and our fears about evil Japs sneaking up on us. . . .

I understand that fear is my friend, but not always. Never turn your back on Fear. It should always be in front of you, like a thing that might have to be killed. My father taught me that, along with a few other things that have kept my life interesting. When I think of him now I think of fast horses and cruel Japs and lying FBI agents.

"There is no such thing as Paranoia," he told me once. "Even your Worst fears will come true if you chase them long enough. Beware, son. There is Trouble lurking out there in that darkness, sure as hell. Wild beasts and cruel people, and some of them will pounce on your neck and try to tear your head off, if you're not careful."

It was a mean piece of wisdom to lay on a 10-year-old boy, but in retrospect I think it was the right thing to say, and it definitely turned out to be true. I have wandered into that darkness many times in my life and for many strange reasons that I still have trouble explaining, and I could tell you a whole butcher shop full of stories about the horrible savage beasts that lurk out there, most of them beyond the wildest imagination of a 10-year-old boy—or even a 20- or 30-year-old boy, for that matter, or even beyond the imagination of a teenage girl from Denver being dragged away from her family by a pack of diseased wolves. Nothing compares to it. The terror of a moment like that rolls over you like a rush of hot scum in a sewer pipe.

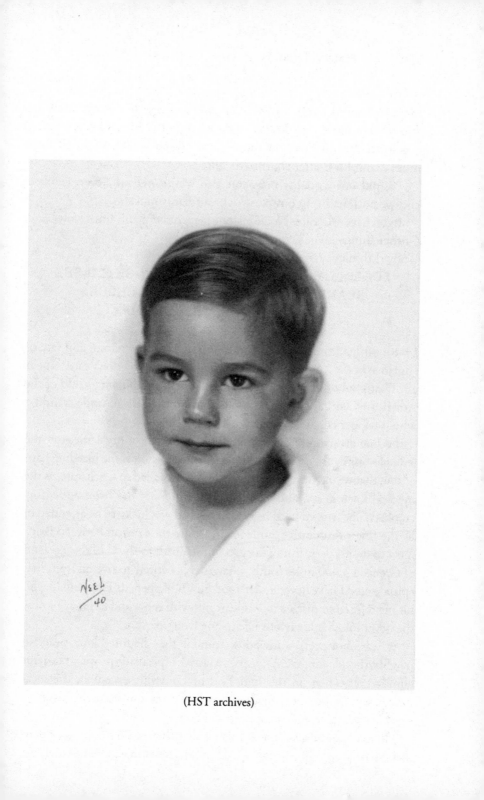

(HST archives)

. . .

Here is a story I wrote for the *Atheneum Literary Association* magazine and tried to insert into *The Spectator* when Porter Bibb was editor—he was a numb-nuts creep in those days, but so what? We loved each other—and I was after all, the Art Director. . . .

We put out a quality magazine and we printed whatever we liked and we both had veto power, which was dangerous.

Except for *this* one. No. This one never saw print, until now. And God's mercy on you swine for reading it.

## SOCIETY HOUSEWIFE EXPOSED IN CHILD-SEX SCANDAL; BLOODY AFTERMATH SHOCKS EAST END NEIGHBORHOOD

I have not had the leisure to brood seriously on the nature and fate of true love in the 21st Century, but that doesn't mean I don't care. Not at all. That kind of flotsam is never far from my mind. I am a child of the American Century, and I feel a genetic commitment to understanding why it happened, and why I take it so personally.

Let me give you one example: In the summer of my 15th year, the wife of a family friend bit me on the face and tore off some bleeding flaps of skin that would never grow back. The tissue failed to regenerate, as the medical doctors say, and ever since then my face has been noticeably crooked. The wound itself healed perfectly. I was lucky to be attended to by the finest Restorative Surgeons in a nine-state region between Baltimore and St. Louis, from Chicago in the north to the Caribbean island of Grenada 3,000 miles south. I have never entirely recovered from that episode, and I have never understood how it happened. The woman who bit me refused to discuss it—at least not with me—and as far as I know she never told her lascivious tale to any living person.

It was, however, a towering scandal that haunted our peaceful neighborhood for many years. Massive speculation was rampant almost everywhere in the East End of Louisville except in the local newspapers, which only made it hotter as truly unspeakable gossip. It was Unacceptable and Irresistible all at once.

Ho ho. Stand back, you churlish little suckfish! I have my own definitions of words like Unacceptable and Irresistible. I remember the slope of her perfect little breasts and the panties she never wore. I remember exactly how she smelled and how she laughed when I sucked her nipples down my throat. I was her pimply sex toy, and she was the love of my life. I worshiped her desperate mouth and prayed at the shrine of her grasping pussy. Why she sunk her teeth into my face I will never know. Perhaps it was God's will or the hex of some heinous Devil.

## Rape in Cherokee Park

I look back on my youth with great fondness, but I would not recommend it as a working model to others. I was lucky to survive it at all, in fact: I was hounded & stalked for most of my high school career by a cruel & perverted small-town Probation Officer who poisoned my much-admired social life and eventually put me in jail on the night of my Class graduation.

Once Mr. Dotson came into my life I was marked as a criminal. He was an officious creep with all sorts of hidden agendas—or not that hidden—and he hounded me all through high school. It was an embarrassment, and it criminalized me long before I ever got to marijuana. All kinds of people who had no reason to be in contact with the Juvenile Court were contacted by this Swine, which accounted for a lot of my reputation. He was out of control, and people like that shouldn't get away with abusing their power.

Especially as I hadn't committed a crime. All we had wanted was some cigarettes.

We ran out of cigarettes on the ride home from Cherokee Park. I was asleep in the backseat passed out, or half passed out, and I remember thinking: *Cigarettes. Cigarettes. Cigarettes.*

Max and Eric (or so I'll call them) were up front. Eric was driving, and I guess it was Max who said, "Well. Let's see if these people have any."

I might have thought of that, too: Here are people, neckers, parked in the park at Neckers' Knob, or whatever. Why not ask for a cigarette? That was Max's logic, anyway.

So we pulled up beside them, which could have frightened some people. And Max got out and went over to a car with two couples in it and asked for cigarettes, and the driver said, "We don't have any."

That seemed fair, but something else was said. The car was seven feet away, and Max was a fairly violent bugger. The next thing I remember is him yelling, "All right, Motherfucker! You give me some cigarettes or I'm going to grab you out of there!"

Then he reached into the car and said, "I'm going to jerk you out of here and beat the shit out of you and rape those girls back here." And that's all it was.

Eric was driving, so I had to get out of the backseat and go over and grab Max, saying, "Fuck this. We don't need any cigarettes." I meant we didn't need any fights. So I got back in the car and we drove off. That's all it was, but they got our license plate number and reported it. . . . Then—you know Cops: a Rape Charge.

# God Might Forgive You, but I Won't

My Probation Officer knew it was wrong, he said later, in late-night chats with my mother, who was by then Chief Librarian at the Louisville Public Library and stocking my books on her shelves. My success was a joyous surprise to her, but she feared for the grievous effect it was having on my old nemesis, Mr. Dotson. He often stopped by our house for coffee, and he desperately begged her forgiveness for all the trouble he'd caused her.

She forgave him, in time, but I didn't. I will spit on his memory forever. The last of many letters I got from him carried a postmark from the Kentucky State Prison at Eddyville. I was not even curious enough to read it and find out if he was a convict or merely a Guard. I had other lessons to learn. My continuing education in the nature of the Criminal Justice System was picking up speed.

I remember Juvenile Court Judge Jull saying, "Well, Hunter. You've made my life a nightmare for four years. You've been in and out of this Court. You've mocked it. And now you're going to get away from me. This is my last chance at you. So now I remand you to the County Jail for sixty days." That was their last shot.

But it was a total outrage. I became good friends with the "victims," and they said the same thing. But this was Mr. Dotson and Judge Jull, and what they did was cause a huge rallying of support behind me. I would never have gone into their jail, except that minors couldn't make bail in Kentucky back then.

The only reason I got out in thirty days was because my eighteenth birthday came in thirty days, so they couldn't hold me: I could make bail. They didn't try to hold me; they had made their point. Last shot. That, and a group of powerful citizens and civic leaders had worked to get me out. But I was a hero while I was in jail—they decided they'd call me "The President," and on my birthday, "Hit the Bricks," they said, "My boy, 'Hit the Bricks.'" It became a cause, and I was a hero there for a while.

. . .

Many wild and desperate years have whirled through my life since my one and only experience as a certified Victim of the law enforcement process. The lesson I learned from those thirty days in jail was never to go back there again. Period. It was not Necessary. My jail mates had called me "The President" and beautiful girls came to visit me on Thursday afternoons, but I had better sense than to feel any pride about it.

The late Pablo Escobar, former kingpin of the powerful Medellín cocaine cartel in Colombia, once observed that "the difference between being a criminal and being an outlaw is that an outlaw has a following"—which he did, for a while, for his willingness to share his huge profits with the working-class Poor of his city. He was a Home-boy, a generous friend of the people. His only real crime, they said, was that the product his business produced was seen as a dangerous menace by the ruling Police & Military establishments of the U.S. and a few other countries that were known to be slaves and toadies of U.S. economic interests.

When I got out of jail, in fact, I went immediately to work for the rest of the summer for Almond Cook, the Chevrolet dealer in town. I'm not sure what I thought I was going to do that fall—maybe go to the U.K. I didn't know, but I was in no mood really to take up anything conventional. Mr. Cook was the father of one of my longtime girlfriends, and I was given a job driving a brand-new Chevrolet truck, delivering parts around town. It was a wonderful job—I'd just take things all over town, driving constantly, sort of a very large version of those bicycle messengers in New York, but in a brand-new fucking V-8 truck.

I got very good with the truck. I was driving all the time, and it was wonderful, like being given a rocket. And I had no trouble and got to be such a good driver that something was bound to happen . . . the numbers were getting bad. Then one Saturday morning—a very bright, very sunny day—I was speeding down an alley behind some kind of a car repair emporium on Second Street. I'd gone down this particular alley many times, and had gotten to the point where I could put this huge V-8 Chevy pickup through a burning hoop without it being touched—at sixty or seventy miles an hour.

I remember coming down that alley. It was bright. I could see it was all bricks on either side, and here was this big truck, say a ton and a half, like a big Ryder delivery truck, only blue or green, and it had one of those tailgates that hangs down on chains, made of pointed lead or hard steel. The tailgate was pointing out by a few degrees; had it been parked parallel I would have had room to go through with about three inches to spare. But instead of being parallel to the wall, it was parked at a slight angle, and I remember thinking, *Shit. I can make that.* But I knew it was bad.

I hit the accelerator so hard that I went through the alley at about sixty—so fast that I barely felt the impact. Sort of a click, more than a crash. . . .

I knew immediately that I hadn't made it clean, and I stopped. Another inch and I would have made it . . . two inches, maybe. But I missed it by those two inches: The tailgate had kicked in, just to the right of the front headlight. The truck had a big chrome stripe all along it, and right on top of it, about three inches above, was another stripe, this one dark in color. I looked at it and thought, What the fuck? What's that? There was no other damage. I hadn't crashed anything. Nothing bent. So I stared at the dark stripe again, and as I looked at it I realized that the tailgate had caught the front headlight right there and opened up the truck like a can opener—the whole length, front to back, about two inches wide—but clean, like a sardine can. You put one on both sides and people would think that's the way new Chevy trucks were.

I thought, Oh, fuck. But nobody had seen it. It didn't make any noise; there was no crash. Just a hairline miss. Hubris! I knew I should learn from the thing. I knew the damned track was not what it looked like, literally: a two-inch racing stripe. But it was so clean that I thought for a minute that I might get away with it.

I went into the diner across the street and sat drinking coffee and beer, thinking, What the Hell do I do? . . . Do I tell anybody? I parked the truck out in the lot with the bad side right next to a fence so nobody could see it, then finally decided what to do.

I went in and told the parts manager, "Come out here, Hank. I've got something to show you." He was in charge of such things, and he was a good friend. I took him out to the lot in the hot noonday sun and said, "Now, I want you to be calm here, but I just want to show you this. I don't know what to do about it, and I need some advice." I took him around to the other side, between the fence and the truck, and he almost passed out.

I said, "What should I do about this?"

And he said, "We'll have to tell Mr. Cook."

That's fair, I thought. It was right before lunch. Hank then called and said he needed to talk to Mr. Cook, but he wasn't there, Thank God, which gave me another hour or so. I was going nuts with this. Something was coming down.

We just happened to be right across the street from the main Louisville Post Office, and I thought, Ah, hah! I bet the draft office is still open there. So I went right across the street at lunch and volunteered for the draft, which a lot of my friends had done. It was kind of a nice resting place between stops—and there was a six-month waiting list. I thought, Oh, fuck, time's way down and I have to go back and see Almond Cook at one-ten.

I had an appointment.

So I just went next door to the Air Force. It happened to be next door. And I took the pilot training test and scored like 97 percent. I didn't really mean to go in there, but I told them I wanted to drive jet planes, and they said I could with that test. So I said, "When can I . . . when can I leave?"

And the recruiting officer said, "*Well*. Normally it takes a few days to check out, but you go Monday morning"—allegedly to flight school at Lackland Air Force Base in San Antonio, Texas.

I thought, Ah, hah! I'm out of here.

I went back and apologized to Almond Cook and told him that I had to admit I had failed at driving the truck.

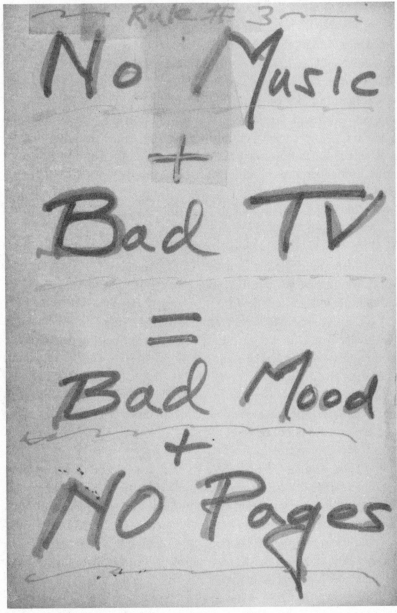

(HST)

. . .

And where is my old friend Paul Hornung, now that we need him? Paul was the finest running back of his time: All-State at Flaget High in Louisville, All-American at Notre Dame, and All-Pro for the Green Bay Packers. He was a big handsome boy from Louisville's gamey West End, a longtime breeding ground for sporting talent, which also produced a flashy young fighter with extremely quick hands named Cassius Clay, who would become even more famous than Hornung.

That would be my old friend Muhammad Ali, the Heavyweight Champion of the World. He beat the shit out of me once, for no good reason at all, and Paul Hornung ran over me in a car, just because I couldn't get out of his way. . . . Yes sir, those boys stomped on the terra.

They were also serious flesh-tasters, as working Libertines were sometimes called in those days. They were . . .

Fuck this, I feel weak.

Get your hands off me, Harold! What the fuck is wrong with you?

Okay. You're the boss. Do anything you want, but please don't hurt my animals! That is all I ask.

Oh Yes Oh Yes! Praise Jesus, don't *hurt* them. They are creatures of God, and so am I. Oh god, pain is everywhere I feel. . . . "Bend over, honey," he said. "I'm going to put this Eel up your ass, so try to relax."

Ho ho, eh? Balls! There *are* no jokes when we start talking about introducing saltwater Eels into people's body cavities. Some of them are nine feet long. That is over the line, if it's done against their will. That would be rape of some kind.

Whoops! How about a break, people? How about some Music? Yes. Music is where it's at, so consider this:

I am a confused Musician who got sidetracked into this goddamn Word business for so long that I never got back to music—except maybe when I find myself oddly alone in a quiet room with only a typewriter to strum on and a yen to write a song. Who knows why? Maybe I just feel like singing—so I type.

These quick electric keys are my Instrument, my harp, my RCA glass-tube microphone, and my fine soprano saxophone all at once. That is my music, for good or ill, and on some nights it will make me feel like a god. Veni, Vidi, Vici. . . . That is when the fun starts. . . . Yes, Kenneth, this *is* the frequency. This is where the snow leopards live;

"Genius, all over the world, stands hand in hand, and one shock of recognition runs the whole circle round. . . ."

Herman Melville said that, and I have found it to be true, but I didn't really know what it *felt* like until I started feeling those shocks myself, which always gave me a rush. . . .

So perhaps we can look at some of my work (or *all* of it, on some days) as genetically *governed* by my frustrated musical failures, which led to an overweening *sublimation* of my essentially musical instincts that surely haunt me just as clearly as they dominate my lyrics.

## The New Dumb

*Something is happening here,*
*But you don't know what it is,*
*Do you, Mr. Jones?*
                        —Bob Dylan

No sir, not a chance. Mr. Jones does not even pretend to know what's happening in America right now, and neither does anyone else.

We have seen Weird Times in this country before, but the year 2000 is beginning to look *super* weird. This time, there really is nobody flying the plane. . . . We are living in dangerously weird times now. Smart people just shrug and admit they're dazed and confused.

The only ones left with any confidence at all are the New Dumb. It is the beginning of the end of our world as we knew it. Doom is the operative ethic.

. . .

The Autumn months are never calm in America. Back to Work, Back to School, Back to Football Practice, etc. . . . Autumn is a very Traditional period, a time of strong Rituals and the celebrating of strange annual holidays like Halloween and Satanism and the fateful Harvest Moon, which can have ominous implications for some people.

Autumn is always a time of Fear and Greed and Hoarding for the winter coming on. Debt collectors are active on old people and fleece the weak and helpless. They want to lay in enough cash to weather the known horrors of January and February. There is always a rash of kidnappings and abductions of schoolchildren in the football months. Preteens of both sexes are traditionally seized and grabbed off the streets by gangs of organized Perverts who traditionally give them as Christmas gifts to each other as personal Sex Slaves and playthings.

Most of these things are obviously Wrong and Evil and Ugly—but at least they are Traditional. They will happen. Your driveway *will* ice up, your furnace *will* explode, and you *will* be rammed in traffic by an uninsured driver in a stolen car.

But what the hell. That is why we have Insurance, eh? And the Inevitability of these nightmares is what makes them so reassuring. Life will go on, for good or ill. The structure might be a little Crooked, but the foundations are still Strong and Unshakable.

Ho, ho. Think again, buster. Look around you. There is an eerie sense of Panic in the air, a silent Fear and Uncertainty that comes with once-reliable faiths and truths and solid Institutions that are no longer safe to believe in. . . . There is a Presidential Election, right on schedule, but somehow there is no President. A new Congress is elected, like always, but somehow there is no Congress at all—not as we knew it, anyway, and whatever passes for Congress will be as helpless and weak as Whoever has to pass for the "New President."

If this were the world of sports, it would be like playing a Super Bowl that goes into 19 scoreless Overtimes and never actually Ends . . . or four L.A. Lakers stars being murdered in different places on the same day. Guaranteed Fear and Loathing. Abandon all hope. Prepare for the Weirdness. Get familiar with Cannibalism.

Good luck, Doc.

*November 19, 2000*

# In the Belly of the Beast

*Although I don't feel that it's at all necessary to tell you how I feel about the principle of individuality, I know that I'm going to have to spend the rest of my life expressing it one way or another, and I think that I'll accomplish more by expressing it on the keys of a typewriter than by letting it express itself in sudden outbursts of frustrated violence. I don't mean to say that I'm about to state my credo here on this page, but merely to affirm, sincerely for the first time in my life, my belief in man as an individual and independent entity. Certainly not independence in the everyday sense of the word, but pertaining to a freedom and mobility of thought that few people are able—or even have the courage—to achieve.*

—from a letter to Joe Bell
October 24, 1957
Eglin Air Force Base
Fort Walton Beach, Florida

(Tom Corcoran)

## Sally Loved Football Players

I was halfway through training in the Air Force when I saw my first AF flying-team disaster. That was down in Florida, at Eglin AF Base, at a *practice* run for the annual "Firepower Demonstration." Arthur Godfrey was there, as I recall, and it made him Sick. He didn't do any more PR for the Air Force.

Help! Now I'm having flashbacks about when my best photographer went to cover the once-famous 24-Hour Formula One Grand Prix at Sebring & never came back to work. His name was George Thompson, a very talented boy. He was smashed into hamburger when he was trotting across an "Exit ramp" with his camera. Jesus! I had to write his Obituary for the Sports Section that night. . . . It happened about two weeks after that ungodly disaster at the Firepower Demonstration. I almost went crazy—drunk & AWOL for two (2) months, in Tallahassee & Mobile & New Orleans. I went from Top Gun to Psychiatric Observation Status in what seemed like the Speed of *Light*.

Sad story, eh? Yeah, but I was Young then. I could bounce like a gum rubber ball. It was Fun. Girls loved me and queers gave me "speed" in New Orleans. I had a fast MG/A sports car that I would drive out on the beach in Destin & swim naked with Officers' wives at midnight. Colonel Hugo's beautiful daughter let me stay for two weeks at her slick condo in Mobile while the Air Police were looking for me. She had a swimming pool shaped like a football in her backyard, and the neighbors called the Police on us when we ran around naked & fucked like sea-weasels on the diving board. . . . Sally loved football players. She thought she could stay Young forever by sucking the juice of Eternal Life out of hard young bodies. She called it "The Milk of Paradise" and she rubbed it on her face every night.

Sally was 25 years old & she looked like one of those racy Brazilian girls who play volleyball on the beach in Rio on Sunday mornings. Her father was a bird-Colonel at the Air Force base, and her mother was a Southern Debutante. She had a very young son who laughed crazily when I would pick him up by his ankles and swing him around in fast circles like a pinwheel. . . . I forget his name now, but he liked me & he thought my name was Air-Man. His mother took me to dinner at fancy bars and Yacht Clubs in Mobile. She drove a sky-blue Cadillac, and she loved to get naked & drive fast at night on the Pensacola Highway—in my car or hers, which was far too heavy to drive out on the beach & park between the sand dunes while we swam in the Gulf of Mexico on moonlit nights.

Sally had a day job somewhere in downtown Mobile, but she would always call in sick when I came to visit. She would say that she'd "hurt her back on the diving board" and she could hardly walk, for the pain. She would take off five or six days at a time when I was there, but she never worried about it. She said they could do without her for a few days, and they knew she had a Bad Back—which was true, but not because she was crippled.

No. It was because of that nasty sandpaper surface on the diving board at her pool. It rubbed her spine raw when we got drunk and screwed on it at night for two or three hours at a time. We would wake up in the morning with blood all over the sheets from bouncing around on that goddamn diving board all night. . . . The pain made her cry, and I could barely walk the next day because of the bleeding wounds on my knees and my elbows. I had bleeding scabs on my knees for most of that summer, and when I finally went back to work on the newspaper, I had trouble walking around the office. The other editors laughed at me, but my boss Colonel Evans was a serious Military Man and he hated the sight of a man with fresh blood on his pants limping around his office.

"Goddamnit, Hunter!" he would scream. "What in the name of Shit is wrong with you? There's blood all over the floor in the bathroom! I slipped and almost *fell down* when I went in there to piss!"

I told him it was because I had to play football on the weekends, and the Base football field was in such bad shape that I sometimes fell down when I was running out for a pass from Zeke Bratkowski or Max McGee.

"O my God!" he would scream. "You're a goddamn Fool, aren't you! Why in Shit are you trying to play *football* at this time of year? Do you have *Shit* for brains? . . . This is goddamn *baseball* season. . . . Are you too stupid to know that it's *baseball* season? . . . Are you some kind of Human JACKASS?"

"No," I would say. "I'm the *Sports Editor*." (Which was true.) The Colonel hated it, but his hands were tied. The Eglin Eagles were the defending Champions of what was the U.S. Worldwide Military Command, in those days, and we expected to win it again. Football was *Big* at Eglin Air Force Base, very big. The football team was a perennial powerhouse, famous all over the world—at least everywhere in the world where the United States of America had a functioning military base, and that was just about Everywhere.

Playing for Eglin was like playing for the Green Bay Packers, and star players were no less pampered. ROTC was a mandatory course for all student/athletes at taxpayer-funded universities in the nation, back then—even for All-American football stars at schools like Alabama & Ohio State—and all ROTC student/athletes were required to serve for at least two (2) years of active duty in the U.S. Armed Forces. . . . They had No Choice—unless they qualified for a Draft Exemption for Moral or Medical reasons, which carried a life-long, career-crippling Stigma—so most of them did their 2 years "in uniform" & then got on with their lives in the Real World, like everybody else.

## Paris Review #156

GEORGE PLIMPTON: *Reading* The Proud Highway, *I got the impression you always wanted to be a writer.*

HUNTER S. THOMPSON: Well, wanting to and having to are two different things. Originally I hadn't thought about writing as a solution to my problems. But I had a good grounding in literature in high school. We'd cut school and go down to a café on Bardstown Road where we would drink beer and read and discuss Plato's parable of the cave. We had a literary society in town, the Athenaeum; we met in coat and tie on Saturday nights. I hadn't adjusted too well to society—I was in jail for the night of my high school graduation—but I learned at the age of fifteen that to get by you had to find the one thing you can do better than anybody else . . . at least this was so in my case. I figured that out early. It was writing. It was the rock in my sock. Easier than algebra. It was always work, but it was worthwhile work. I was fascinated early on by seeing my byline in print. It was a rush. Still is.

When I got to the Air Force, writing got me out of trouble. I was assigned to pilot training at Eglin Air Force Base near Pensacola in northwest Florida, but I was shifted to electronics . . . advanced, very intense, eight-month school with bright guys . . . I enjoyed it, but I didn't want to end up on the DEW line—the "distant early warning" line—somewhere in the Arctic Circle. Besides, I'm afraid of electricity. So I went up to the base education office one day and signed up for some classes at Florida State. I got along well with a guy named Ed and I asked him about literary possibilities. He asked me if I knew anything about sports, and I told him I had been the editor of my high school paper. He said, "Well, we might be in luck." It turned out that the sports editor, a staff sergeant, of the base newspaper, the *Command Courier,* had been arrested in Pensacola and put in jail for public drunkenness, pissing against the side of a building; it was the third time, and they wouldn't let him out.

So I went to the base library and found three books on journalism. I stayed there reading until it closed. I learned about headlines, leads: who, when, what, where, that sort of thing. I barely slept that night. This was my ticket to ride, my ticket to get out of that damn place. So I started as an editor. I wrote long Grantland Rice–type stories. The sports editor of my hometown *Louisville Courier-Journal* always had a column, left-hand side of the page—so I started a column.

By the second week I had the whole thing down. I could work at night. I wore civilian clothes, worked off base, had no hours, but I worked constantly. I wrote not only for the base paper but also the local paper, *The Playground News.* I'd put things in the local paper that I couldn't put in the base paper. Really inflammatory shit. I wrote for a professional wrestling newsletter. The Air Force got very angry about it. I was constantly doing things that violated regulations. I wrote a critical column about how Arthur Godfrey, who'd been invited to the base to be the master of ceremonies at a firepower demonstration, had been busted for shooting animals from the air in Alaska. The base commander told me: "Goddamnit, son, why did you have to write about Arthur Godfrey that way?"

When I left the Air Force I knew I could get by as a journalist. So I went to apply for a job at *Sports Illustrated*. I had my clippings, my bylines, and I thought that was magic—my passport. The personnel director just laughed at me. I said, "Wait a minute. I've been sports editor for *two* papers." He told me that their writers were judged not by the work they'd done, but where they'd done it. He said, "Our writers are all Pulitzer Prize winners from *The New York Times*. This is a helluva place for you to *start*. Go out into the boondocks and improve yourself."

GP: *You eventually ended up in San Francisco. With the publication in 1967 of* Hell's Angels, *your life must have taken an upward spin.*

HST: All of a sudden I had a book out. At the time I was twenty-nine years old and I couldn't even get a job driving a cab in San Francisco, much less writing. Sure, I had written important articles for *The Nation* and *The Observer*, but only a few good journalists really knew my byline. The book enabled me to buy a brand-new BSA G50 Lightning—it validated everything I had been working toward. If *Hell's Angels* hadn't happened, I never would have been able to write *Fear and Loathing in Las Vegas* or anything else. To be able to earn a living as a freelance writer in this country is damned hard; there are very few people who can do that. *Hell's Angels* all of a sudden proved to me that, Holy Jesus, maybe I can do this. I knew I was a good journalist. I knew I was a good writer, but I felt like I got through a door just as it was closing.

GP: *The San Francisco scene brought together many unlikely pairs— you and Allen Ginsberg, for instance. How did you come to know Allen during this period?*

HST: I met Allen in San Francisco when I went to see a marijuana dealer who sold by the lid. I remember it was ten dollars when I started going to that apartment and then it was up to fifteen. I ended up going there pretty often, and Ginsberg—this was in Haight-Ashbury—was always there looking for weed too. I went over and introduced myself and we ended up talking a lot. I told him about the book I was writing and asked if he would help with it. He helped me with it for several months; that's how he got to know the Hell's Angels. We would also go down to Ken Kesey's in La Honda together.

One Saturday, I drove down the coast highway from San Francisco to La Honda and I took Juan, my two-year-old son, with me. There was this magnificent crossbreeding of people there. Allen was there, the Hell's Angels—and the cops were there too, to prevent a Hell's Angels riot. Seven or eight cop cars. Kesey's house was across the creek from the road, sort of a two-lane blacktop country compound, which was a weird place. For one thing, huge speakers were mounted everywhere in all the trees, and some were mounted across the road on wires, so to be on the road was to be in this horrible vortex of sound, this pounding, you could barely hear yourself think—rock 'n' roll at the highest amps. That day, even before the Angels got there, the cops began arresting anyone who left the compound. I was by the house; Juan was sleeping peacefully in the backseat of the car. It got to be outrageous: The cops were popping people. You could see them about a hundred yards away, but then they would bust somebody very flagrantly, so Allen said, "You know, we've got to do something about this." I agreed, so with Allen in the passenger's seat, Juan in the back sleeping, and me driving, we took off after the cops that had just busted another person we knew, who was leaving just to go up to the restaurant on the corner. Then the cops got after *us*. Allen at the very sight of the cops went into his hum, his *om*, trying to hum them off. I was talking to them like a journalist would: "What's going on here, Officer?" Allen's humming was supposed to be a Buddhist barrier against the bad vibes the cops were producing, and he was doing it very loudly, refusing to speak to them, just *"Om! Om! Om!"* I had to explain to the cops who he was and why he was doing this. The cops looked into the backseat and said, "What is that back there? A child?" and I said, "Oh, yeah, yeah. That's my son." With Allen still going, *"Om,"* we were let go. He was a reasonable cop, I guess—checking out a poet, a journalist, and a child. Never did figure Ginsberg out, though. It was like the humming of a bee. It was one of the weirdest scenes I've ever been through, but almost every scene with Allen was weird in some way or another.

GP: *Did any other Beat Generation authors influence your writing?*

HST: Jack Kerouac influenced me quite a bit as a writer . . . in the Arab sense that the enemy of my enemy was my friend. Kerouac taught

Juan, age 3
(HST)

me that you could get away with writing about drugs and get published. It was *possible,* and in a symbolic way I expected Kerouac to turn up in Haight-Ashbury for the cause. Ginsberg was there, so it was kind of natural to expect that Kerouac would show up too. But, no—that's when Kerouac went back to his mother and voted for Barry Goldwater in 1964. That's when my break with him happened. I wasn't trying to write like him, but I could see that I could get published like him and break through the Eastern establishment ice. That's the same way I felt about Hemingway when I first learned about him and his writing. I thought, Jesus, some people can *do* this. Of course Lawrence Ferlinghetti influenced me—both his wonderful poetry and the earnestness of his City Lights bookstore in North Beach.

GP: *What's the appeal of the "outlaw" writer, such as yourself?*
HST: I just usually go with my own taste. If I like something, and it happens to be against the law, well, then I might have a problem. But an outlaw can be defined as somebody who lives outside the law, beyond the law, not necessarily against it. It's pretty ancient. It goes back to Scandinavian history. People were declared outlaws and were cast out of the community and sent to foreign lands—exiled. They operated outside the law in communities all over Greenland and Iceland, wherever they drifted. Outside the law in the countries they came from—I don't think they were trying to be outlaws . . . I was never trying, necessarily, to be an outlaw. It was just the place in which I found myself. By the time I started *Hell's Angels* I was riding with them and it was clear that it was no longer possible for me to go back and live within the law. Between Vietnam and weed—a whole generation was criminalized in that time. You realize that you are subject to being busted. A lot of people grew up with that attitude. There were a lot more outlaws than me. I was just a writer. I wasn't trying to be an outlaw writer. I never heard of that term; somebody else made it up. But we were all outside the law: Kerouac, Miller, Burroughs, Ginsberg, Kesey; I didn't have a gauge as to who was the worst outlaw. I just recognized allies: my people.

*Fall 2000*

Timothey Leary and Neal Cassady, their first meeting at Millbrook N.Y. in Ken Kesey - Merry Prankster's "Further" bus which Neal'd drive Crosscountry S.F. to N.Y. via Texas before Fall 1964 Presidential, with "A vote for Goldwater is a vote for Fun" logo painted large across bus-side, LSD Cool-aid Pitcher in icebox. Neal scratching amphetamine itch in his driver's palm, he'd driven out to bring Kerouac into the city for brief meeting with Pranksters & Kesey a few days before. For Hunter Thompson. Allen Ginsberg

(Allen Ginsberg)

. . .

In the violent years of the Sixties I found myself sinking deeper & deeper into a dangerously criminal lifestyle, along with most of my friends & associates. I was a hardworking professional journalist, at the time, with a wife & a son & extremely smart friends & a brand-new BSA motorcycle that was widely admired as "the fastest bike ever tested by *Hot Rod* magazine." My comfortable pad on a hill above Golden Gate Park was alive, day & night, with the babble of artists, musicians, writers, lawyers, wild bikers & rock 'n' roll stars whose names would soon be famous. . . . San Francisco was the capital of the world, in those years, and we were the new aristocracy. It was like living in the Kingdom of Magic.

But something about it disturbed me. Something was far out of whack. It was impossible not to notice that more & more of my friends were being arrested & locked up in jail. We were doing the same things we had always been doing, but we were suddenly committing more crimes—Felony crimes, in fact, which carried drastic criminal penalties. . . . Like five years in state prison for smoking a joint on a bench in a public park, or ten years for resisting arrest by refusing to be drafted into the Army & sent off to die in Vietnam.

It was the beginning of the Criminalization of a whole generation, and I soon became keenly aware of it. Even Joan Baez went to jail. New laws made possession of LSD a Class I felony and gave all police the right & even the duty to kick down yr. door on a whim. . . . I looked around me one night at a birthday party in Berkeley & saw that we were all committing a felony crime, just by being there. Yesterday's Fun had been officially transmogrified into tomorrow's insane nightmare. Fear led me to retaining a prominent Criminal lawyer; he agreed on one condition, he said—that I would never talk to a cop before he came to my rescue.

## What Marijuana?

Indeed, some of my best friends are lawyers. I have other good friends who are law enforcement professionals, but not many. It is not wise, in my business, to count too many cops among your good friends, no more than it is wise to be constantly in the company of lawyers—unless, of course, you are about to be put on trial in a Criminal Court, and even then you want to be very careful. Your life or your freedom and certainly your sacred fortune will certainly depend on your choice of a criminal lawyer, and if you make the wrong choice, you will suffer. If your attorney is a fool or a slacker, you are doomed. The courts will disdain you, all criminal prosecutors will treat you with contempt, your friends will denounce you, and your enemies will rejoice. You will be taken without mercy into the bowels of the Criminal Justice System.

That is when pleading hopeless insanity begins to look like a pretty good option. The Insane, after all, can be cured, under the law, while the Guilty will be Guilty forever—or until they make enormous money contributions to a friendly second-term President with nothing to lose by tossing a few last-minute Pardons up for grabs. That is when you will need a profoundly expensive Attorney. Justice has never been cheap in America, not even for the innocent.

· · ·

O no. Forget that traditional bullshit about "let the client suffer." *While the lawyer suffers Later, all alone, confronting his own demons in the lavish privacy of his own mansion(s).*

No. None of that. I want him to suffer now, just as I do. You bet! We are Brothers, joined at the Soul. We will suffer together, or not at all.

This is our sacred Vow, our highest mixing of Blood, Truth, and Honor. We will fight back-to-back on the crest of the highest hill—because We are The Brotherhood, the highest tribe of Truth & Law & Justice.

We are few, but we speak with the power of many. We are strong like lonely bulls, but we are legion. Our code is gentle, but our justice is Certain—seeming Slow on some days, but slashing Fast on others, eating the necks of the Guilty like a gang of Dwarf Crocodiles in some lonely stretch of the Maputo River in the Transvaal, where the Guilty are free to run, but they can never Hide.

Their souls will never die, and neither will ours. The only difference will be that when the Great Cookouts occur on the very Selective beaches of the Next Life, it will be their souls that are turning on the long sharp sticks in the fire pit, and ours will be the hands on the spit handles. . . .

. . .

I instructed my attorney to scroll up my personal FBI file the other day, but he laughed and called me a fool. "You will never get your files from those swine," he said. "We can ask, we can beg, we can demand and file civil suits—but they will *never* tell you what they have on you—and in your case, Doc, that shit will be so huge and so frightening that we don't want to see it. The cost would be astronomical."

"Of course," I said quickly. "Thank you for warning me. I must have been out of my mind to mention it."

"Yeah," he replied, "figure at least a million dollars—about what you'd pay for a nice house in New Orleans or two rounds of golf with Tiger Woods."

"Shit on it," I said. "Never mind the FBI. Who else is after me?"

"Nobody," he said. "I can't understand it. This is a dangerous time to get busted. You should knock on wood and enjoy it while it lasts."

"Yes," I replied. "That's why we're going to Africa next month. It is time to get out of this country while we still can!"

"We?" said the lawyer. "Just exactly who is 'we,' Doc? As your attorney, I know not *we*."

"You evil bastard," I said. "Don't worry, I understand the attorney-client relationship. Nobody will ever accuse *you* of Terrorism, will they? I think it's about time some of you bastards got locked up, counselor. That's what *we* means."

He fell silent. It is always wise to have yr. lawyer under control—lest he flee & leave you to sink all alone.

## Lynching in Denver

*First they came for the Jews*
*and I did not speak out—*
*because I was not a Jew.*

*Then they came for the communists*
*and I did not speak out—*
*because I was not a communist.*

*Then they came for the trade*
*unionists and I did not speak out—*
*because I was not a trade unionist.*

*Then they came for me—*
*and there was no one left*
*to speak out for me.*

—Pastor Niemoeller (victim of the Nazis)

## GUILT BY ASSOCIATION AT HEART OF AUMAN CASE
### BY KAREN ABBOTT, *NEWS* STAFF WRITER
### *ROCKY MOUNTAIN NEWS*, APRIL 29, 2002

Colorado's Lisl Auman has one thing in common with the man federal agents say was the 20th hijacker on Sept. 11. They were in custody when others committed the spectacular crimes that got them in the worst trouble of their lives.

Auman was handcuffed in the back of a police car when a man she had known less than a day shot Denver police officer Bruce Vander-Jagt dead in 1997, but she was convicted of the murder and sentenced to life in prison.

Zacarias Moussaoui, a French citizen of Moroccan descent, was in jail last year on immigration violations when others committed the Sept. 11 terrorist attacks for which federal prosecutors want Moussaoui executed.

He's still in jail, awaiting a federal trial in Virginia on charges of conspiring to bring about the attacks that killed thousands.

Auman, 26, is behind bars in a state prison while she appeals her conviction in a case that also has attracted nationwide attention. The Colorado Court of Appeals will hear oral arguments in her case Tuesday.

Moussaoui is not a sympathetic figure in most American minds, but Auman may be.

"The instinctive reaction to the Lisl Auman case is, 'That's not fair,'" said Denver attorney David Lane.

Defense lawyers say both Auman and Moussaoui have been unfairly targeted by authorities eager to punish someone for heinous crimes committed by others who put themselves beyond the reach of the law by dying.

The 19 known hijackers died when the four planes they commandeered hit the World Trade Center towers and Pentagon and crashed in a field in Pennsylvania.

VanderJagt's murderer, Matthaeus Jaehnig, immediately killed himself with the officer's gun.

Both Auman and Moussaoui exemplify a long-standing principle of American law: You don't have to pull the trigger, hijack the plane, be nearby, or even intend to kill someone to face the toughest penalties.

"The theory is that even though you're not a hands-on operative, you're still as culpable as the perpetrator," said Denver defense attorney Phil Cherner, president of the Colorado Criminal Defense Bar.

A Denver jury convicted Auman of "felony murder"—a murder committed during another serious crime or the immediate flight afterward—on the legal theory that she was responsible for VanderJagt's death because she earlier had arranged a burglary.

Auman enlisted Jaehnig's help in burglarizing her ex-boyfriend's apartment in Pine. When the police showed up, the two fled by car. The police chased them to Denver, where they took Auman into custody. But Jaehnig escaped on foot and shot VanderJagt while Auman sat handcuffed in a police cruiser.

Defense lawyers nationwide see Auman's case as their chance to challenge the felony murder statutes under which people who didn't expect anyone to be killed, and weren't present when they were, have been condemned to death.

"The felony murder doctrine is extremely harsh and frequently unjust," Lane said.

The National Association of Criminal Defense Lawyers has filed a brief on Auman's side. The Colorado District Attorneys Council has filed one supporting the government.

"What we are concerned with is the integrity of the felony murder statute statewide," said Peter Weir, the council's executive director.

He said the established public policy in Colorado is that "it's appropriate for an individual to be fully accountable for the consequences of all acts that they engage in."

"Once the acts are set in motion, you're responsible for what happens," Weir said.

An unusual assortment of supporters has gathered in Auman's cause, from "gonzo" journalist Hunter Thompson to conservative U.S. Senate candidate Rick Stanley to one of the jurors who convicted her.

. . .

Peacocks don't move around much at night. They like a high place to roost, and they will usually find one before sundown. They know how many nocturnal beasts are down there looking for food—foxes, coyotes, wildcats, bloodthirsty dogs on the prowl—and the only animal that can get them when they're perched up high is one of those huge meat-eating owls with night vision that can swoop down & pounce on anything that moves, from a water rat to a healthy young sheep.

My own peacocks wander widely during the day, but at night they come back into their own warm cage. Every once in a while they will miss curfew & decide to roost in a tree or on top of a telephone pole—(and that is what happened last week).

It was not a Lightning ball that blacked out my house, but a male peacock that stepped on a power line & caused a short circuit that burned him to a cinder & blew half my Electrics. The power came back, but the bird did not. It was fried like a ball of bacon. We couldn't even eat it. That tragedy occurred at halftime—so let the record stand corrected. Sorry.

I have consulted with many lawyers on the Lisl Auman case—which gets uglier every time I look at it. I don't do this very often—Never, in fact—but this case is such an outrage that it haunts me & gives me bad dreams at night. I am not a Criminal Lawyer, but I have what might be called "a very strong background" in the Criminal Justice System & many of my friends & associates are widely known as the best legal minds in that cruel & deadly business.

It is no place for amateurs, and even seasoned professionals can make mistakes that are often fatal. The System can grind up the Innocent as well as the Guilty, and that is what I believe happened to 20-

year-old Lisl Auman, who was unjustly found guilty of murder and sent to prison for the rest of her Life Without Parole.

In all my experience with courts & crimes & downright evil behavior by the Law & the Sometimes criminal cops who enforce it, this is the worst & most reprehensible miscarriage of "Justice" I've ever encountered—and that covers a lot of rotten things, including a few close calls of my own. Which might easily have gone the other way if not for the help of some hammerhead Lawyers who came to my aid when I was in desperate trouble.

I learned a lot about Karma in those moments, and one thing that sticks with me is a quote from Edmund Burke that says: "THE ONLY THING NECESSARY FOR THE TRIUMPH OF EVIL IS FOR GOOD MEN TO DO NOTHING."

That is what got me into the Lisl Auman case, and that is why I will stay in it until this brutal Wrong is Righted. That is also why the first contribution to the Lisl Auman Defense Fund came from Gerald Lefcourt of New York, then the President of the National Association of Criminal Defense Lawyers. "This is not going to be easy," he said with a wry smile. "But what the hell—count me in."

Indeed. It is no small trick to get a "Convicted cop killer" out of prison—but it will be a little easier in this case, because Lisl no more killed a cop than I did. She was handcuffed in the backseat of a Denver Police car when the cop was murdered in cold blood by a vicious skinhead who then allegedly shot himself in the head & left the D.A. with nobody to punish for the murder—except Lisl.

*February 5, 2001*

## The Felony Murder Law—Don't Let This Happen to You

I don't think that people across the board necessarily identify with Lisl Auman as much as, God help them, they might identify with me. I've often frankly thought that Lisl's case is possibly the worst case I've ever decided to get involved in. We've got a convicted cop killer—Help. It doesn't matter who she is.

The few real facts in the case that were, and have been, and remain, evident—as opposed to the avalanche of hate-crime propaganda and "Off the Skinheads" hysteria that came with the conviction . . . along with the clear violations in the court record, and the police procedures at the time of the crime—are this: Somebody got killed. We know that. Two people came out of there dead. Beyond the vicious political circumstances surrounding Lisl's case, we've got the vicious skinhead, Matthaeus Jaehnig, and the cop, Bruce VanderJagt, and Lisl, the supposed perpetrator. . . .

We may have to go outside the characteristics of the city of Denver for this. The points of the law that are going to be decided, once again, however vaguely, in this appeal hearing—and hopefully the retrial—are overwhelmingly odious and spurious. There was a carelessness in the way this case was handled that led us to a witchbag of strange problems within the law-enforcement system. We have the effective abuse of Lisl's rights—but they were abused not by the cops necessarily, who were part of it; her rights were abused by all parties in the system. Lisl's end of the case was taken very lightly: President Clinton was actively campaigning against cop-killing at the time; then his Hate Crimes bill passed in Congress, and the Denver police were understandably up in arms about the death of one of their own.

But we want to remember that two people came out of this thing dead, and there was no real explanation for it during the legal process, in Lisl's first trial. That leaves critical questions: It's not even known exactly *who* shot Officer VanderJagt and who shot Matthaeus, who was an over-the-line thug—I'm not convinced that he shot himself. Questions remain about Who Did What during this encounter, this weird encounter, which should not have happened, basically, because Matthaeus had a rap sheet as long as his arm; he should have been shot yesterday. "I should have killed you a long time ago"—is it a case like that? If the cops had paid any attention to the dangers of the streets instead of weird chickenshit complaints, Lisl might not be in jail. The actions and behavior of the police in this berserk episode involving forty or fifty officers at one time were not examined—even the crime scene itself has never been developed. At least it has never been tested in any kind of court, because Lisl's confession to a lesser crime is what avoided any examination of the case. This thing was guided through the system so that there *was* no examination. I'm not calling for an investigation—though I could, and I might. I am calling for a retrial.

The proper workings—and I say "proper" in the sense that it's almost religiously vital to all of us—within the law-enforcement system, the judicial system, the court system, the system of right and wrong, who is responsible, that system has to function for all of us, because anybody could get involved in it at any time. A simple traffic ticket you don't even know about if you run a red light and there's a camera on you could get you into that system, and sometimes the system doesn't work . . . and if it doesn't, then everybody suffers—even Matthaeus and VanderJagt. Even me, or the publisher of *The Denver Post*, Dean Singleton—he and his family might suffer from the failure of the American judicial system to work as it should have, and as it was set up. With the way it's working now—the way it's dysfunctioning now—we're in serious trouble.

Surrounded by a public and political atmosphere that supports the U.S.A. Patriot Act, the Lisl case suddenly stands up as a classic example of the one that fell through the cracks, or the one that was too awkward at the time to confront. A case of a college student who got mixed up with the wrong crowd, who was a good, orderly middle-class girl until—well, Lisl Auman was an anonymous person, and will remain so. Yet the question of her guilt or innocence is indelible. How could she be guilty of a crime that would put her in state prison for the rest of her life without parole, when she was locked up and handcuffed in the back of a police car at the time the murder was committed?

And that gets us into *attenuation*. This is clearly a crime that this woman didn't commit, a crime that any one of you might be guilty of, every time you drive to a 7-Eleven, say, and the person next to you in the car—a friend perhaps, wife, lover, stranger—gets out of the car and says, "Okay, I'll run right in and get it. We've had a hard day and night with this goddamn legal stuff, I'm about to flip, we're under terrible pressure, so I'll go in and get us some more beer. I just wish they had a lot of gin in here, man, I feel like drinking gin."

That's what you're dealing with: the kind of everyday attitude of a good friend, or a stranger, who gets out of your car and goes into a 7-Eleven store. It's 11:30 at night, and you have a long night's worrying ahead of you about some matter, maybe an addiction, who knows, but you're not solving it, and your friend—say, Curtis—well, you can see he's been agitated for a while about something, maybe everything, things are not going his way or necessarily yours, so he gets out of the car and you give him some money. Curtis says, "Oh, never mind, I have some," but he takes your twenty anyway and gets out of the car, walking just like a normal person going into a 7-Eleven store on Christmas Eve, just part of the big American buying system. He goes inside and, let's say, we add to Curtis's life the fact that his sister, many years ago, married a Korean man, and that over the years Curtis has developed some *issues*—we may not want to revisit that story right now, so let's just say that the marriage between the Korean gentleman and Curtis's sister did not bear fruit, and in fact Curtis has hated Koreans ever since. (This guy who married his sister once belted him in the side of the head.)

So Curtis gets out of your car, and you're relaxing, reading the paper; he's being an old friend journalist who's pissed off and has this tic about Koreans. He goes inside this 7-Eleven store, and there's a Korean behind the counter. All Curtis wants is some beer, and he's already pissed off that it's only 3.2 beer anyway, it's not real beer, and now he's looking for the one thing he wants: He's thinking that maybe there's something in here that might have some alcohol, or, you know, *don't they have any gin?* So he asks the Korean guy that: "Don't you have any gin, Sport? Bubba?" And the guy says, "Gin? You want me to call the police? What do you mean? Of course I don't have any gin. What do you want? Get out of here."

Curtis—who just happens to have gotten his permit two weeks ago from the local sheriff to carry a concealed weapon—is packing a 10-millimeter Glock, a very powerful handgun; it's a little hotter than the 9, it takes a bigger bullet and it packs a punch, but it's the same-looking gun; and he's been getting comfortable with it for a while. He may have pulled it on some Arab who he thinks may have been looking at his car too long in an underground garage, and when he pulled it, the guy fled, so he has confidence in it. And the Korean man behind the counter is suddenly extremely rude to him, and his mind dissolves into his sister . . .

You'd once shared something with Curtis that your father had explained to you in a moment of curiosity: You had asked him, "What's the difference between a Korean, a Japanese, and a Chinese person?" It was during the Korean War, and you wondered why the Koreans were fighting—you didn't know who they were, or what the difference was. And your father said, "Son, let me put it this way: The Japanese are clean on the outside and dirty on the inside; and the Chinese are dirty on the outside but clean on the inside. But Son, I really hate to tell you this, the Koreans are dirty *on both sides*." You've spoken to Curtis about this—it puts him into kind of a flare—so you can identify with what happens when Curtis goes in there and gets fucked with by a foul-mouthed, apparently speeded-up, wiggy Korean. . . . And then the guy refuses his credit card; he says it's not magnetic. You know, *This doesn't say shit; this doesn't ring my bell.* So, he can't get the beer.

You know how Curtis is, with that redheaded temper spiral he gets into, where suddenly he goes from first floor to seventh floor, when you're still going to floor two and you forget, talking to him, that he's already spiraled up to seven. . . . So Curtis forgets about the money you gave him. He figures, *Fuck This;* he doesn't really even think. The guy has pushed him in areas he's unfamiliar with—and with his temper he gets properly angry. Let's say the guy threatens him: "What are you going to do about it, Fat Man?" (I had a cop do that to me once, in Mobile: "Go back and sit down, Old Man." That was when I was forty years old.) And here's Curtis: His mind is on this frog-eyed Korean who hit his sister, beat her repeatedly, destroyed her beautiful life that Curtis was once morbidly in love and involved with, and he has every flare that's possible sitting right there in that hot box on a Saturday afternoon in the sun. And BANG! He goes—as we all do from time to time, we lose it—and it's his muscle memory operating now, he's done this enough, he's slapped leather, and he jerks the Glock out of his belt and points it at the guy; and then he senses some menace from the back of the store. Somebody else—an extremely large guy, the guy's brother, his cousin—comes out of the back and the guy says, "Come here and help me get this bastard, this fat bastard."

Curtis is suddenly aware of what appears to be two or three more attackers, maybe one, maybe a friend in the aisles, some movement behind him—he feels threatened by more than this one foulmouthed bastard—and due to his self-defense instincts, he sees himself surrounded. So Curtis shoots the guy in front of him, in order to teach the attackers a lesson, and sure enough, they swing away. Then the guy makes a lunge at him, so Curtis pops him two more times. Not quite the best judgment. Since the beer is on the counter in front of him, and he was trying to pay for it with a credit card, let's say Curtis leaves his card and takes the beer—that's the kind of thing that could happen, even in our professional journalism ranks.

You hear the shots, but you don't really hear them; you're listening to the radio. You aren't watching in there, necessarily; let's say a cop car had pulled into the far side of the parking lot where the light didn't reach, and you're aware of that. You think, *Hmm, a cop, where's Curtis,* and you look up just in time to see him kind of scurrying back, not galloping or fleeing, but in a hurry back to the car with a six-pack in his hand. He hurriedly jumps in, and he tells you, "Get out of here, man." And you say, "What happened, what's wrong?" He says, "Never mind, just get out of here, get out of here." You mention the cops at the other end of the 7-Eleven parking lot, and that really freaks him out. The next time you have a thought you're three or four blocks away. And Curtis is trembling, and then you start to tremble too, because you have a right to, because the next thing he's going to tell you is "I think I shot that guy; I shot that guy. Goddamn that bastard, they attacked me in there, I had to shoot."

And you're starting to think, *Whoops. Uh-oh. Say what? Oh my God.* Because you are then almost certain to go to prison for Murder One. In the state of Colorado, the state of California, and most others, attenuation involves the felony murder law. You are an accessory, you're held liable for the crime of your friend, you're a conspirator—and conspirators, under that law, go to death, or to jail forever. Murder One. So does that describe, more or less, our situation?

(to be continued)

## Jesus Hated Bald Pussy

Let's face it—the yo-yo president of the U.S.A. knows *nothing*. He is a *dunce*. He does what he is *told* to do—says what he is *told* to say—poses the way he is *told* to pose. He is a *Fool*.

This is never an *easy* thing for the voters of this country to accept.

No. Nonsense. The president cannot be a Fool. Not at this moment in time—when the last living vestiges of the American Dream are on the line. This is not the time to have a *bogus rich kid* in charge of the White House.

Which is, after all, *our* house. That is our headquarters—it is where the heart of America lives. So if the president lies and acts giddy about other people's lives—if he wantonly and stupidly endorses *mass murder* as a logical plan to make sure we are still Number One—he is a Jackass by definition—a loud and meaningless animal with no functional intelligence and no balls.

To say that this goofy child president is looking more and more like Richard Nixon in the summer of 1974 would be a flagrant insult to Nixon.

Whoops! Did I *say* that? Is it even vaguely possible that some New Age Republican *whore-beast* of a false president could actually make Richard Nixon look like a Liberal?

The capacity of these vicious assholes *we* elected to be in charge of our lives for four years to commit terminal damage to our lives and our souls and our loved ones is far beyond Nixon's. Shit! Nixon was the *creator* of many of the once-proud historical landmarks that these dumb bastards are savagely *destroying* now: the Clean Air Act of 1970; Campaign Finance Reform; the endangered species act; opening a Real-Politik dialogue with China; and on and on.

The prevailing quality of life in America—by *any* accepted methods of measuring—was inarguably freer and more politically *open* under Nixon than it is today in this evil year of Our Lord 2002.

The Boss was a certified monster who deserved to be impeached and banished. He was a truthless creature of former FBI Director J. Edgar Hoover—a foul human monument to corruption and depravity on a scale that dwarfs any other public official in American history. But Nixon was at least smart enough to understand why so many honorable patriotic U.S. citizens despised him. He was a *Liar*. The truth was not in him.

Nixon believed—as he said many times—that if the president of the United States does it, it *can't* be illegal. But Nixon never understood the much higher and meaner truth of Bob Dylan's warning that "To live outside the law you must be honest."

The difference between an *outlaw* and a war criminal is the difference between a pedophile and a Pederast: The pedophile is a person who thinks about sexual behavior with children, and the Pederast *does* these things. He lays hands on innocent children—he penetrates them and changes their lives forever.

Being the object of a pedophile's warped affections is a Routine feature of growing up in America—and being a victim of a Pederast's crazed "love" is part of dying. Innocence is no longer an option. Once penetrated, the child becomes a Queer in his own mind, and that is not much different than *murder*.

Richard Nixon crossed that line when he began murdering foreigners in the name of "family values"—and George Bush crossed it when he sneaked into office and began killing brown-skinned children in the name of Jesus and the American people.

When Muhammad Ali declined to be drafted and forced to kill "gooks" in Vietnam he said, "I ain't got nothin' against them Viet Cong. No Cong ever called me *Nigger*."

I agreed with him, according to my own personal ethics and values. He was *Right*.

If we all had a dash of Muhammad Ali's eloquent courage, this country and the world would be a better place today because of it.

Okay. That's it for now. Read it and weep. . . . See you tomorrow, folks. You haven't heard the last of me. I am the one who speaks for the spirit of freedom and decency in you. Shit. *Somebody* has to do it.

We have become a Nazi monster in the eyes of the whole world—a nation of bullies and bastards who would rather kill than live peacefully. We are not just Whores for power and oil, but killer whores with hate and fear in our hearts. We are human scum, and that is how history will judge us. . . . No redeeming social value. Just whores. Get out of our way, or we'll kill you.

Well, shit on that dumbness. George W. Bush does not speak for me or my son or my mother or my friends or the people I respect in this world. We didn't vote for these cheap, greedy little killers who speak for America today—and we will not vote for them again in 2002. Or 2004. Or *ever*.

Who *does* vote for these dishonest shitheads? Who among us can be happy and proud of having all this innocent blood on our hands? Who are these swine? These flag-sucking half-wits who get fleeced and fooled by stupid little rich kids like George Bush?

They are the same ones who wanted to have Muhammad Ali locked up for refusing to kill gooks. They speak for all that is cruel and stupid and vicious in the American character. They are the racists and hate mongers among us—they are the Ku Klux Klan. I piss down the throats of these Nazis.

And I am too old to worry about whether they like it or not. Fuck them.

*HST, 2002*

# PART TWO

The artist at work, with Deborah, in the kitchen, 1994
(Paul Chesley)

# Politics Is the Art of Controlling Your Environment

*I know my own nation best. That's why I despise it the most.*
*And I know and love my own people too, the swine. I'm a*
*patriot. A dangerous man.*

—Edward Abbey

## Running for Sheriff: Aspen 1970

On Wednesday night, seven days before the 1970 sheriff's election, we hunkered down at Owl Farm and sealed the place off. From the road the house looked stone dark. The driveway was blocked at one end of the circle by Noonan's Jeep, and at the other end by a blue Chevy van with Wisconsin plates. The only possible approach was on foot: You could park on the road, climb a short hill, and cross the long front yard in the glare of a huge floodlight . . . or come creeping down from behind, off either one of the two mesas that separate the house from the five-million-acre White River National Forest.

But only a fool or a lunatic would have tried to approach the place quietly from any direction at all . . . because the house was a virtual fortress, surrounded by armed crazies. Somewhere off to the left, in a dry irrigation ditch about two hundred yards beyond the volleyball court, was Big Ed Bastian, a onetime basketball star at the University of Iowa . . . limping around in the frozen darkness with a 12-gauge pump shotgun, a portable spotlight, and a .38 Special tucked into his belt. Big Ed, our long-suffering campaign coordinator, was growing progressively weaker from the ravages of his new macrobiotic diet. On top of that, he had recently snapped one of the bones in his left foot while forcing his legs into the lotus position, and now he was wearing a cast. The temperature at midnight was 12 above zero and sinking fast. There was no moon.

On the other side of the house Mike Solheim, my campaign manager, was patrolling the western perimeter with a double-barreled 12-gauge Beretta and a .357 Colt Python Magnum. We suspected that Solheim was probably turning on very heavily out there—caving in to the Vietnam-sentry madness—and we were vaguely concerned that he might get wiggy and blow Bastian's head off if they happened to cross paths in the darkness.

But they weren't moving around much despite the bitter cold. From the spots they'd selected they were both perfectly positioned to deal not only with the threat from the rear or either side of the house, but also to catch anyone approaching from the front in a deadly cross fire of 00-buckshot . . . thus tripling the terror for any poor bastard coming up from the road and straight into the muzzle of Teddy Yewer's 30-30.

Teddy, a wild young biker with hair hanging down to his waist, had driven out from Madison to have some fun with the Freak Power sheriff's campaign . . . and he'd arrived just in time to get himself drafted into the totally humorless role of 24-hour bodyguard. Now, with the original concept of the campaign long gone and forgotten in this frenzy of violence, he found himself doing dead-serious guard duty behind a big window in the darkened living room, perched in the Catbird seat with a rifle in his hands and a fine commanding view of anything that could possibly happen within one hundred yards of the front porch. He couldn't see Solheim or Bastian, but he knew they were out there, and he knew that all three of them would have to start shooting if the things we'd been warned about suddenly began happening.

The word had come that afternoon from the Colorado Bureau of Investigation (CBI), and the word was extremely grim. Tonight—sometime between dusk on Wednesday and dawn on Thursday—Mr. Thompson, the Freak Power candidate for sheriff, was going to be killed. This intelligence had come from what the CBI investigator described as "an extremely reliable informant," a person they had every good reason to believe because he (or maybe she; we weren't told) had "always been right in the past." The informant had not been able to learn the identity of the assassins, the CBI man told us. Nor had he/she been able to learn what means or methods they planned to use on this job. Shooting was of course the most logical thing to expect, he said. Maybe an ambush at some lonely spot on the road between Aspen and Woody Creek. And if that failed . . . well, it was widely known that the candidate lived in a dangerously isolated house far out in the boondocks. So perhaps they would strike out there, by fire . . . or dynamite.

Indeed. Dynamite. RDX-type, 90 percent nitroglycerine. Two hundred and ten sticks of it had been stolen just a few days earlier from an Aspen Ski Corp. cache on Ajax Mountain—according to a report from the Ski Corp.—and the thieves left a note saying, "This [stolen dynamite] will only be used if Hunter Thompson is elected sheriff of Aspen." The note was signed "SDS."

Right. Some ignorant dingbat actually signed the note "SDS." The CBI man hadn't smiled when we laughed at the tale: He quickly unfolded another sheet of notes and told us that his "reliable informant" had also told him that half the town was about to be destroyed by dynamite—the County Courthouse (meaning the Sheriff's Office), City Hall (the Police Station), the Hotel Jerome (our campaign headquarters), and the Wheeler Opera House (where Joe Edwards and Dwight Shellman, our attorneys, had their offices).

Only a cop's brain could have churned up that mix of silly bullshit . . . and although we never doubted that, we also understood that the same warped mentality might also be capable of running that kind of twisted act all the way out to its brutally illogical extreme. It made perfect sense, we felt, to assume that anybody stupid enough to spread these crudely conceived rumors was also stupid enough to try to justify them by actually dynamiting something.

At that point in the campaign it was still a three-way race between me, the incumbent (Democratic) sheriff, and the veteran undersheriff who'd resigned just in time to win the GOP primary (over the former city police chief) and emerge as a strong challenger to his former boss—first-term sheriff Carrol Whitmire, a devious, half-bright small-town cop whose four years in office had earned him a reservoir of contempt and neo–public loathing on the part of the local Bar Association, the District Attorney, his own Undersheriff and former deputies, the entire City of Aspen police force and everybody else unlucky enough to have had any dealings with him.

When the campaign began, Whitmire had virtually no support from the people who knew him best: the county commissioners, the former mayor, the city manager, the ex-D.A., and especially his former employees. He spent the first two weeks of the conflict beseeching both the CBI and the FBI to turn up at least one recorded felony conviction on me . . . and when that effort failed, because I have no criminal record, the evil bastard brought in undercover federal agents to try to provoke both me and my campaign workers into felony violence that would have given him an excuse to bust us before the election.

At one point he hired a phony outlaw biker from Denver—Jim Bromley, a veteran of two years of undercover work for the feds—who boomed into town one day on a junk chopper and first threatened to dynamite my house if I didn't drop out of the race at once . . . then apologized for the threat—when it failed—and tried to hire on as my bodyguard . . . then spread rumors that people on my staff were in touch with Kathy Powers and a gang of Weathermen who planned to blow all the bridges into town . . . then tried to sell us automatic weapons . . . then offered to stomp the shit out of anybody we aimed him at . . . then got himself busted, by accident, when the city cops found a completely illegal sawed-off 20-gauge pump action shotgun in his car—which they happened to tow away from a no-parking zone.

The sheriff panicked at that point and blew Bromley's cover by instructing the city cops to give his illegal weapon back to him because he was a "federal agent." This was done. But instead of leaving town, Bromley came back to our headquarters—unaware that a friendly city cop had already tipped us off—and hung around offering to run the mimeograph machine or anything else we needed done. Meanwhile, we were trying to compel the assistant D.A. to have the bastard arrested on charges ranging from felony conspiracy to threatening the life of a political candidate to carrying an illegal weapon—and offering to wreak violence on innocent people—but the assistant D.A. refused to act, denying all knowledge of the man or his motives, until the sheriff unexpectedly admitted that Bromley was actually working for him.

Meanwhile, Bromley had once again lost his sawed-off shotgun—this time to a city cop who went out to his motel room at the Applejack Inn to seize the weapon for the second time in 36 hours, after a desk clerk we'd assigned to get a photo of Bromley called us to say that one of the maids had found a "vicious-looking gun" in his room. . . . But even then the D.A.'s office refused to move, not even to pick up the shotgun again. So we had to send a cop out on our own—Rick Crabtree, a dropout English major from Columbia—and even after Crabtree seized the weapon, the D.A.'s office snarled petulantly at our demands that Bromley be picked up and booked. He'd returned to the Applejack with a girl, they said, and they didn't want to disturb him until morning.

This was too much for the frustrated crew of Left-bikers, Black Belts, White Panthers, and assorted local heavies who'd been calling for open season on Bromley ever since he showed up. They wanted to soak him down with Mace, then beat him to jelly with baseball bats . . . and they didn't give a flying fuck if he was a federal agent or not. I was still on the phone with the assistant D.A. when I noticed the room emptying around me. "We're on our way to the Applejack," somebody yelled from the doorway. "You can tell that chickenshit pig of a district attorney that we decided to make a citizen's arrest . . . and we'll dump his fink at the jail in about thirty minutes, in a plastic bag."

I translated this to the D.A. . . . and thirty minutes later Bromley was moving down the highway in a rented car. He left so fast that we couldn't even get a good snapshot of him, so the next morning we called the "White Panther photo agency" in Denver, and they assigned a young, harmless-looking Black Belt to go out to Bromley's suburban home with a camera. Paul Davidson got the picture we needed by knocking on the agent's door and saying that he was so impressed with the wonderful chopper outside that he just had to get a shot of it—along with the proud owner. So Bromley—ever alert—posed for the photo, which ran a day later in the *Aspen Times* along with a detailed exposé of his brief but hyperactive flirtation with the local Freak Power movement. We sent Bromley a copy of the published photo/story . . . and he responded almost instantly by mailing me a threatening letter and another, very personal, photo of himself that he said was a hell of a lot better than the one our "funny little photographer" had conned him out of. Even the CBI man was stunned at this evidence of total lunacy on the part of a veteran undercover agent. "This is hard to believe," he kept saying. "He actually signed his name: He even signed the photograph! How could they hire a person like this?"

How indeed?

(Paul Harris)

. . .

The story began in 1968, when Random House gave me $5,000 and my editor there said, "Go out and write about 'The Death of the American Dream.'" I had agreed without thinking, because all I really cared about, back then, was the money. And along with the $5K in front money came a $7,500 "expenses budget"—against royalties, which meant I'd be paying my own expenses, but I didn't give a fuck about that either. It was a nice gig to get into: Random House had agreed, more or less, to finance my education. I could go just about anywhere I wanted to just as long as I could somehow tie it in with "The Death of the American Dream."

It looked easy, a straight-out boondoggle, and for a long time I treated it that way. It was like being given a credit card that you eventually have to pay off, but not now. I remember thinking that Jim Silberman, the editor, was not only crazy but severely irresponsible. Why else would he make that kind of deal?

I went a few places for reasons that I can't even recall now, and then I went to Chicago in August of 1968, on my Random House tab with a packet of the finest, blue-chip press credentials—issued by the Democratic National Committee—for the purpose of covering the Convention.

I had no real reason for going—not even a magazine assignment; I just wanted to *be there* and get the feel of things. The town was so full of journalists that I felt like a tourist . . . and the fact that I had heavier credentials than most of the working writers & reporters I met left me vaguely embarrassed. But it never occurred to me to seek an assignment—although if anybody had asked me, I'd have done the whole story for nothing.

Now, years later, I still have trouble when I think about Chicago. That week at the Convention changed everything I'd ever taken for granted about this country and my place in it. I went from a state of Cold Shock on Monday, to Fear on Tuesday, then Rage, and finally Hysteria—which lasted for nearly a month. Every time I tried to tell somebody what happened in Chicago I began crying, and it took me years to understand why.

I wasn't beaten; I spent no time in jail. But neither of these things would have had much effect on me, anyway. It takes a real expert (or experts) to beat a person badly without putting him into a state of shock that makes the beating meaningless until later . . . and getting dragged into jail with a bunch of friends is more a strange high than a trauma; indeed, there is something vaguely dishonorable in having lived through the Sixties without having spent time in jail.

Chicago was the end of the Sixties, for me. I remember going back to my room at the Blackstone, across the street from the Hilton, and sitting cross-legged on my bed for hours at a time. Trembling, unable to make any notes, staring at the TV set while my head kept whirling out of focus from the things I'd seen happen all around me . . . and I could watch it all happening again, on TV; see myself running in stark terror across Michigan Drive, on camera, always two steps ahead of the nearest club-swinging cop and knowing that at any instant my lungs would be shredded by some bullet that would hit me before I could even hear the shot fired.

I was standing at the corner of Michigan and Balboa on Wednesday night when the cops attacked . . . and I remember thinking: No. This can't be happening. I flattened myself back against a wall of the Blackstone and fished a motorcycle helmet out of my friendly blue L.L. Bean kit bag . . . and also the yellow ski goggles, thinking there would probably be Mace, or at least gas . . . but that was the only time they didn't use any.

On Wednesday evening they used clubs, and it was a king-hell bitch of a show. I stood against the wall, trying to put my helmet on while people ran past me like a cattle stampede. The ones who weren't screaming were bleeding, and some were being dragged. I have never been caught in an earthquake, but I'm sure the feeling would be just about the same. Total panic and disbelief—with no escape. The first wave of cops came down Balboa at a trot and hit the crowd in the form of a flying wedge, scattering people in all directions like fire on an anthill . . . but no matter which way they ran, there were more cops. The second wave came across Grant Park like a big threshing machine, a wave of long black truncheons meeting people fleeing hysterically from the big bash at the intersection.

Others tried to flee down Balboa, toward State Street, but there was no escape in that direction, either—just another wave of cops closing off the whole street in a nicely planned pincer movement and beating the mortal shit out of anybody they could reach. The protesters tried to hold their lines, calling back and forth to one another as they ran away: "Stay together! Stay together!"

I found myself in the middle of the pincers, with no place to run except back into the Blackstone. But the two cops at the door refused to let me in. They were holding their clubs out in front of them with both hands, keeping everybody away from the door.

By this time I could see people getting brutalized within six feet of me on both sides. It was only a matter of seconds before I went under . . . so I finally just ran between the truncheons, screaming, "I live here, goddamnit! I'm paying fifty dollars a day!" By the time they whacked me against the door I was out of range of what was happening on the sidewalk . . . and by some kind of wild accidental luck I happened to have my room key in my pocket. Normally I would have left it at the desk before going out, but on this tense night I forgot, and that key was salvation—that, and the mad righteousness that must have vibrated like the screeching of Jesus in everything I said. Because I *did* live there. I was a goddamn *paying guest*! And there was never any doubt in my mind that the stinking blue-uniformed punks had no RIGHT to keep me out.

I believed that, and I was big enough to neutralize one of the truncheons long enough to plunge into the lobby . . . and it was not until several days or even weeks later that I understood that those cops had actually *planned* to have me beaten. Not me, personally, but Me as a member of "The Enemy," that crowd of "outside agitators" made up of people who had come to Chicago on some mission that the cops couldn't grasp except in fear and hatred.

This is what caused me to tremble when I finally sat down behind the locked & chained door of my hotel room. It was not a fear of being beaten or jailed, but the slow-rising shock of suddenly understanding that it was no longer a matter of Explaining my Position. These bastards knew my position, and they wanted to beat me anyway. They didn't give a fuck if the Democratic National Committee had issued me special press credentials; it made no difference to them that I'd come to Chicago as a paying guest—at viciously inflated rates—with no intention of causing the slightest kind of trouble for anybody.

That was the point. My very innocence made me guilty—or at least a potential troublemaker in the eyes of the rotten sold-out scumbags who were running that Convention: Mayor Richard J. Daley of Chicago, Lyndon Baines Johnson, then President of the United States. These pigs didn't care what was Right. All they knew was what they wanted, and they were powerful enough to break anybody who even thought about getting in their way.

Right here, before I forget, I want to make what I think is a critical point about the whole protest action of the 1960s. It seems to me that the underlying assumption of any public protest—any public disagreement with the government, "the system," or "the establishment," by any name—is that the men in charge of whatever you're protesting against are actually listening, whether they later admit it or not, and that if you run your protest Right, it will likely make a difference. Norman Mailer made this point a long time ago when he said that the election of JFK gave him a sense, for the first time in his life, that he could actually communicate with the White House. Even with people like Johnson and Mac Bundy—or even Pat Brown or Bull Connor— the unspoken rationale behind all those heavy public protests was that our noise was getting through and that somebody in power was listening and hearing and at least weighing our protest against their own political realities . . . even if these people refused to talk to us. So in the end the very act of public protest, even violent protest, was essentially optimistic and actually a demonstration of faith (mainly subconscious, I think) in the father figures who had the power to change things—once they could be made to see the light of reason, or even political reality.

This is what the bastards never understood—that the "Movement" was essentially an expression of deep faith in the American Dream: that the people they were "fighting" were not the cruel and cynical beasts they seemed to be, and that in fact they were just a bunch of men like everybody's crusty middle-class fathers who only needed to be shaken a bit, jolted out of their bad habits and away from their lazy, short-term, profit-oriented life stances . . . and that once they understood, they would surely do the right thing.

A Willingness to Argue, however violently, implies a faith of some basic kind in the antagonist, an assumption that he is still open to argument and reason and, if all else fails, then finely orchestrated persuasion in the form of political embarrassment. The 1960s were full of examples of good, powerful men changing their minds on heavy issues: John Kennedy on Cuba and the Bay of Pigs, Martin Luther King Jr. on Vietnam, Gene McCarthy on "working behind the scenes and within the Senate Club," Robert F. Kennedy on grass and long hair and what eventually came to be Freak Power, Ted Kennedy on Francis X. Morrissey, and Senator Sam Ervin on wiretaps and preventive detention.

Anyway, the general political drift of the 1960s was one of the Good Guys winning, slowly but surely (and even clumsily sometimes), over the Bad Guys . . . and the highest example of this was Johnson's incredible abdication on April Fool's Day of 1968. So nobody was ready for what began to happen that summer: first in Chicago, when Johnson ran his Convention like a replay of the Reichstag fire . . . and then with Agnew and Nixon and Mitchell coming into power so full of congenital hostility and so completely deaf to everything we'd been talking about for ten years that it took a while to realize that there was simply no point in yelling at the fuckers. They were born deaf and stupid.

This was the lesson of Chicago—or at least that's what I learned from Chicago, and two years later, running for the office of sheriff, that lesson seemed every bit as clear as it did to me when I got rammed in the stomach with a riot club in Grant Park for showing a cop my press pass. What I learned, in Chicago, was that the police arm of the United States government was capable of hiring vengeful thugs to break the very rules we all thought we were operating under. On Thursday night in the Amphitheatre it was not enough for me to have a press pass from the Democratic National Committee; I was kicked out of my press seat by hired rent-a-cops, and when I protested to the Secret Service men at the door, I was smacked against the wall and searched for weapons. And I realized at that point that, even though I was absolutely right, if I persisted with my righteous complaint, I would probably wind up in jail.

There was no point in appealing to any higher authority, because they were the people who were paying those swine to fuck me around. It was LBJ's party and I was an unwelcome guest, barely tolerated . . . and if I couldn't keep my mouth shut, I would get the same treatment as those poor bastards out on Michigan Avenue, or Wells Street, or Lincoln Park . . . who were gassed and beaten by an army of cops run amok with carte blanche from the Daley-Johnson combine—while

Hubert Humphrey cried from tear gas fumes in his twenty-fifth-floor suite at the Hilton.

A lot of people felt that way after Chicago. And in my case it was more a sense of shock at the sudden understanding that I was on the ground. I went there as a journalist; my candidate had been murdered in Los Angeles two months earlier—but I left Chicago in a state of hysterical angst, convinced by what I'd seen that we were all in very bad trouble . . . and in fact that the whole country was doomed unless somebody, somewhere, could mount a new kind of power to challenge the rotten, high-powered machinery of men like Daley and Johnson. Sitting in a westbound TWA jet on the ramp at O'Hare, waiting for a takeoff slot, it occurred to me that I was suddenly right in the middle of the story I'd been sent out to look for. What had begun as a dilettante's dream was now a very real subject.

That was the way it began. And for the first few weeks of October, the 1970 sheriff's campaign was a colorful, high-powered replay of the previous year's "Joe Edwards for Mayor" uprising, which lost by only six votes. But the secret of our success, that year, was the failure of the local power structure to take us seriously . . . and by the time they understood what was happening to them, they almost croaked. Only a last-minute fraud with the absentee ballots—and our inability to raise $2,000 to challenge that fraud in court—prevented a 29-year-old bike-racing freak from becoming mayor of Aspen. And in the wake of Edwards's loss, we created a completely new kind of power base, the first of its kind anywhere in American politics. It was a strange combination of "Woodstock" vibrations, "New Left" activism, and basic "Jeffersonian Democracy" with strong echoes of the Boston Tea Party ethic. What emerged from the Joe Edwards campaign was a very real blueprint for stomping the Agnew mentality by its own rules—with the vote, instead of the bomb; by seizing their power machinery and using it, instead of merely destroying it.

The national press dug it all—mainly on the basis of a *Rolling Stone* article I wrote about the 1969 election (*Rolling Stone* #67, October 1, 1970) which laid it all out, step by step. My idea, when I wrote it, was to line out the "freak power" concept for massive distribution—with the blueprint and all the details—in the hope that it might be a key to weird political action in other places.

(Michael Montfort)

. . .

So it was hard to know, on that jangled Wednesday night before the sheriff's election, just what the fuck was happening . . . or even what might happen. The local power structure appeared to have gone completely crazy.

There was not much doubt that we had Owl Farm completely fortified. And our rotating "outside triangle of fire" was only the beginning. Behind that, waiting to take their turns outside in the moonless, bitter-cold night, was a whole house of wired-up freaks—all armed to the teeth. The only light visible from the road was the outside flood, but inside—behind shrouded windows in the big wooden kitchen and downstairs in the soundproof, windowless "war room"—a rude mix of people drifted back and forth on the nervous tides of this night: eating, drinking, plotting, rehashing the incredible chain of events that had plunged us into this scene . . . all of us armed, nobody ready to sleep, and none of us really believing that what we were doing was sane. It was all too weird, too unlikely, too much like some acid-bent scriptwriter's dream on a bad night in the Château Marmont . . . some madman's botch of a Final Politics movie.

But it was all insanely real. And we knew that, too. Nobody in the house was stoned or twisted that night. Nobody was drunk. And when it had first become clear, a few hours earlier, that we were headed for a very wild and menacing kind of night, we ran a very discreet sort of staff shakedown and carefully selected the half dozen or so people who seemed capable of dealing with the kind of madness the Colorado Bureau of Investigation had told us we were likely to deal with before dawn.

Clearly we were all doomed. Half the population would never live to vote, and the other half would perish in the inevitable election-night holocaust. When NBC-TV showed up about midway in the campaign, I advised them to stick around. "There'll be a bloodbath if I win," I said, "and a bloodbath if I lose. The carnage will be unbelievable either way; you'll get wonderful footage. . . ."

That was back when we could still laugh about the hideous Freak Power challenge. But now the laughter was finished. The humor went out of the campaign when the Aspen establishment suddenly understood that I looked like a winner. Pitkin County, Colorado, was about to elect the nation's first Mescaline sheriff . . . a foul-mouthed bald-headed freak who refused to compromise on anything at all, even his taste for wild drugs, and who didn't mind saying in public that he intended to hamstring, flay, and cripple every greedy plot the Aspen power structure held dear . . . all their foul hopes and greedy fascist dreams.

. . .

Sometime around midmorning on Election Day the *Life* correspondent rushed into our Hotel Jerome headquarters suite with a big grin on his face and announced that we were sure winners. "I've been out on the streets," he said, "taking my own poll. I must have talked to two hundred people out there—all different types—and all but about two dozen of them said they were going to vote for you." He shook his head, still grinning. "It's incredible, absolutely incredible, but I think it's going to be a landslide." Then he opened a beer and began helping his photographer, who was busy wiring strobe lights to the ceiling, so they could shoot the victory celebration in color.

It was going to be a hell of a story—and especially for *Life* because they had an angle that nobody else could touch. They'd only been in town about 24 hours, but when they arrived at our headquarters on Monday morning they were confronted with a really mind-bending scene. Here was the candidate, the next sheriff of Aspen and indeed all of Pitkin County, Colorado, raving crazily about Armageddon and pounding on a desk with a big leather sap. We had been up all night dealing with a violent personal crisis that would have blown the whole campaign out of the water if we hadn't contained it, and by ten o'clock on Monday we were half hysterical with fatigue, drink, and a general sense of relief that there was nothing else to be done. At least by me: Pierre Landry had the poll-watching teams organized, Bill Noonan was still getting our sample ballots printed, Solheim had a full schedule of radio ads laid out for Monday and Tuesday, and Ed Bastian was putting together a vast telephone network to get the vote out.

That Monday was the first day in a month that I felt able to relax and let my head run—which is precisely what I was doing when the *Life* team walked in and found me laughing about Freak Power and what a fantastic shuck we had run on the liberals. "We'll put those fuckers on trial, starting Wednesday!" I shouted. "Paul, do you have the list? Maybe we should start reading it on the radio today." Paul Davidson grinned. "Yeah, we'll start rounding the bastards up tomorrow night. But we need money for Mace; do you have any?"

"Don't worry," I said. "We have plenty of money—and plenty of mescaline to sell if we need more. Get the Mace—get several gallons, and some double-ought buckshot."

. . .

Within two hours after the polls closed, the Battle of Aspen was over . . . at least that's how it looked at the time, from the eye of the shit rain. Freak Power bombed early that night, and we didn't need an RCA 1060 to project the final result—even after the early returns showed us winning. But not by enough. The early returns came from our hard-core freak strongholds in the middle and east end of town. We won handily in precincts One, Two, and Three, but our voter turnout was too light and the margin it gave us was not nearly enough to overcome the landslide that we knew was about to come down on us from suburban Agnewville and the down-county trailer courts. The backlash vote was kicking in, and the doom message was obvious in the eyes of our poll watchers about halfway through the day. They refused to confirm it, but I think we all knew. . . .

So somewhere around dusk we began loading up on mescaline, tequila, hash, beer, and whatever else we could get our hands on . . . and after that, it was only a matter of fucking with the national press and waiting for the axe to fall. Our elegant Hotel Jerome headquarters was a total madhouse. Everybody in the place seemed to have a long black microphone the size of a baseball bat, and all those without microphones had cameras—Nikons, Nagras, Eclairs, Kodaks, Polaroids, there was even a finely equipped videotape team from the California Institute of Arts.

The floor was a maze of cables, there were strobe lights taped to the ceiling. . . . The photographer from *Life* was muscled out of the way by two CBS thugs from Los Angeles; the chief cameraman on *Woodstock* got ugly with the director of the British TV crew . . . there was constant, savage jostling for camera positions around the phone desk and the fatal blackboard where Alison and Vicky Colvard were putting the numbers together. Bill Kennedy, a writer from *Harper's*, was maintaining his position in front of the telephone desk with a nasty display of elbow tactics summoned up, on instinct, from memories of covering the riot squad in Albany and San Juan.

Writers from *Life, LOOK, Scanlan's, Ski, The Village Voice, Fusion, Rat*—even a Dutch correspondent from *Suck*—moved constantly through the crowd, hassling everybody. The phones jangled with long-distance calls from AP, UPI, the TV networks, and dozens of curious strangers calling from Virginia, Michigan, and Oregon demanding to know the results. One of the best quick descriptions of the chaos came later from Steve Levine, a young columnist for *The Denver Post* who had spent half the day as one of our poll watchers:

"It was madness and sadness and drinking and dope and tears and anger and harsh plaster smiles," he wrote. "Parlor B in the old Jerome was jammed from wall to fading, flowered wall with partisan strugglers, both full freak and moderate freak, and the press from London and L.A., and well-wishers, and many people were rip-smashed and optimistic, but some knew better. . . ."

Indeed . . . and the solemn, smoke-filled hideaway for those who really knew better was room Number One, about two hundred feet down the crowded hallway from the vortex-madness in Parlor B. It was Oscar Acosta's room. He had been there for two weeks, dealing with one crisis after another and rarely sleeping in his complex, triple-pronged role of old friend, bodyguard, and emergency legal advisor to what *The New York Times* called "The most bizarre (political) campaign on the American scene today." But the *Times*man didn't know the half of it; he had come to town early in October, long before the campaign turned so crazy and vicious that *The New York Times* couldn't possibly have told the real story.

By the time Acosta arrived the Aspen political scene looked like some drug-addled Mafia-parody of a gang war scene from *The Godfather*. And a week before the election we actually went to the mattresses. Oscar, a prominent Chicano civil rights lawyer from Los Angeles, stopped in Aspen after a Denver visit with his client Corky Gonzales—the Chicanos' answer to Huey Newton or maybe H. Rap Brown in the old days. In mid-November Corky was scheduled to go on trial in L.A. on dubious charges of "carrying a deadly weapon" during the East Los Angeles riot the previous August, which resulted in the murder of Ruben Salazar by an L.A. County sheriff's deputy. Oscar would be the defense attorney in that trial, but in mid-October he found himself in Colorado with not much else to do, so he decided to stop by his old home in Aspen to see what the Honky/Gabachos were up to . . . and the nightmare scene that he found here seemed to convince him that white middle-class Amerika was truly beyond redemption.

HST and Oscar Acosta on election night in Aspen, November 1970
(Bob Krueger)

. . .

On election night Oscar's small room in the Jerome filled quickly with people—both locals and "outsiders"—who shared his dreary conviction that this Aspen election had serious implications in the context of national politics. From the very beginning it had been a strange and unlikely test case, but toward the end—when it looked like a Radical/Drug candidate might actually win a head-on clash with the Agnew people—the Aspen campaign suddenly assumed national importance as a sort of accidental trial balloon that might, if it worked, be tremendously significant—especially to the angry legions of New Left/Radical types who insisted, on good evidence, that there was no longer any point in trying to achieve anything "within the system."

But obviously, if an essentially Republican town like Aspen could elect a sheriff running on a radical Freak Power platform, then the Vote might still be a viable tool . . . and it might still be possible to alter the mean, fascist drift of this nation without burning it down in the process. This was the strange possibility that had brought Dave Meggyesy out of San Francisco. Meggyesy, a former linebacker for the St. Louis Cardinals, had recently abandoned pro football and plunged into radical politics. . . . The first serialization of his book, *Out of Their League,* was on the newsstands in *LOOK* that week, and he had just come back from a New York gig on *The Dick Cavett Show.* But *LOOK* was a bit too cerebral for the kind of people who voted against us in Aspen; to them, Dave Meggyesy was just another one of those "dirty Communist outsiders that Thompson was importing to take over the town."

It's hard to communicate when they don't speak your language, so Meggyesy reverted to type and signed on as a bodyguard, along with Teddy Yewer, the wild young biker from Madison; Paul Davidson, the Black Belt White Panther from Denver; and Gene Johnson, a super-wiggy ex–painting contractor from Newport Beach . . . all Communists, of course, every one of them on salary from Peking.

These treacherous perverts—and others—were among those who gathered in Oscar's room that night to ponder the wreckage of Amerika's first Freak Power campaign.

. . .

There was certainly no shortage of reasons to explain our defeat. A few were so brutally obvious that there is not much point in listing them except for the record—which is crucial, because the record will also show that, despite these apparently suicidal handicaps, we actually carried the city of Aspen and pulled roughly 44 percent of the vote in the entire county. This was the real shocker. Not that we lost, but that we came so close to winning.

The record will also show that we learned our political lessons pretty well, after coming to grips with the reasons for Joe Edwards's six-vote loss in 1969. Our mistake, of course—which was actually my mistake—was in publishing what we learned in a national magazine that hit the newsstands just in time to become a millstone around our necks in 1970. The local appearance of the October 1, 1970, issue of *Rolling Stone* was a disaster of the first magnitude, for several reasons: 1) because it scared the mortal shit out of our opposition; 2) because it got here just a week or so too late to be effective in our crucial "freak-registration" campaign; and 3) because it outlined our campaign strategy in such fine detail that the enemy was able to use it against us, with hellish effectiveness, all the way to the end.

Among other damaging revelations, the article went into great detail to show that we couldn't possibly win in 1970 unless the Democrats and the Republicans effectively split the "establishment vote," as they had a year earlier. Here is a word-for-word excerpt from "The Battle of Aspen" (*Rolling Stone* #67, October 1, 1970):

> *The root point is that Aspen's political situation is so volatile—as a result of the Joe Edwards campaign—that any Freak Power candidate is now a possible winner.*
>
> *In my case, for instance, I will have to work very hard—and spew out some really heinous ideas during my campaign—to get less than 30 percent of the vote in a three-way. And an underground candidate who really wanted to win could assume, from the start, a working nut of about 40 percent of the electorate—with his chances of victory riding almost entirely on the Backlash Potential: or how much active fear and loathing his candidacy might provoke among the burghers who have controlled local candidates for so long.*

With Sandy, in Aspen
(Bob Krueger)

. . .

So it was no surprise, when it finally became apparent that the Freak Power slate was going to get no less than 40 percent of the vote, to find our local GOP brain trust scrambling to arrange a last-minute emergency compromise with their "archenemies" in the other party. The difference, in Aspen, was like the difference between Nixon and LBJ on the national level: Beyond the personalities and patronage squabbles, there was no real difference at all. Not on the issues.

What happened, however, is that about halfway through the campaign both establishment parties found themselves hawking a local version of the Black Panthers' "theory of the greater fear." As much as they might detest each other personally, they hated "freak power" more—and they agreed that it had to be stopped, by any means necessary.

The unholy agreement they forged, less than 48 hours before the election, was that each party would sacrifice one of its two major candidates (in the sheriff and county commissioner races) so as not to split the vote. This assured massive bipartisan support for both incumbents: Sheriff Carrol Whitmire, a Democrat, and Commissioner J. Sterling Baxter.

The trade-off was effected by a sort of chain-letter telephone campaign on election eve, an effort so frantic that one man, a Republican, got eighteen calls that night telling him that the final word from headquarters was to "split your ticket; we're dumping [GOP sheriff candidate] Ricks and the Democrats are dumping Caudhill."

. . .

What we learned in Aspen was that if you "work within the system," you'd damn well better win—because "the system" has a built-in wipe-out mechanism for dealing with failed challengers.

If the Freak Power brain trust learned anything serious in that election, it was that "working within the system" is merely a lame euphemism for "playing by their rules." Once you do this, and lose—especially in a small town with a voting population of just under 2,500—you're expected to hunker down like a natural gentleman/politician and take your beating, the inevitable consequences of running a failed challenge on a deeply entrenched Power Structure.

Like the laws of Physics, the laws of Politics in America seem based on the notion that every force creates a counterforce of exactly equal strength. Our bizarre voter-registration campaign mobilized a vast number of local "freaks" who had never registered, before, to vote for anything—and many of them said afterward that they would never register again. They insisted all the way to the voting booths that they "hated politics" and especially "politicians."

But the Freak Power platform—and indeed the whole campaign—was so far above and beyond anybody's idea of "politics" that in the end we found most of our strength among people who were proud to call themselves Non-Voters. In a town where no candidate for any public office had ever considered it necessary to pull more than 250 votes, a stone-bald and grossly radical Freak Power candidate for sheriff pulled 1,065 votes in 1970, yet lost by nearly 400 votes.

The Freak Power election so polarized Aspen that we managed, in the end, to frighten up enough Negative/Scare votes to offset our shocking and unprecedented success in mobilizing the "freak" vote. We frightened the bastards so badly that on Election Day they rolled people in wheelchairs—and even on stretchers—into the polling places to vote against us. They brought out people, young and old, who thought "Ike" Eisenhower was still president of the U.S.A. "It was the goddamnedest thing I've ever seen," said one of our poll watchers. "I was out there in Precinct One, where we thought things were cool, and all of a sudden they just rolled over us like a sheep drive. I've never seen so many pickup trucks in my life."

We are still seeing those pickups. And anybody who challenges them had better be ready to die. That's what they told me, over and over again, when I ran for sheriff: That even if I won, I would never live to take office. And when I lost, they instantly got down to making sure that nobody like me could ever run for office again.

With George McGovern in Washington, 1972
(Stuart Bratesman)

## Sunday Night at the Fontainebleau

Sunday night at the Fontainebleau: Hot wind on Collins Avenue. Out in front of the hotel, facing the ocean, teams of armed guards and "police dogs" were patrolling the beach & pool area to make sure nobody sneaked in to feel the water. Not even the guests. It was illegal to use the ocean in Miami Beach at night. The beach itself was technically public property, but the architects of this swinish "hotel row" along what the local Chamber of Commerce called the "Gold Coast" had managed to seal off both the beach and the ocean completely by building the hotels so they formed a sort of Berlin Wall between Collins Avenue and the sea.

There were ways to get through, if you didn't mind climbing a few wire fences and seawalls, or if you knew where to find one of the handful of tiny beach areas the city fathers had quietly designated as "public," but even if you made it down to the beach, you couldn't walk more than 50 or 60 yards in either direction, because the hotels had sealed off their own areas . . . and the "public" areas were little more than rocky strips of sand behind hotel parking lots, maintained as a grudging, token compliance with the law that said hotels had no legal right to fence the public away from the ocean. This was a touchy subject in Miami then, because many of the hotels had already built so close to the high-tide line that their pools and cabanas were on public land, and the last thing they wanted was a lawsuit involving their property lines.

The Doral, for instance—headquarters for both George McGovern and Richard Nixon in that mean "Convention summer" of 1972— had been built so close to the sea that at least half of its beachfront cabanas and probably half of its so-called Olympic-size pool were built on public property. A test case on this question could have precipitated a financial disaster of hellish proportions for the Doral, but the owners were not losing much sleep over it. They had me arrested on four consecutive nights during the Democratic Convention that August for swimming in the pool "after hours." Usually around three or four in the morning.

After the first two days it got to be a ritual. I would appear on the moonlit patio and say hello to the black private cop while I took off my clothes and piled them on a plastic chair near the diving board. Our conversation on the first night was a model for all the others:

"You're not supposed to be out here," the private cop said. "This area is closed at night."

"Why?" I said, sitting down to take off my shoes.

"It's against the law."

"What law?"

"The one they pay me to enforce, goddamnit. The one that says you can't go swimmin' out here at night."

"Well . . ." I said, taking off my watch and stuffing it into one of my crusty white basketball shoes. . . . "What happens if I just jump into the pool and swim, anyway?"

"You gonna do that?"

"Yeah," I replied. "I'm sorry to hassle you, but it's necessary. My nerves are all twisted up, and the only way I can relax is by coming out here by myself and swimming laps."

He shook his head sadly. "Okay, but you're gonna be breakin' the law."

"I doubt it."

"What?"

"The way I see it," I said, "about twenty feet of this pool over there on the side near the ocean is on public property."

He shrugged. "I'm not gonna argue with you about that. All I know is the law says you can't swim out here at night."

"Well, I'm going to," I said. "What happens then?"

He turned away. "I'll call the cops," he said. "I'll get fired if I don't. And I'm sure as hell not comin' in after you."

"You could shoot me," I said, walking over to the edge of the pool. "Blow me out of the water; claim you thought I was a shark."

He smiled and turned away as I dove into the pool . . . and 15 or 20 laps later I looked up to see two city cops with flashlights pointing down at me. "Okay fella," said one, "come on outta there. You're under arrest."

"What for?"

"You know," said the other. "Let's go."

They took me up to the lobby to see the night manager, who declined to press charges when he realized I was a paying hotel guest.

My bill was running around $85 a day at that point and, besides that, I was registered as "press." So the matter was dismissed without rancor when I agreed to go back to my room.

We went through the same motions 24 hours later, and also on the third & fourth night . . . but on the fifth night, for some reason, the pool guard said nothing at all when I appeared. I said "hello" and started taking off my clothes, expecting him to head for the house phone on that pole out in the middle of the patio that he'd used on the other nights . . . but he just stood there and watched me dive in. Then he spent the next 45 minutes pointedly ignoring me . . . and at one point, just as dawn was coming up, he chased a videotape crew away from the pool when they tried to film me swimming. When they asked why I could swim and they couldn't even walk around on the patio, he just shook his head and pointed his billy club toward the exit door.

I never asked him why. When I finally felt tired enough to sleep, I climbed out of the pool and yelled "thanks" as I waved to him and went back inside. He waved back, then resumed his bored pacing around the patio. Moments later, up in my oceanfront room on the sixth floor, I looked down and saw him leaning on the railing and staring out to sea at the sunrise, his billy club dangling idly from his right wrist and his cop's hat pushed back on his head. I wondered what he was thinking about: A young black "private" cop, maybe 25 or 30 years old, spending every night of the week, all night—8:00 P.M. to 8:00 A.M.—enforcing a bogus law that probably didn't even say, if you read it carefully, that nobody could swim in a big empty pool built illegally on public property (his beachfront) by the wealthy white owners of a Miami Beach hotel. During one of my conversations with the night manager at the Doral, he had hinted that the "no swimming" rule had its origins more in the hotel's insurance policy than in any municipal law.

I watched the cop for a while, wondering if George McGovern upstairs in the penthouse might also be looking down at him . . . but probably not, I thought: McGovern might be up there, but if he was, I figured he was probably looking out to sea, squinting through the glass sight of that big .358 Weatherby Magnum he liked to use on sharks. It was a strange vision: the Democratic nominee, braced at sunrise on the ledge of his penthouse in Miami, scanning the dawn surf for the cruising, thin gray edge of a Hammerhead fin; his rifle cocked, with the strap curled around his left arm and a Bloody Mary on the table beside him, killing sharks to keep his mind loose on his morning of triumph.

Indeed. McGovern had become The Candidate, and as the senior correspondent in the McGovern press corps, I felt a certain obligation to know exactly what he was doing and thinking at that hour. What would he have said if I had called up there on the phone and said I was about to go on NBC-TV and say McGovern had spent his morning blasting sharks with a huge Weatherby Magnum from the patio of his penthouse on top of the Doral Beach Hotel?

I had been tempted to make the call, if only to jerk him around a bit and make him get Frank Mankiewicz out of bed to draft a denial for the press conference that would almost certainly have followed such an ugly revelation . . . but I decided against it; I needed some sleep, and if I had made a call like that, I knew sleep would be out of the question. It would have generated trouble, and I figured it would probably result in getting myself publicly denounced as a Dangerous Dope Addict, a man given over in extremes to multiple hallucinations and other forms of aggressive personal dementia. . . . Between Mankiewicz and South Dakota Lieutenant Governor and McGovern crony Bill Dougherty, they would have hashed up a story that would not only have caused me to be discredited, but probably would have gotten me locked up indefinitely at the expense of The State, forced to undergo the Hickory Cure and perhaps even Shock Treatments. . . .

WHAT? Don't mention that word!

Shock treatments? Shark-shooting? Well. . . . I get a sudden sense that we're pushing it a bit here, so why not change the subject?

*July 1972*

HST addressing a voter registration ralley in Aspen with
Sheriff Bob Braudis (center) and Mayor John Bennett
(Steve Skinner)

# Memo from the Sheriff

*Hunter asks a lot of his friends, but he gives so much.*
—Anonymous

One early winter morning, I looked out the window to see Hunter walking to my door. I've never seen Hunter before 10:00 A.M., except, maybe, in court. He had come to ask me if I'd accompany him to Louisville, where he'd be honored with a key to the city the following day. I immediately agreed.

At 7:30 the next morning, Hunter was getting ready. We had an 8:30 flight. At eight he asked me what time I had. I said, "Eight." He said, "Christ, I've got 7:30! That's anti-airport time." I knew what he meant.

We passed twenty cars in a row on a snow-packed mountain two-lane to make the plane. Hunter complimented my driving. I had a premonition that this road trip might involve some work.

It took all day to get to Louisville. Wayne Ewing had been on the ground, and the event seemed well organized. We checked into the hotel with pseudonyms: A. Lincoln. D. Boone. Hunter's suite had a dining room and forty or fifty shrimp cocktails.

The next day the only obligation before the evening event was a "sound check" at the auditorium. Warren Zevon, Johnny Depp, Hunter's son, Juan, many more of Hunter's friends, and I were parts of the "show."

Hunter was happy. He shot Zevon in the back with a huge fire extinguisher while Warren rehearsed at the piano. Scared the shit out of him.

We had a Sedan de Ville delivered to the auditorium so Hunter could "get away" at will. He wanted to buy a bullwhip to snap during the show. Two coeds from the university who had been assigned to assist guided us to a huge leather store.

Hunter didn't like the action of any of the whips but bought the coeds shoes and jackets. We spent the afternoon cruising Basketball Alley, Cherokee Park, and memories from Hunter's youth. No trouble, yet.

Shotgun art with Warren Zevon, Owl Farm, 1994
(Daniel E. Dibble)

Just before the big show, Hunter asked me to tell the organizer that he wouldn't appear onstage until a brown paper bag, stuffed with cash, was delivered. Jesus. I started my request by saying: "I'm not used to this, but . . ." Two minutes before kickoff, I gave Hunter the bag. He asks a lot of his friends.

The ceremony was a high-quality love fest. A poetess read her ode to Hunter, and he became entranced. At 4:00 A.M., Hunter was behind the wheel, on the way to drop the woman off at her door.

Hunter threaded the pride of Detroit between granite retaining walls and huge elms with $\frac{1}{32}$ of an inch to spare, driving on the goddamn sidewalk. I saw trouble everywhere.

"Hunter, get back on the street! Every yuppie in these antebellum mansions is dialing 911. What will you say to the cops?"

Hunter told me that I worry too much. We dropped the poetess off and went to the hotel. No trouble. No arrests.

On our last day in Louisville, Hunter visited Virginia, his mother, at her nursing home outside of the city. Juan and I and Bambi, a stripper, drove out with him. Bambi wanted Hunter to sign her ass so she could replicate it with a tattoo.

I dropped Juan and Hunter at the Episcopal Care Center and said I'd kill an hour in a bar with Bambi. I spent the hour looking for a bar in a *dry* county. Life is a gradual release from ignorance.

When we got back to the assisted living center, I escorted Bambi to the bathroom through the large day room. Her micro-skirt, high boots, and makeup caused a lot of old dudes to skid-stop their walkers.

Virginia had invited most of her relatives to visit with her and Hunter. He was ready to bolt from this "quality time" with Mom. We went back to the hotel, Bambi disappeared sans autograph, and Zevon and I had dinner. No trouble. No arrests.

The journey home started to get strange when, during climb-out, with the plane aimed at the sun at a forty-five-degree angle, Hunter clawed his way to the forward first-class head. Even though the cabin was full of United personnel, nobody said anything. Maybe it was because, just prior to this walk, Hunter let out a thirty-second, two-octave, head-splitting rebel yell. "Just what people like to hear during takeoff," he said. After we got to flight level and the seat belt sign went off, a line formed at the door to the restroom. The flight attendant came to me and asked, "Just what is your friend doing in there?"

Without hesitation, I lied. "He's had bad diarrhea all day."

"Oh, no problem," she said, and herded the line, with whispers, aft.

A half hour later the door opened and Hunter sat down to my left. "Just what were you doing in there?" I asked. "Oh, I took a little bath, shaved, changed clothes. Any problem?" No. No trouble, no arrest.

Hunter said that traveling with me was like traveling with Superman. Oliver always said that if Hunter got crazy at his own home, we could just leave. I couldn't leave him in Louisville, I never would. It didn't get that crazy.

*Bob Braudis, Pitkin County Sheriff*

# Dealing with the D.A.—Before and After

(EDITOR'S NOTE)

Dr. Thompson was again arrested for political reasons in 1995 for leading a finely organized Voters Rebellion against the long-dominant Aspen Skiing Company, which was planning to enlarge and expand the local airport to accommodate huge new jetliners designed for "industrial tourism." The SkiCo was allied with United Airlines and the local real-estate bund and corporate interests ranging from General Dynamics to Enron.

With these Goliaths of global industry behind them, the SkiCo anticipated no opposition at all to its November ballot initiative that would make the glorious new airport a legal, tax-payer-funded reality before the year 2000. . . . And there *was* no opposition, in fact, until the ever-contentious Woody Creek Caucus suddenly reversed itself and declared war on the new airport and everything it stood for—which included, by presumably universal agreement, giving the SkiCo and its corporate money changers the right to exploit the valley on a scale previously undreamed of in the ever-shrinking ski-resort business. Aspen is doomed, they warned, without drastic expansion, modernization, and a total commitment to a "new age commercialization." It was a matter of life or death, economically.

Thompson's epic eleventh-hour crusade *against* the airport expansion is a classic of Twentieth Century political organizing and catapulted the "No" vote from zero on October 1, to 50 percent on the night before the November 7 election—when the Doctor was arrested and jailed after addressing a rip-roaring Get Out the Vote rally in downtown Aspen that also featured the mayor, the sheriff, and a naked woman from Malibu who sold kisses.

News of Thompson's arrest spread rapidly and generated a huge voter turnout that swamped the new airport proposal by a 2–1 margin. The SkiCo was humiliated and never entirely recovered from the defeat. The Aspen ski business remained stagnant.

The following three (3) documents tell the story of that merciless 2-year legal struggle that eventually resulted in an unprecedented solution called the *Sharp Necklace Agreement* that broke the power of the local police forever—or at least until the Attorney General overrules it for antiterrorism reasons.

As always, Dr. Thompson's legally aggressive courtroom behavior is cited as a *matter of record* & not necessarily as recommended behavior for others. There are always risks in challenging excessive police power—but the risks of *not* challenging it are more dangerous, even fatal. Never do it impulsively. The Law can be cruel and unforgiving, especially of careless stupidity. The rule of thumb is BEWARE, and be quiet. You are Innocent until *proven* guilty, so act that way. And remember the Felony Murder Law. You may have been in Chicago when that poor woman got butchered by some runaway slave on speed; it won't matter. Get ready for prison. Abandon all hope, even if you are innocent. . . . It is a weird and brutal law, created *by* prosecutors *for* prosecutors, because it eliminates the need for Proof or even Evidence.

## THOMPSON, COPS COME TO SHARP NECKLACE AGREEMENT

I did not ask for this fight. It came to me on a lonely road at the end of a wild night of politics, and it's been a shame and a travesty ever since. From its horrible beginnings, this case has been less about one person charged with a misdemeanor and more about the soul of the Aspen Police Department.

I despise drunk drivers just as much as I hate crooked cops. I fear anybody on the road who is out of control for any reason—and that would have to include, by universal agreement, public servants who use their badge and authority to settle personal grudges or enforce their political beliefs.

This agreement we're executing today will serve as a Sharp Necklace to crooked cops as well as dangerous drunkards and brings an end to the cheap, low-rent, back-alley pile of scum that this case has been.

*H. S. Thompson, April 1997*

*December 12, 1995*
LAWSON WILLS
Dep. District Atty.
Pitkin Cty. Courthouse

Dear Mr. Wills,

I am given to understand that you want me to come into the courthouse and officially surrender to you, in front of witnesses, so that you can formally re-arrest me on some kind of vague, chickenshit charge cooked up by Officer Short on the night of Nov. 7–8, '95, in the course of our bizarre encounter on Cemetery Lane as I was very skillfully driving home (on an utterly deserted road) after delivering the keynote address at a major political rally full of people who planned to wake up the next morning (Election Day) and kick the shit out of the Aspen Ski Co.

Is my information correct? Did that vengeful dingbat actually fail to serve me with a valid, legal summons? Did he botch *everything* that night? Was he so crazy that he couldn't even *arrest* me properly? And is *that* why you want me to drive at top speed into town so you can get yr. picture in the papers while you slap handcuffs on me and swell up like a toad for the cameras?

Ah, Lawson, have you *no* shame? Are you a Nazi? Are you nuts with lust for yr. upcoming 15 minutes of fame? Has it come to *this*—that you have to beg, bitch & cajole yr. victims to turn themselves in & abandon all hope for anything except humiliation and jail?

How long, O Lord, how long? You should be deeply ashamed of yourself. I talked with a journalist who said you reminded him of William Jennings Bryan at the Scopes "Monkey Trial" in 1925. It was a horrible thing to hear. (Bryan, as you recall, was whipsawed by Darrow & wound up testifying, under oath, that a whale is not a mammal & therefore, neither was he.)

Ah, but don't get me wrong, Lawson: I'm on Your side—or at least I was until that bungling dunce harassed me for 3 ½ hours on Election Day and made an ass of himself in the Jail. It was ugly. He went haywire when he finally understood that I was *not* Drunk and none of his high-tech Drunk-Buster machines were going to give him the numbers he wanted. He was like an ape trapped in chains. His fellow Officers were mortified, and so was I. It is shocking to see Aspen's long and honorable tradition of quality law enforcement being sullied by these charges about "rogue cops" and "stalkers" and "dumb Watersuckers with six-guns" who strut like John Wayne and think like Mark Fuhrman. There ain't many, as we know, but we also know in our bones that one rotten apple ruins the whole bushel, and that is why I feel real sympathy for you, because I know the people you work for, and I know how sick they are.

But don't worry, Lawson: The pigs will soon be out of the poke. Yessir. The fat is in the fire. Today's pig is tomorrow's bacon.

Whoops. Sorry. But rest easy. I *will* come in (probably today) and surrender again—and a whole legion of falsely accused drunkards will come with me. And they *all* hate Mark Fuhrman. But not me, Lawson. I don't hate anybody. I am a child of god of the new-age Buddhist persuasion, and I love to go to court. Because that is where Justice lives, and you know how I feel about Justice.

Indeed. Yr. time is coming, Whore-face. When I get yr. lame ass in court, you'll wish you'd been run over and killed by a Buick when you were six years old. We will skewer those swine on worldwide TV and put them in prison for Perjury. Nobody in this valley will ever see them again.

You filthy stinking animal. Do you know what *Misprison of a Felony* means? Or *Aggravated Conspiracy to Obstruct Justice*? Are you aware of the *terrible punishment that awaits* a Main Pig like you?

Okay. That's it. I'll surrender at noon on Wednesday.

## THE SHARP NECKLACE AGREEMENT

*The parties to this case agree to the following:*
1. That driving while one's ability is impaired by alcohol is dangerous to the health and safety of the public and must be avoided at all costs.

2. That statements by police officers which are inaccurate or untruthful are dangerous to the administration of justice and must be avoided at all costs.

3. That it is an important function of police officers to enforce Colorado law prohibiting alcohol-impaired driving and that failure to enforce those laws vigorously would comprise a serious breach of duty and violation of public trust on the part of police.

4. That it is an essential quality of police officers to be free of enmity or bias against any individual or group of individuals in the community they serve and that for any officer to act or even appear to act out of any such enmity or bias would constitute an abuse of power and a violation of public trust.

5. That although Colorado law does not prohibit driving after drinking anything, clearly the wisest choice is not to drive after having anything alcoholic to drink, including after drinking a sufficient amount to obtain a blood alcohol concentration of .08.

6. That decency, security, and liberty alike demand that government officials shall be subjected to the same rules of conduct that are commands to the citizen. In a government of laws, existence of the government will be imperiled if it fails to observe the law scrupulously. Our government is the potent, the omnipresent teacher. For good or ill, it teaches the whole people by its example. Crime is contagious. If the government becomes a lawbreaker, it breeds contempt for the law; it invites every man to become a law unto himself; it invites anarchy. To declare that in the administration of the criminal law the end justifies the means—to declare that the government may commit crimes in order to secure the conviction of a private criminal—would bring terrible retribution.

7. The parties agree mistakes and/or errors in judgment have been made by all parties, that each party will strive to avoid any such errors in the future, and that it is in the best interest of justice to go forward with the tendered agreement.

*(Signed) Hunter S. Thompson and*
*H. Lawson Wills,*
*Chief Deputy District Attorney*

Forging the landmark Sharp Necklace Agreement
at home with noted criminal lawyer
(Deborah Fuller)

## Saturday Night in Aspen

Saturday night in Aspen and the road out of town is empty in both directions. The only things moving on Main Street are me and one slow-rolling cop car. No people on the street, no local traffic. I wave to him, as I normally do, but he ignores me & picks up his radio squealer, probably to run my plate and maybe get some action. . . . I can see him back there, in my mirror, and I instinctively make a right turn & speed up, gripping the wheel with both hands and hearing a sudden roar of music all around me. It is "Walk on the Wild Side." Ah yes:

> *Candy came from out on the Island*
> *In the back room she was everybody's darlin',*
> *But she never lost her head*
> *Even when she was givin' head,*
> *She says, Hey babe, take a walk on the wild side*
> *Said, Hey babe, take a walk on the wild side,*
> *And the colored girls go—*
> *Doo, do doo, do doo, do do do . . .*

Right. And thank you, Lou Reed, for that one. You bet. Every once in a while, but not often, you can sit down and write a thing that you know is going to stand people's hair on end for the rest of their lives— a perfect memory of some kind, like a vision, and you can see the words rolling out of your fingers and bouncing around for a while like wild little jewels before they finally roll into place & line up just exactly like you wanted them to. . . . Wow! Look at that shit! Who wrote that stuff?

What? Me? Hot damn! Let us rumble, keep going, and don't slow down—whatever it is, keep doing it. Let's have a little Fun.

Even writing feels like fun when you catch a moment like this. You feel Pure and natural—Yes sir, I am a Natural Man tonight. Bring it on. Fuck those people. Tonight we walk with the King. . . . That is My kind of fun, and I like to spread it around. You can't Hoard fun. It has no shelf life.

And so much for that, eh? I started off writing about Aspen, but I wandered off into the definition of Fun, which is always dangerous. So, to hell with Fun. I shit on the chest of Fun. Look what it did to Charles Manson. He had Too much fun—no doubt about that—so they put him away for life. He was a Monster, and he still is. Put him Down. Shove him off the Bridge with a wire around his neck and bowling balls chained to his feet. Drown the bastard. What if it was your daughter he got hold of?

What indeed? I have no daughters, thank God, so I don't have to worry about it. I have always loved women of all ages, but they have always been Other people's daughters. If I had a daughter and she came home with a creature like Manson, my heart would fill with Hate. I would not kill him instantly, but my brain would start moving that way—Okay, how do we do this, without being busted for Murder?

First, get rid of the Witness. Send her upstairs to her room and make sure nobody else is around. That is a basic Rule in this business. . . . The next step is to grab a loaded shotgun off the wall and lure him into the kitchen by stomping heavily on the floor & screaming crazily while you dial up 911. That will put your situation on the Record.

Keep screaming, "Get away from me, Charley! Don't come any closer!" until he comes running into the room with wild eyes & you can blast him straight in the chest with both barrels. . . . Do not miss, or things will turn queer in a hurry. Make sure he's stone dead when he drops, because you will not get another chance. He will be on you with a butcher knife. . . . But if you do it Right, you will be hailed as a Hero, and yr. daughter will think long & hard before she comes home with another creep like Manson.

Death Bomb, Thanksgiving, 1992

(Deborah Fuller)

# Witness II

## Woody Creek, August 2002

I am not a religious man in any formal sense, but in truth I am far more *theologically conscious* than anyone I know—except perhaps my monkish brute of a neighbor, Ed Bastian, who conducts big-time Spirituality seminars on Aspen mountain and rides a huge black BMW motorcycle that was once blessed by the Dalai Lama, who also gave me the diaphanous white silk scarf that hangs across the room on my storyboard.

That is what I mean by "theologically conscious," but so what? I *enjoy* the company of religious scholars and even Jesus freaks from time to time, as long as they have a sense of humor and a bit of fine whiskey to oil the exotic machinery of speculations about the Meaning of God in Modern America, or Why Child Rape is *good* for Catholic priests and punishable by DEATH in the suburbs of San Diego. . . .

Smart boys from Tibet or the Society of Jesus are always fun for this kind of banter, and I am always on the lookout for these people, but rarely for anything except as sparring partners. There is nothing like a corrupt Jesuit or a high-rolling Buddhist to sharpen up with. And some are even *wise* in their own shrouded way.

Big-time lawyers and Appeals Court judges are also a morbid

kind of fun in times of personal darkness. I have many close friends on that side of the law, and I derive a lot of grim pleasure from them. They have a good sense of what is *possible* within the law, and what is probably Not. . . . That is what lawyers are all about. Most of them have spent enough time in Law School to have at least a rudimentary understanding of how the Judicial system operates.

*Never Be Late for Court When You Are the Person on Trial* is a good one to remember, for instance, and another is *The Cops Will Never Play Fair.*

*Justice Is the Whim of the Judge* is an axiom that I picked up a long time ago at the Columbia Law School in New York, where I also learned how to handle large sums of money and how to smoke marijuana in polite company without making a scene and acting like a junkie.

## DR. HUNTER S. THOMPSON AND THE LAST BATTLE OF ASPEN
### BY LOREN JENKINS, SMART MAGAZINE, JAN./FEB. 1990
### (INTERVIEW TOOK PLACE IN SEPTEMBER 1989, 3 ½ MONTHS BEFORE GAIL PALMER CAME TO VISIT.)

The Rocky Mountain night is cold and still except for the occasional screeech [sic] of the peacocks that stalk the darkness just off the wooden deck where Hunter S. Thompson sits drinking under the iron bat sculpture that decorates his front porch. A week earlier, he had been caught out in the dead of night firing an assortment of weaponry over the house of a neighbor and had just barely avoided a felony indictment on gun charges. Now, with the September stars twinkling overhead, he is trying judiciously to explain the exact nature of the fear and loathing that have crept into the lush, quiet valley of Woody Creek, where he has made his home for the past two decades.

"I ran for sheriff in Aspen years ago to try to
stop the greed heads from ruining the place,"
Thompson says in his singular stop-start, mumbling
cadence. "Now . . . uhhh . . . they're . . . trying to move on me right here where I live."
Indeed, land developers, the final plague of all
paradises lost, have pretty much overwhelmed the
once-funky mountain town. . . . And now the developers are reaching downvalley to Thompson's own
pastoral backyard, disrupting his life and work
and bringing him quixotically to center stage in a
drama that the more sentimental locals have taken
to calling the "last battle in the lost war for
the soul of Aspen."

. . . That's why Thompson has become embroiled
in a bitter dispute—nay, a modern-day range war—
with a newcomer named Floyd Watkins, who, for
Thompson, embodies all that is evil in Aspen. A
rich man with a dubious past and the habit of getting his way, Watkins moved upstream of Hunter's
house four years ago like a bad omen. Nothing has
been the same since. Until then, Woody Creek was
in a Western time warp, a valley of blue-collar
bartenders and construction workers, a couple of
aging hippies, and one famous writer. It was a
place where locals prided themselves on their
rural individualism, their isolation from increasingly ostentatious Aspen, and their unpaved roads
and rough-hewn log houses.

The community center was a log post office and
the adjoining Woody Creek Tavern, a smoky bar
where cowboys and construction workers played
pool, gambled on ball games, and occasionally
brawled. Thompson used the tavern as a kind of
office, a semipublic haven for his eccentricities.
Taking calls, meeting people who flew in to see him
on business, he set a hilarious, outlaw tone that

his neighbors sympathized with immediately. He was a lot of fun, even if he did set off the occasional smoke bomb and raise his voice from time to time. It was a real Western.

In a valley where individualism and personal freedom are the reigning ideology, Floyd Watkins should have a lot of friends. He is the type of person who, at one point, made the West what it is. . . . A self-made man who had amassed millions in Florida and California in the heady world of high-level bill collecting (his company, which he sold for millions in 1985, was called Transworld Systems), Watkins came here expecting the respect he enjoyed in his Miami home. To that end he set out to build a multimillion-dollar estate that would rival those that have turned Aspen into an alpine Palm Springs over the past decade.

. . . [But] in fact, Watkins's insensitivity to the traditions of the old West in general and to the etiquette of Woody Creek in particular could not help but offend. He surrounded his spread with intimidating urban chain-link fences, built a massive rock-and-concrete gateway, laid tons of cement on his driveways, and began pushing to have the Woody Creek road paved to keep the dust out of his parlors. Worse, in a land where water is valued as much as gold, Watkins ran bulldozers through streambeds that his downstream neighbors used to water their cattle and fields and rerouted the creek through his front lawn; he planned to build artificial trout ponds, in defiance of official county disapproval, that he would turn into a commercial fishing camp.

Thompson later fictionalized these developments in his weekly column in the *San Francisco Examiner,* suggesting that nothing short of a Hatfield-and-McCoy feud was about to engulf the valley. . . .

It was an adolescent act of common vandalism that

brought matters to a head. As Floyd Watkins later told the story, his work crews had hardly finished pouring a new driveway at his Beaver Run Ranch when someone unseen and unknown inscribed "Fuck you, prick" on his black-tinted concrete and an anonymous telephone call warned him: "No more concrete is going to be poured in Woody Creek." Watkins said it was the final straw, coming as it did after a series of other incidents that he claimed ranged from an attempted poisoning of his dog, the shooting out of his night-lights, the sawing down of a Beaver Run Ranch sign on the main road, and the scrawling of graffiti on his imposing rock gateway labeling the place "Fat Floyd's Trout Farm."

"I called the sheriff's office to complain, but they said they had only two deputies on duty and couldn't send anyone up here," Watkins said when I visited him to hear his side of the dispute. "I told the sheriff then and there that I was going to take care of things myself."

The first sign that Watkins had gone on the warpath came that evening, when Gaylord Guenin, an amiable former journalist who runs the Woody Creek Tavern, was driving to his home, two miles up the creek beyond the Beaver Run Ranch. Watkins chased down Guenin's pickup and forced him to pull over.

"He was furious and fuming and threatening," Guenin recalls. "He talked about having Uzis and infrared scopes at his home and his ability to 'take care of people' and be three thousand miles away when it happened. It was clear that I had been chosen to deliver a message." Still shaken when he got home, Guenin called the Tavern and warned everyone that Watkins was on a tear. What no one knew, of course, was that Watkins had decided to spend the night well armed in his car, near his endangered driveway.

Watkins recalls some fifteen or twenty cars driving up the road that night, "all honking and jeering" as they passed his hidden four-wheel drive. Around 4 A.M., he fell asleep. Then, "at about 4:30, I heard five blasts of a shotgun. At first I thought Roberto, my foreman, had shot a coon by the shed where I keep some ducks, and I started to go over there, when there were about twenty shots from an automatic weapon of some kind, then six shots from a pistol. I realized the shots came from down the road. I saw car lights from either a Jeep Cherokee or a Wagoneer. I started after them, and there was a high-speed chase in the dark." Three miles down the road, the escaping vehicle slowed down and turned in to the Flying Dog Ranch, owned by George Stranahan, a respected physicist turned cattle rancher who also owns the tavern and is the valley's most influential citizen. He is a very old friend of Thompson's.

There were two people in the car, according to Watkins, and one—a girl—ran up to Stranahan's house while the other started to get out on the driver's side. "I had these spotlights on the car," Watkins says. "I turned them on and saw Hunter Thompson. I said, 'What the fuck do you think you're doing, Hunter?' And he came up to me, jabbed me in the chest, and said, 'You have been given a warning; there is to be no trout operation or any more concrete poured in Woody Creek.'"

The official version that Thompson later gave to the *Aspen Times Daily* from my kitchen telephone was somewhat different. Thompson denied that he was firing at Watkins or his house or delivering any personal warning. He said, instead, that he was heading up to Watkins's ranch when he came face to face with a giant porcupine. "Don't laugh," Hunter told the reporter Dave Price. "Look at Jimmy Carter. He was attacked by a killer swamp rabbit and had to beat it off with his oar. I was attacked by this huge porcupine. I stopped to look at it and it attacked me, so I blasted it." The porcupine, alas, was never found.

That there was a confrontation with Watkins in the driveway of Stranahan's Flying Dog Ranch is not in dispute. Thompson maintains, however, that he was the master of diplomacy, telling Watkins that he, Hunter, was his only friend. "I even offered him my last beer and invited him to come down to my place later in the day to watch the ball game." But Watkins went home, called Sheriff Bob Braudis, and demanded that Thompson be prosecuted for what Hunter later said was "everything from the Manson family killings to shooting his mules."

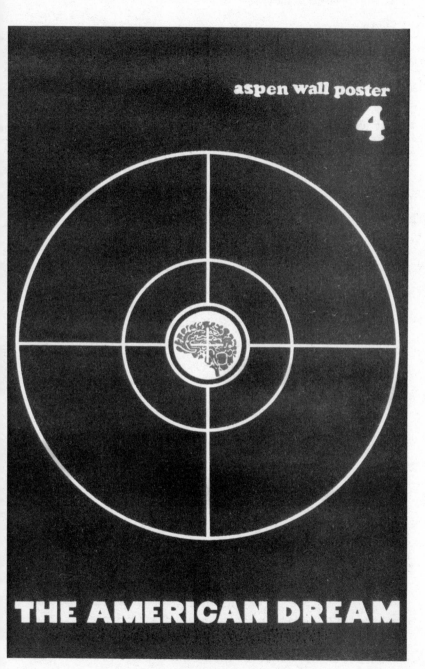

(Tom Benton)

That was an exaggeration. But Mac Myers, the deputy district attorney whose office conducted the investigation, came within a hairbreadth of bringing charges against Thompson for firing an automatic weapon. In the end, he couldn't prove such a weapon had been fired. Thompson had a permit for a nonfunctioning automatic weapon, and when he was asked to turn in the gun for inspection, he presented a destroyed machine gun that had been packed in viscous antitrust naval jelly that rendered ballistics tests inconclusive.

Three days after the shooting, while the district attorney's office debated whether to press charges against Thompson, Watkins woke to a nightmare. The ponds he had stocked with trophy-sized trout during the past three years were shimmering with the silver bellies of dead fish. More than six hundred trout, some weighing up to twenty pounds, were dead. The waters had been poisoned in the night, and Watkins immediately blamed the slaughter on his neighbors, charging them with employing "terrorist tactics" against him because they didn't like his tastes and style. He went on to say that the multimillion-dollar, seventeen-thousand-square-foot main house of his estate would not be completed for another two years, but he'd be damned if he was going to let anybody scare him off his land. "I'm just gearing up to get tough," he told reporters, warning that he would hire gunmen, and "if I have to, I will put guards all along that road. I can afford it."

. . . The level-headed Stranahan shared the sheriff's concern, and they issued joint statements calling for everyone to calm down before someone was hurt. Down at the Tavern, where talk of Watkins's problems was normally greeted with raucous jokes, there was disbelief that someone from the valley would actually poison Woody Creek's waters, Watkins or no Watkins. This is the West, after all, and water isn't messed with. The new mood was illustrated by the large glass that appeared on the Tavern's bar, accompanied by a sign that said: "We're sorry the trout died. Your $ can put a trout back in Floyd's ponds. Woody Creek wants the world to know we don't think killing trout is a way to solve the problems. Let's put the trout back, and then we will talk about the differences." Thompson, resentful of innuendos that he might have been behind the fish poisoning, offered a $500 reward to anyone who could clear up the mystery and said that perhaps he should poison some of his peacocks.

The collection jar had just begun to fill with bills when Watkins's fish story began to unravel. A disaffected Beaver Run Ranch employee quit his job, and soon he was signing a sheriff's affidavit testifying that the night before the trout kill, Watkins's twenty-three-year-old son, Lance, and Roberto, the Mexican foreman, poured from four to five gallons of an algaecide called Cutrine Plus into the fish ponds. Cutrine Plus is a copper-based chemical normally used to control algae growth.

"Chemists have told us that the water from the ponds had a copper content that was a zillion times the lethal level for trout," Sheriff Braudis reported at a Tavern meeting of the Woody Creek Caucus, an informal assembly of valley landowners and residents that includes both Watkins and Thompson. The sheriff's investigation concluded that the ponds had been poisoned not by antisocial outsiders but "by accident," by Watkins's own son and his Mexican majordomo.

"We have a difference of opinion here," Watkins defiantly told his neighbors, to hoots of derisive laughter. Refusing to accept the sheriff's verdict, he cited his own fish biologist, Dr. Harold Hagen, who insisted that the level of Cutrine Plus in the water could not have been enough to massacre the trout. More hoots. "My ranch is different from George Stranahan's or yours, but it doesn't make any difference," Watkins finally blurted out. "Do you mean I don't have the right to paint my house pink if I want to? And you have a right to paint your house blue?" Referring to one of Thompson's accusations that only a "vampire or a werewolf" would want to live in his house, Watkins said, "Well, I'm neither a vampire nor a werewolf, but I can tell you one thing: I sure as hell wouldn't want to live in Hunter's house. But I don't care if he lives there."

Everyone cracked up, and in the spirit of goodwill that reigned until the end of the meeting, Thompson withdrew his original charge about the Watkins house. "I apologize for the vampire thing," he said. "I was in a weird mood. But we are not talking about whether we like or dislike your house. No one is oppressing you. It is not about individual rights. We all live in this valley; this is a one-road community. We all have to live here, you included, and we are sliding into weird squabbles here. But the point is that we don't want to see the life of this valley poisoned—that is as bad as poisoning fish."

. . . "The truth is that Woody Creek has become urbanized in the last twenty years," Sheriff Braudis says rather sadly. "I've told Hunter that, and I've told him he can't be out shooting on the road as he used to. His neighbors are complaining more and more about his peacocks screeching and the gunshots in the night. Today Woody Creek is

different. What is happening now is that the bil-
lionaires are pushing out the millionaires."

Thompson knows this, of course, and says that perhaps if he could afford to move—and could find somewhere as interesting to move to—he would. But he
can't and he won't. Sometimes, though, he gets
tired. "Living out here like this doesn't go with
being pushed around and run over by yo-yos," he
says. "It isn't that you can't win against them—it
is that you don't want to fight them all the time. I
don't mind fucking with Floyd, but that is not my
job. If both of us are going to continue to live in
this valley, he is going to have to learn that he has
to live with us more than we have to live with him."

As of this writing, Watkins has imported two
Bengal tigers to inhabit the new caged run along
his driveway. "Everyone is holding their breath
while we wait to find out what's going to be next,"
says Guenin. "We have reached the ultimate in
ridiculousness." Hunter S. Thompson, meanwhile, is
talking about getting some elephants.

---

That is the famous story of Floyd and the Giant *Porcupine,* as told
by my good friend Loren Jenkins, Pulitzer Prize–winning war correspondent for *Newsweek* and *The Washington Post* and currently
Foreign News Editor for NPR. . . . Back then, in 1990, he was editor-
owner of the venerable *Aspen Times* and I was a major stockholder
in a slick new magazine he started in New York called *SMART.*

In truth, I was probably a minor stockholder, but I had a keen
personal interest in it—a profoundly *vested* interest, which I
immediately put to good use when I was suddenly threatened
with the possibility of going to Federal Prison on RICO charges of
attempted/premeditated Murder with Intent to Kill, felony possession and public use at midnight of automatic weapons, and a fist-
ful of other degrading charges ranging from Dangerous Drugs to
Animal Cruelty and Gross Sexual Imposition.

It was an extremely bad moment, on its face, and many people said I was *done for.* "He's gone too far this time," they said. "What kind of dangerous maniac would attack a man's home with machine guns in the dead of night and then poison all of his fish the next day?"

. . .

Well, shucks. Only a *real* vicious dope fiend, I guess, some white-trash shithead with nothing left to lose. The jails are full of those bastards. Kill them all at once, for all I care.

It was not easy for me to retain a reputable attorney under those circumstances. Nobody wanted to touch it.

A mood of desperation settled over the Owl Farm. My girlfriend went off to Princeton, and I was left alone to barricade myself inside the compound and wait for the attack I knew was coming. I was receiving daily ultimatums from the ATF and the District Attorney. They wanted *all* my guns immediately or they would come out with a SWAT team and get them. The fat was in the fire.

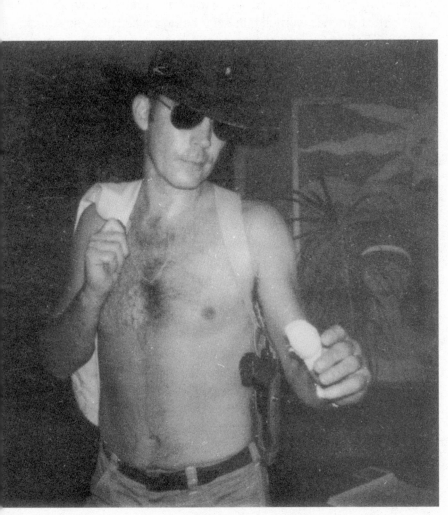

(Lalia Nabulsi)

. . .

My mood became dangerously confrontational in those weeks. I was angry and lonely and doing a lot of target shooting day and night. My friends worried that I was being pushed over the edge by this constant barrage of threats and sudden death by violence. I was always armed and sullen, living from moment to moment and ripped to the tits on my own adrenaline. I look at Deborah's photos from that feverish time and think, Ye fucking gods. This man appears to be criminally insane. It looks like some horrible flashback from *Reefer Madness* and *The Crays* and *Scarface* and *Boogie Nights* all at once. The photos still give me the creeps.

God damn it. I have bitten the front of my tongue again! Why? What have I eaten tonight that would cause me to draw blood from my own tongue? Where is the Percodan? Where is Anita? What is that noise in the bushes? Why am I so crazy all the time?

There was a time when I was vaguely worried by questions like these, but no longer. There are some questions that you can only worry about for *so* long, until finally they become meaningless . . . and it is never healthy to start questioning your own sanity. Being free and happy on the street is evidence enough of sanity these days.

Why is it that so many people have gone insane since the end of the American Century and the horrible Bush family was restored to power? Why is the teenage suicide rate going up? Is the President a clone? Is my car going to explode? Why does my sweetheart suddenly have all these lewd tattoos on her body?

### (EDITOR'S NOTE)

Wait a minute. Time out! Why am I writing all these things on this primitive red electric typewriter when I can read them all in real time on the goddamn overloaded Internet with the flick of a mouse or a button? Am I a Fool? Have I been bogged down in Alzheimer's all these years? What does it all mean, Homer?

. . .

Okay. Back to business. The Giant Porcupine story did not go away. Finally, to avoid deadly violence and another five years in prison, I was compelled to sacrifice my precious Smyser Nazi machine gun— I chopped it up with a heavy industrial grinder and had it formally delivered to the forces of law and order in a large white bag filled with poison grease that would eat the flesh off of anyone who touched it.

And that was that, as I recall. It was never mentioned again, and neither was the Porcupine. My new assistant arrived on Xmas—on loan from the University of Florida's College of Journalism and Communications—and I settled down, as it were, to finishing my long-overdue book, *Songs of the Doomed,* which was still only half written—another deadline agony. They are always painful. . . .

. . .

Christmas came and went in a frenzy of work. The big snow fell and the thermometer plunged to 10 or 15 below zero. The Democrats had lost another election and Bush was still the new President. But not much had changed since the 80s, when the looting of the Treasury was running in high gear and the U.S. Military was beginning to flex its newfound money-muscle. When, everywhere you looked, the flag-suckers were in charge.

We invaded a bunch of tiny helpless countries like Lebanon, Grenada, and Panama, just for the practice, and it was about that time that I went to work as a columnist for the Hearst-owned *San Francisco Examiner* and discovered feminist pornography and moved to Sausalito with Maria.

It was a wild and savage time, Bubba. All hell broke loose, in a phrase. . . . Moving down the mountain has always been dangerous for me, because of the Space problem, but San Francisco in the 1980s was a genuine Adult Dose.

I was shocked. In 1981 I was 44 years old and I saw myself in the mirror as a grizzled veteran of many wars, untold violence, a respectable eight or nine jails all over the world. I had ridden the wild beast of Passion through so many jungles and nightmares and devastating personal disasters that I felt about 200 years old. My heart was strong, but my body was scarred and broken and warped from a life-

time of dangerous confrontations. . . . I was old beyond my years, as
they say, and I had developed a curious habit of survival. It was the
only way I knew, and I was getting pretty good at it, on the evidence. . . .

I had even survived my time as Night Manager of the depraved
O'Farrell Theatre, along with being arrested seven times in six
weeks for crimes that you can't avoid committing when the Police
are admittedly tracking you 24 hours a day and routinely busting
you for things like Open Container and running yellow lights and
being naked at night in Golden Gate Park for no apparent reason.

Ho ho. Of course there were reasons. There are always *reasons*.
Even the blood-thirsty Manson family had reasons. They were stu-
pid murdering swine, for one, and they also had way too much
Time on their hands.

My own situation was exactly the opposite. I had too much
Action on my hands. I was a notorious best-selling author of weird
and brutal books and also a widely feared newspaper columnist
with many separate agendas and many powerful friends in government, law enforcement, and sociopolitical circles.

I was also drunk, crazy, and heavily armed at all times. People
trembled and cursed when I came into a public room and started
screaming in German. It was embarrassing. . . . Maria and I spent
more and more time hiding out in obscure places like Stinson Beach
or Harding Park in the fog belt and even the Crime-ridden San
Bruno Municipal Parking Garage.

It was a sweet time, all in all. In some ways it was a depraved
and terrifying adventure in the darkest side of life, and at least half
the time it was like being shot out of a beautiful cannon in some
kind of X-rated Peter Pan movie. I would definitely *do it again*. . . .

. . .

Hi folks, my name is Marvin and I'm here to sell you this amazing
beautiful old typewriter, which is guaranteed to do for you exactly
what it has done for me. This one is a *monster*, folks. Writing a
book with this thing is like sitting in a pool of LSD-25 and suddenly
feeling yr. nuts on fire. . . . Yes sir, that is a *lifetime guarantee*. Think
about it. . . .

So let me ask *you* a fat little question, friends, and I want you to *think* about this real carefully before you spit out yr. answer—this one is BIG. This is the one query you are going to *have* to answer when you come face to face with GOD ALMIGHTY!

He will ask: "What can I *do* for you, boy? What is the *one* thing you could ask me to do for you *right now*??? What *is* it? WHAT? *Speak up!* NOW! Or I will send you straight to Hell. . . .

What will you *say*, brother? What is the one true answer you will give to Almighty God when you get your final chance? And *remember*—he will Judge you by yr. answer. He will *JUDGE you*! And if you say the wrong thing, you will *suffer* for it. You will eat shit and *die*.

(Long pause filled with weeping and babbling and noise of chairs being pushed around. . . .)

OKAY! OKAY, brother—Relax and feel happy. Fear not, for I am with you and *I will tell you the answer*! Hallelujah *Mahalo*. You are saved!

THE ANSWER YOU WILL GIVE TO GOD ALMIGHTY WHEN HE COMES TO JUDGE YOUR FATE IS Yes Yes Yes, yr. honor. I thought you'd never ask. What I want, of course, is a BRAND-NEW WILD AND SUPERCOOL MODEL 22 IBM SELF-CORRECTING FIRE-ENGINE RED MAGNUM SELECTRIC TYPEWRITER exactly like this one! JUST LIKE MINE. . . . That is what you will say in yr. magic moment of judgment.

. . .

Help me, Lord, for I am watching Gail Palmer's movies again. It is a desperate habit that I formed many years ago when I was preparing to go to Trial. That is always an awkward moment in a smart man's life. I was looking down the barrel of the end of the world, as I knew it. And I understood that I was coming to a major Fork in my road of life—to live *free* like an otter, or to die like a stupid young bee in the web of the federal law-enforcement system. There was no middle way. I had no choice. The deal was going down.

I have known a few magic moments like these—red dots on a sea-green map—and I treasure them. They are the high points of my life, my moments of total Function, when I felt like a snow leopard fighting for life on its own turf.

Whoops. Let's not get maudlin, Doc. Don't embarrass the breed
with some drunken hillbilly hubris. The joke is over. They are coming after your heart this time, so behave accordingly. At the top of
the mountain we are all snow leopards.

. . .

Right, and now let's get back to the Witness who came into my
house that night and almost put me in prison.

She was clearly a refugee from the sex film industry—a business
I had covered as a journalist, regrettably arousing her interest.

In 1985 I ventured to San Francisco to do an article for *Playboy*
on "feminist pornography." Nobody knew what it was, but I was
telling *Playboy* what it was and that was why they gave me the
assignment. Feminist porn was really just couples' films—sex films
made for couples to which you could take a date.

It was a new genre, and I had happened to run into some of the
women who appeared in these films when I was in San Francisco
for the Democratic Convention in '84. They kind of adopted me.
Most of the girls were at least bisexual, and they were fun. A lot of
them were the stars of this new style of films. Juliet Anderson, later
famous as Aunt Peg, was a big one. Veronica Hart was another—
she is still making films and is pretty good at her trade.

. . .

Now we arrive at the complicated part of the story.

I understand situations like the one I am about to tell you, and I
know how strange they can get. I have spent more time in the belly
of that beast than I can ever admit, and certainly not in print. I have
never felt tempted to tell these stories in public—or even in private,
for that matter, except on some moonless nights when I start feeling lonely and sentimental and strung out on combat or pussy or
fear, like our old friend from Arkansas.

But tonight might be that kind of night, so what the hell?

. . .

I had never heard of Gail Palmer. I didn't need to hear about her,
but I got a letter one day telling me that I was off, that I didn't really

get it. I had written that the new feminist pornography was going to take over; she wrote arguing that I didn't understand the sex business, and she said she wanted to explain it to me. I didn't give a fuck.

I got several more letters from her, leading up to the infamous Hallmark card (which my defense attorneys later presented in court) that was full of lewd, tiny, very dense handwriting. The front of it said, "Sex is a dirty business." When you opened it up, it read: "But somebody has to do it." She took up every white surface inside the card with her little tense handwriting, telling me all the fun we could have—more fun than a barrel of monkeys in heat—and that she could really straighten me out about what I knew and thought about the sex business.

Meanwhile, she had also sent me a thick sheaf of press clippings and two films. In one, she is wearing a bodysuit and skipping rope in a high office building, looking out on what appears to be Long Beach Harbor. While she is skipping rope, she is singing to her own little song, repeating the stanzas once or twice:

> *Porno queen, porno queen*
> *It's not a seamy scene*
> *Porno queen, porno queen*
> *You think that sounds funny?*
> *Then why am I*
> *Making so much money?*

It was sickening. She thought it was a very sexy come-on and that she was irresistible, but she was wrong.

I got another letter not long afterward, telling me she would be in town in February and would be staying at the Stonebridge Inn in Snowmass, and that she wanted to get together with me. Her presumption was as telling as the rest of it. I had a lot of sex-film girls coming on to me during that period. A lot of people had noticed what I had done for girls like Bambi and Jo Ann at the O'Farrell. I was a favorite there—I was the people's Night Manager.

I didn't think much about Gail Palmer's upcoming visit. But Deborah, my majordomo, put it on the calendar, just in pencil—I guess she thought I wasn't having enough fun. Which could have been true, but Gail Palmer didn't fit the bill; I had no interest in her—a big, hefty hustler—or in her side of the story.

. . .

On the night of Georgetown vs. Syracuse—a big basketball game— Tim Charles, an old friend and a Georgetown fan, came over to watch the game and to fix my Macintosh amplifier. There were two exterior fuses on the back of the amp, and I somehow knew, or sensed, that there was a third interior fuse, which Tim did not believe. He refused to give up the idea that he knew better, so he took the amp apart on the kitchen floor, like a watch all in pieces. Semmes Luckett, the grandson of the great Confederate Admiral Rafael Semmes, was also here—he was here all the time.

I was in a work frenzy, still trying to finish *Songs of the Doomed*, which had recently been interrupted by Floyd Watkins and the giant porcupine. Cat, my assistant from the University of Florida, was here as well. We had the whole book spread out on the living room table. Cat was in charge of keeping the three manuscript copies identical—they changed every day, and the changes had to be transferred to the other two. I was not plotting to seize her, but I was thinking that later we could go in the hot tub together and have some fun. I had just finished an article for some women's magazine, like *Elle*—it was sort of a celebratory moment. I wanted to clear the house and unwind for a night.

There are some subtle details in this story that you have to appreciate to understand what happened. I wanted to watch the Georgetown game—I would have watched it anyway with just Cat; she was fun to watch sports with because she would bet—but then Tim or Semmes brought up the fact that the Grammys were coming on after the game; Jimmy Buffett was going to be on and they wanted to watch it. I didn't want to watch the fucking Grammys and did not plan to.

Meanwhile, the amplifier was still in pieces on the floor. It was not going to get fixed until Tim figured out that there was an internal fuse, which was very deep in the middle. I knew that, Tim did not, and Semmes didn't care. Semmes was drinking a lot of beer;

he had been planning to go into town—he wanted to go dancing. Tim was eventually going home to dinner and his wife, Carol Ann.

The game was very good—a two-point game. Georgetown won. I was waiting for them to get the fuck out. I think we were smoking some weed. I was ready to let my hair down, but not with them around. Cat may have known what I was thinking—we hadn't planned anything, but she probably understood it.

Tim was getting cranked up, fixated on the fucking machinery, and Semmes was getting sloppy drunk and starting to sink into the winged chair, slumped over. Semmes was not a fun drunk; he was constantly worried about his fucking probation. In my desperation, I looked up at the calendar (maybe I remembered her pending visit) and saw the note Deborah had written: "Gail Palmer . . ." It was just a quick scan—then, CLICK. I thought for a minute how Semmes had been complaining that the women in Aspen all eat shit—just a bunch of whores—nobody to go dancing with. He was a dancing fool.

It seemed like a solution, and before I thought it all the way through, I said, "Semmes, I got a solution to your fucking problem." He had started to look like he might be discouraged over the fact that he couldn't get a date. I was trying to push him out, edge him out, encourage him out.

He didn't jump right on it, but I insisted. *I've got a date for you! This is a really hot, wild woman . . .* I had the file. I showed him the press clippings. I was doing a real selling job on her—I said, "You just call her and she'll be your date. She'll whoop it up with you. I'll even pay for the drinks."

I convinced him to go in the other room and call the Witness. I could hear him talking, but I didn't care to hear what he was saying. As far as I was concerned, he was leaving to go meet her. Suddenly he appeared at the kitchen door, leaving the phone in the living room, and said: "She wants to meet you. She wants to meet *you* before we go dancing."

To resolve it took three different calls and three visits from Semmes to the kitchen. The Witness wanted to meet me, and I was really unhappy about that. On Semmes's second trip to the kitchen, I finally said, "Oh fuck, all right Semmes, you tell her to get in a cab and come here but tell the cab to wait."

She wouldn't agree to the date without meeting me, and it pissed me off. When Semmes came back in the kitchen for the third time and said, "She wants to know if she can bring her husband," I said, "Fuck no! Absolutely not. Not even for a drive-by." It took half an hour more of dickering and fucking around before she accepted that.

I could see Semmes had a weird setup coming with a husband in the picture. She wanted an interview with me—she wanted to talk to me about the sex business. She thought of herself as the Ralph Nader of the sex business, and she wanted to form a partnership with me and put out a line of sex toys—perhaps a high-quality line of dildos. I wanted no part of that, of course; I had no need, no interest, and my experience with her up to that point made her nothing but a negative, dishonest face. I can see now, telling this story, that I lost control of it little by little.

. . .

About twenty minutes later, there was a knock on the door. I had arranged with Semmes—out of laziness, I guess—that he could bring her into the kitchen and I would shake hands with her, and then he was taking her off dancing. I even gave him money . . . and that is where we lost it.

I stood up and said "Hello" to the Witness, and she began babbling with all sorts of questions she wanted to ask me: "What's your sex life like? What do you think of fever-fresh nightgowns?" Gibberish and bullshit, which I wanted no part of. "Quiet. Quiet. Be QUIET!" I said. I stressed that to Semmes, too: "She has to be quiet here." Semmes wanted to continue watching the Grammys, and somehow the Witness ended up sitting in the armchair—just to watch the Grammys.

I kept her quiet for a while: If she started to talk, I was harsh with her—barking "Shut up." During commercials, she would start babbling and pestering me. When she continued to ask me about my sex life, I made her read *Screwjack* out loud: "All right," I said, "you're curious? Here's a story I just wrote."

She never finished *Screwjack*; it really disturbed her. I said, "What's wrong with you? Keep going. Can't you read?" She read about half of it, and said, "Wow. What the shit is this? What kind of a pervert . . . " It got to her, directly, but I forced her to continue. I knew that book would tell her something, and I could tell she learned from the experience. She was not as loud afterward. Meanwhile, we were waiting for Buffett to come on, and I was getting very edgy.

It is true that the night may have been a little boring; it was boring to me. Up to that point all kinds of yo-yos and nymphomaniacs and fiends with plenty of dope to lay out had visited my home. I have had assholes of serious magnitude, including senators, in my house. I should make a list of the most horrible assholes ever to visit . . . but if I did, Gail would not be at the top of that list. I had sympathy for her when I realized that she was being run by this "husband," who was probably a pimp for the Detroit Lions. She was a blemish, even on the sex trade.

We were stuck in the Grammys, and I was stuck with her. Semmes was irresponsible, and I was full of annoyance—as I would be with any loud stranger that somebody else brings into my kitchen. The Witness was hard to insult; she was dumb and also professionally inured from the sex business to caring what people really thought or felt. The triple-X brand will make you a little thick-skinned after a while, like an armadillo. Maybe I'm like that.

It is a mystery why it bothered me, but this woman also had no sense of humor. She was the unwanted stranger; that was her position in the room. I didn't say more than ten words to her—including "Be quiet." I was damn careful to keep people and things between us. I may have shaken her hand, but that was it. I remember telling the *Aspen Times* later that I could not even have imagined having her in the hot tub with me (as she alleged I tried to), because she would have displaced too much water.

The basketball game had been interesting. The Grammys were not. This irritant had been introduced into the social fabric, but I was as much of a Southern gentleman as I could be. I knew what I was eventually going to do that night, but it was not going to be with this woman. The only question was how soon I could get her out.

I kept trying to get her away from the phone in the office—she was constantly leaving the room to call her husband "in private." I had appointed Semmes to watch her, but Semmes failed; I'm never going to forgive Semmes for this. It was an utter failure of a performance, as a friend and a protector. I don't blame Tim, but he could see weird shit brewing. Tim read the situation and saw it was like a game of musical chairs.

. . .

My support system fell apart when those swine left me alone with the Witness. When Semmes got up, I said, "Goddamnit, this is your date, what are you doing? What do you mean you're leaving?" but he just got up and left. He'd been on the nod for a long time. Tim, who had failed to fix the amplifier, was also planning to leave. I said, "Tim, you gotta take this woman somewhere. You gotta take her . . ." But he couldn't; "No no no," he said, "Carol Ann would kill me." That was true, of course—I had meant for him to give her a ride to the Tavern. I couldn't take her anywhere. She was very pushy, butting into other people's conversations and assuming they were enjoying her gibberish—she was almost professional in that way. You might have thought she had done this kind of work before. She was a little bit like a cop.

Later, she described to the cops how she knew we were dope fiends because we were all asking her, "Are you sure you're not a cop?" I didn't really *think* she was a cop . . . that is how stupid I was. I thought she was just one more dingbat, one more groupie who was unusually determined.

. . .

I had been making cranberry and tequila, because the margarita mix had run out. I was in that kind of mood. *Let's all have a few margaritas.* And she—that sot—she belted them down. We all did, no doubt; that's what it was all about. Some margaritas to celebrate. . . . We were on about the third jug in the blender, or fourth jug, or fifth perhaps, when we switched to cranberry juice, and she had been getting louder and more randy. She was making open cracks to Cat, asking: "Who are you to Hunter?" She grabbed me and said, "Who's this girl? Why is that other girl here? We don't need her around."

Shortly after Tim left, I reached for the phone and told the Witness, "Let's call a goddamn taxi for you." As I dialed the "T"—in 925-TAXI—she rushed over, knocking the phone down, and cut me off. It was a quick, startling movement. She leaped, surprisingly fast for a rhino, from five or six feet away.

"Oh no, don't let it end like this," she pleaded. "You were always my hero." I was curt with her; she had no business here. I had not encouraged her in any way.

I tried to call for the taxi a second time. She immediately reached over, a long reach, with her hairy tentacle of an arm to hang up the phone, and I was shocked that anybody would dare to do that. I screamed at her: "Get the fuck away!" and I think Cat actually restrained her. That was the second rush; she made three rushes on the phone. On this second one, the cabbie heard a bit of the ruckus. Later, we had to get him to testify, and it was very tricky—to establish that I did call and that she had cut it off.

She was warned twice, and then she had a pretty clear shot at me on the third attempt. I was trying desperately to get through to the taxi company. I could see her coming as I began to call again; this time I had just started to stand up. As she came rushing at me, her hip crashed into the cutting board and the cranberry juice fell onto the tile floor. The juice bottle went bouncing around and interfered with her rush. I was cursing her: "You goddamn idiot, what the fuck are you doing?" I was trying to get up, and she came at me then, angry, very angry now—she had hurt herself, hitting the cutting board.

I remembered the "prefrontal lift," which is my most dependable way of ending an argument, particularly when somebody is coming at you. In this move you hit them in both shoulders with the heels of your hands, using a lifting motion. She was coming at me with speed, so I applied a little force. . . . Considerable motion was employed. Usually the attacker helps you a lot, because you can't do a prefrontal lift on anybody who's not coming at you. It doesn't work and looks like a fag punch.

The prefrontal lift stopped her, although her feet were still moving, and she went back on her large butt with a kind of THUMP and ended up sitting on the floor against the refrigerator. I was satisfied. I had been cursing her for an hour. Everything she did was rotten;

her questions were stupid. "I want you out of here," I said. There was never any pretense about this. She had a hideous penchant for coming in my area, hassling me, and she was very stupid. Big, stupid, and I was never entirely sure whether she had her own police agenda or not.

. . .

It was five days later at about ten o'clock in the morning when my neighbor appeared outside, right below the kitchen window. He was very agitated, and he looked like he had come in a hurry. I walked out and said, "Hi, come on it. Have a beer." He said, "No, I can't do that now." He had left his car running. He seemed agitated and afraid of me. He was parked far away from where he usually did, with his car almost backed into the bushes.

"They're going to come and search your house," he said. I walked down the driveway, to get closer to him, and he mumbled, "Those bastards are . . . they're coming out here . . . they're gonna come get you with a search warrant." I couldn't put it together, so I asked, "What crime? What for? What are you talking about?"

The Night Manager, 1985

(Michael Nichols / Magnum Photos)

# Seize the Night

*The night does not belong to Michelob; the night belongs to Hunter Stockton Thompson.*

—Curtis Wilkie, *The Boston Globe*

## The Night Manager

The noonday flight out of Denver is running late today, another brainless jam-up on the runways at Stapleton International—but no matter. The passengers are mainly commercial people—harried-looking middle-aged businessmen wearing blue shirts with white collars and studying Xerox copies of quarterly sales reports.

Across the aisle from me is a rumpled-looking potbellied wretch who looks like Willy Loman, slumped in his seat like two bags of rock salt and drinking Diet Coke. He is reading the money section of *USA Today*.

In front of me are two giddy young boys wearing matching Walkman machines with built-in mikes that allow them to talk to each other through the headphones. They have removed the armrest between them and are now necking shamelessly and bitching occasionally at the stewardess about the lateness of our arrival. . . . The San Francisco airport is closed by violent weather and we are into a long holding pattern, which will cause them to miss an important business appointment. . . .

So What? We are all businessmen these days. Ray Stevens said it twenty years ago—"Take care of business, Mr. Businessman."

. . .

The bell rang for me last night—about 13 hours ago, in fact, and now I am slumped and jittery like some kind of lost polar bear across two first-class seats on UAL #70, from Denver to San Francisco, and my business on this trip is definitely not the kind of all-American nuts-and-bolts hokum that I feel like sharing with my fellow businessmen across the aisle.

There is not a bull market for raw sex, amyl nitrites, and double-ended Greek dildos in the friendly skies of United.

Some people sell U-joints and others are in the meat service and human commodity business. But I have nothing in common with these people.

I am in the sex racket, which is worth about $10 billion a year on anybody's computer—and I am flying to San Francisco to take on the whole city government; the mayor, the D.A., and the police chief.

(And now into SF again—the sleek green hills and the wretched white salt flats beyond the Berkeley Hills, etc.)

The Mitchell Brothers—Jim and Artie—will be waiting for me at the gate, along with my personal road manager, Jeff Armstrong, who is also executive vice president for The Mitchell Brothers Film Group.

These people drive big Mercedes-Benz sedans, the kind of cars favored by Josef Mengele and Ed Meese.

This is the fast lane, folks . . . and some of us like it here.

. . .

Whoops. We are out of gas now, dropping into Fresno like a falling rock—full flaps, reverse engines, then into full glide.

The pilot comes on the intercom and blames "crosswinds at SF International." Bullshit. This is just another routine air-traffic control emergency. Free enterprise—a quick little taste of what's coming in the next four years.

The passengers whine and moan, but nobody except me gets off in Fresno to make a phone call—even though the ramp sergeant makes a special effort to open a door.

Like sheep—and when I come back on the plane with a *Chronicle,* they turn their eyes away, shunning me. . . .

Finally the salesman sitting next to me asks if he can borrow the business section.

Why not? We are all businessmen these days. I am on my way to SF to market a rare porno film, and I am three hours late for a crucial screening with the Mitchell Brothers at their embattled headquarters on O'Farrell Street. The driver is waiting for me at the airport with an armored car and two fat young sluts from Korea.

. . .

We were somewhere on a main street in San Francisco, headed for the waterfront, when a woman walked directly in front of the car on her way across the street. I felt myself seizing up, unable to speak—until Maria poked my leg and whispered urgently: "Oh my god, Hunter, look at that beautiful spine!"

I was looking. We were halted for a red light, and the woman was walking briskly, also toward the waterfront, and now we were both watching her with unblinking eyes, not moving the car until some bastard honked and called me a *shithead.* . . . I honked my own horn and signaled as if I were stalled, waving him to come around me in the other lane, because I was helpless.

Just then the girl with the beautiful spine paused to examine what appeared to be a menu in the window of Vanessi's, or perhaps the glass tank filled with seawater and large unhappy lobsters. Wonderful, I thought. I knew Vanessi's well—and if this spine of a princess was going in there for dinner, so were we. I honked again, just to crank up the traffic confusion, and waved three more cars around me.

"You dirty motherfucker!" a well-dressed man screamed at me as he passed. "Eat shit and die!" He zoomed his huge SUV into low and roared away down the hill. But the other traffic had quickly adjusted to the problem and now ignored me, as if I were some kind of goofy construction project, leaving me in peace to keep an eye on this woman. It was good karma at the right moment, and I told Maria to make a note of it. I was feeling warm all over. "You asshole," she said. "Get this car started! She is moving again. She is crossing Broadway and picking up speed, almost running. God, look at that spine."

"Don't worry," I told her, reaching across the seat to grasp her thigh. "Hot damn, sweetie, what do you want to do with her?"

"*Nothing* yet," she hissed. "I just want to *look* at her."

Indeed. It was just before dusk on Wednesday. The sun was still bright, the Bay was mildly choppy, and we were mercifully unburdened with appointments or professional responsibilities at the time. The day was a brand-new canvas. *Carpe diem.*

. . .

The Goldstein situation developed very quickly, with no warning at all, about halfway through lunch at Pier 23 on a gray afternoon in mid-April, just a few days before the trial was set to begin. We had come through the general hysteria surrounding the "world premiere" on *The Grafenberg Spot,* and no disasters had happened. No scandals had erupted, nobody had been arrested, no personal or professional tragedies of any kind. I had lost my temper in public a few times and been rude to the local press, but so what? It was not my job to be nice. I was, after all, the Night Manager of the most notorious live sex theater in America, and my job was to keep it running. It was a strange obligation that I had somehow taken on, for good or ill, and if I failed, we might all go to jail.

Certainly the Mitchell Brothers would go, and the theater would probably be padlocked and all the fixtures sold to pay off the fines and the court costs. The lawyers painted a grim picture of disgrace, despair, and total unemployment for everybody, including me. Our backs were all to the wall, they said; Mayor Dianne Feinstein, now a senator, was full of hate and not in a mood to compromise. She had been trying to close the O'Farrell for most of her ten years in politics, and now she had everybody from Ed Meese and God to Militant Feminists and the president of the United States on her side. The deal was about to go down, they said. No more lap dancing in San Francisco, and never mind the busloads of Japs.

It was about this time, less than a week before the trial, that Al Goldstein arrived in town for a personal screening of the new film. It was bad timing, but there was no cure for it. Al is one of the certified big boys in the sex racket. He is the publisher of *Screw,* the film critic for *Penthouse,* and perhaps the one man in America whose opinion can make or break a new sex film. *Penthouse* alone sells 4 million copies a month, at $2.95 each, and the prevailing retail price for X-rated video-cassettes is $69.95.

The wholesale net to the producer is about half that, or something like $3.5 million on sales of 100,000 in the first year—which is no big trick, with the combined endorsement of *Penthouse, Screw,* and Al Goldstein. So if only one percent of the people who buy *Penthouse* buy an X-rated videocassette that comes highly recommended by the magazine, the wholesale gross is going to be $1.5 million, before rentals. The retail gross will be about twice that—on a total investment of $100,000 or so in production costs and another $100,000 for promotion.

That is not bad money for a product that any three bartenders from St. Louis and their girlfriends can put together in a roadside motel across the river in Memphis. There is no shortage of raw talent in the industry, and posing naked in front of a camera is becoming more and more respectable. The line between Joan Collins and Marilyn Chambers is becoming very hazy. Not everybody on the street these days can tell you the difference between Jane Fonda in leotards and Vanessa Williams in chains.

I can. But that is a different matter, and it will take a while to explain it. We are dealing, here, with a genuinely odd contradiction in the social fabric. At a time when not only the new attorney general of the United States, and the president of the United States, and the president's wife, and the president's favorite minister, along with the Moral Majority and the Militant Feminists and the *TV Guide* and also the surly fat brute of a manager at the 7-Eleven store in Vernal, Utah, who refused to sell me a copy of *Playboy* at any price & then threatened to have me arrested when I asked why . . .

. . . At a time when all of these powerful people and huge institutions and legions of vicious dingbats who don't need sleep are working overtime to weed out and crush the last remnants of the "Sexual Revolution" that was said to grip the nation in the 1960s and '70s . . . And at a time when they appear to be making serious public progress with their crusade.

This is also a time of growth, vigor, and profit for the American sex industry. Business has never been better. A wino from Texas made a fortune selling Ben-Wa balls; he is now a multimillionaire and listed in big-time money magazines. He shuns publicity and lives alone in the desert. Women write him letters, but he has never had much luck with them. He has no friends and he will never have any heirs, but he is rich and getting richer. One of his agents who recently visited him said he was "weirder than Howard Hughes."

Most of these stories never get out. Nobody knows, for instance, who holds the patent on the penis-shaped, soft-plastic vibrator that sells for $9.95 in drugstores all over the world. There are stores in San Francisco that sell a hundred of those things every day. When I asked the night clerk at Frenchy's in San Francisco who had the dildo concession, who collected the royalties, he said it was an elderly Negro gentleman from Los Angeles. "We've known him for years," he said, "but he never mentioned the patent. He comes by every week in a green Mercedes van and drops off five or six cases of dildos—sometimes nine or ten. He's a good man to do business with. We don't know him at all."

That is how it works in the sex business, which is generally estimated—without much argument from anybody connected with the business, pro or con—to be worth between eight billion and ten billion dollars a year in America. The true figures are probably much higher, but only the IRS really cares. Ten billion dollars a year would just about equal the combined earnings of Coca-Cola, Hershey, and McDonald's.

. . .

Most nights are slow in the politics business, but the night we flogged Al Goldstein on the wet rug floor off the Ultra-Room was not one of them. It was a fast and cruel situation, a major problem for the Night Manager. It was the first real test of my crisis-management skills, and I handled it in my own way.

The immediate results were ugly. It was so bad that there were not even any rumors on the street the next day. Any high-style fracas at the O'Farrell Theatre will normally rate at least a colorful slap from Herb Caen, or at least a few warning calls from the District Attorney's office—but in this case, there was nothing. Nobody wanted any part of it, including me.

But I was blamed, the next morning, for everything that happened, from the shame of the flogging, to the presence of innocent bystanders, to a million-dollar loss on the books of The Mitchell Brothers Film Group.

My job was in jeopardy and my reputation as a "blue" political consultant was called into serious question.

But not for long. It took about 44 days, as usual, for the truth to finally come out—and in the meantime, life got weirder and weirder. I was arrested seven times in six weeks—or at least charged, or accused, or somehow involved with police and courts and lawyers so constantly that it began to seem like my life.

And it seemed almost normal, for a while. Going to court was part of my daily routine. At one point I had to appear in the dock twice in 72 hours and take a savage public beating in the national press, simply because the Judge had changed his mind.

"That's impossible," I told my lawyer Michael Stepanian. "The judge *cannot* change his mind. He would be overruled on appeal." Which proved to be true.

A week or so later the police stole my paddle-tennis racquets—causing me to forfeit my challenge for the championship of the West Coast—and then subpoenaed me to testify against a nonexistent burglar in exchange for giving my racquets back.

That case is still pending, along with a civil complaint from the neighbors about "beatings and screaming."

The Sausalito police are also still holding my personally engraved Feinwerkbau brand Olympic championship air pistol—the most accurate weapon, at 10 meters, that I've ever held in my hand. It was one of those extremely Rare pistols that would shoot exactly where you pointed it, and it didn't really matter who you were. Women and children who had never aimed a pistol at anything could pick up the Feinwerkbau and hit a dime at 15 feet. Beyond that range, or in a wind on the end of a long bamboo pole off the balcony, we would use slightly larger targets, about the size of a quarter, which were tin buttons showing a likeness of San Francisco Mayor Dianne Feinstein with eight tits, like the wolf mother of Rome.

The Mitchell Brothers had printed up 10,000 of these—for some reason that I never quite understood—in the months of angst and fear and hellish legal strife before the trial. I still have about 1,000 of them, and there are maybe another 2,000 in the bushes and on the huge flat roof of Nunzio Alioto's house at the entrance to Sausalito. Nunzio, a close relative of former San Francisco mayor Joe Alioto, was one of my closest neighbors in Sausalito. He was right below me, the next stop down on the tramway. We lived on a very steep cliff, looking out on San Francisco Bay.

I am Lono
(Lalia Nabulsi)

The apartment is gone now, so we can talk about it freely. It will never again be for rent. The reasons for this are complex, and it is not likely that they will ever be made totally clear—but I like to think that I lived there in a style that honored the true spirit of the place, that if the redwood beams and sliding glass walls and the bamboo stools in my Tiki bar could vote for president, that they would vote for me.

Maybe not, but I feel pretty confident about this. Every once in a while you run across a place that was built in a certain spirit, and even the walls understand that it was meant to be used that way.

There were fires and there was breakage. We had a homemade waterfall in the oak trees out in front of the Tiki bar, and we wandered around naked half the time, drinking green chartreuse and smoking lethal Krakatoa cigarettes, and I built a world-class shooting range that hung in midair from an elegant 22-foot rod off the balcony looking out on Angel Island and Alcatraz.

My attorney called it "the best room in the world."

## 16 Alexander

*July 31, 1985*
*Owl Farm*
To: Michael Stepanian, Esq.
819 Eddy Street
San Francisco, CA 94109

Dear Michael,

The (enc.) letters from Judith to your new client, Ms. Laryce Sullivan, at 16 Alexander Ave. in Sausalito, where I lived with Maria, should give us a nice handle on a $33 million slander suit—against Judith and her quarrelsome husband Norvin, a thus-far unindicted co-conspirator, and the computer company that brought them up here from Orange County and caused them to live in a situation (16 Alexander) that they were unable to handle personally and which led them to eventually file a law-suit (against Ms. Sullivan) that names me in a provably false, wrong, hurtful, and personally (and financially) troublesome characterization—i.e.: "Beatings and screaming . . ."

What Beatings? You were there—you met Jacques (the "husband") in the hallway when you were trying to beat down my door.

In any case, my new book—*The Night Manager*—will be cast in a shadow of ugliness by these charges—which Judith and Norvin have filed, repeat "filed."

So in addition to stealing my air pistol and my binoculars and my jock-straps and my custom-built SORBA paddle-tennis racquets and my Job-Related video tapes and two or three packs of my Dunhills on some cheap Nazi scam that nobody believes—now the fuckers want to bash me in civil court (and the public prints) for beating Maria—night after night while the neighbors fled in terror.

Whoops—a bit of a creative outburst there. I couldn't resist. The elegant hum of that title. A smart writer could have fun with a notion like that.

Why not me?


Okay—back to business. I am deep in debt to you and Joe and Tanya and Patty and everybody else who suffered through the hellbroth of lost sleep and character-testing that accompanied my recent attempt to come down from the mountains and live even vaguely like a normal, middle-aged, middle-class, criminally inclined smart urban male with a job (and a few habits—okay. Ask Nancy for details here . . .).

It was a disaster. We (you and me) had enjoyed no legal or even human congress for many years (for reasons of sloth and dumbness, no doubt, but . . .).

Yeah. And I didn't even come to you with a case or a crime or a problem—except that I had, for reasons of my own, recently taken on the job as Night Manager of the weird and infamous O'Farrell Theatre—which happened to be right around the corner from your office, and also a nice, nice headquarters, a suitable place to invite my best and most trustworthy friends for a drink, from time to time.

(One thing we want to keep in mind about the Mitchell Brothers is that they were utterly dumbfounded by most of what I did while I was there—

They are good boys. And I kept them out of jail. The good Lord didn't make seesaws for nothing.)

My job, as I saw it in the beginning, was merely to interview the Brothers as part of a long-overdue assignment from *Playboy* on "feminist pornography"—which was beginning to bore me, by that time, and in fact the only reason I went to see the Mitchell Brothers was the chance that they might be interesting enough—for 48 hours—to sustain my interest in the Feminist porno story long enough for me to crank out the necessary 6,000 or 7,000 words.

Jesus Christ! That *is* how it all started. I was bored with the article after watching five or six triple-X films a day for most of the football season. . . . I became a connoisseur—a knowledgeable critic in the field; I compiled my own Top Ten list—and the Mitchell Brothers were not on it—which is one of the things I told Jim (the elder) when I called him one night in the autumn.

"You want to talk?" he said. "Good. We will talk for 48 hours. You will be our guest. Just get on a plane."

Well . . . shucks. You don't get many offers like that—48 straight hours, just for openers, eyeball-to-eyeball with the rotten Mitchell Brothers.

"We know who you are, Doc," he said. "Normally we don't give interviews—but in your case, we're going to allot 48 hours, because we hear you're a player."

I have all this on tape. I taped everything—from the first high-macho phone arrangements to our first berserk meeting at the San Francisco airport to broken bones and craziness and limousines full of naked women and relentless orgies at the Miyako Hotel—being rolled around the lobby on a baggage cart with people screaming somewhere behind me in the distance, far down the hall in the direction of my suite with the deep green water tub and the bamboo walls and strange women in the bathroom putting lipstick on their nipples. . . .

Whoops, again.

But so what? I may as well get this memo down somewhere—and why not to You?

Why indeed? A hideous streak of six (6) insanely complex legal confrontations—sudden war on all fronts: open container (work-related), Red Light (ditto), Maria crashes two National Rental cars at the Oakland airport, HST burglarized by Sausalito police, HST crushes three negroes on a ramp near the Hall of Justice . . . ugly financial claims; *après moi le déluge* . . . Getting to know Mr. Wrench, Boz Scaggs, and Diane Dodge . . . Insurance claims and driving school, constant Jeopardy. THE JUDGE HAS CHANGED HIS MIND.

Hundreds of hours, thousands of dollars, light-years of frantic attention . . .

Even Bondock was consulted: the best minds of our generation, tied in knots by the vagaries of an irresponsible jurisdiction. That is how I explained it to Joe Freitas—"You were once the D.A. in this town," I said to him, "which is all I need to know."

If Joe was still the D.A., I'd be doing 30 days of SWAP and he would be coming to visit me with the occasional bottle of Absinthe and asking around the office for Maria's phone number in Phoenix.

I warned you about liberals. . . .

It was a weird time. Not many people could have taken that series of shocks and come out of it thinking, "Yes, we are champions." When the Great Scorer comes to write against your name, he will ask my advice. . . .

And I will tell him about many things—no details will be spared; I owe you that. . . .

So I will tell him about Leonard Louie and how you had the insane balls to run me right between Andre's eyes on the night before the first trial and about the otherworldly madness that enveloped us when that giddy chink changed his mind . . .

. . . And about getting my $86 check back from the court

clerk in Sausalito, after my secretary had already plead guilty for me . . . and about the floating horror of that 15 mph red light violation in the midst of the drunk-crash nightmare. . . .

And the time when the cops stole my finely engraved air pistol because my neighbor, Al Green, complained.

Okay. I'll call you on this and other matters—and if in the meantime I happen to speak as I do, from time to time, with the Great Scorer—you can bet all three of your eyes that I am going to tell him how you ripped and pounded me out of my happy bed one morning at 16 Alexander and dragged me—and poor innocent Maria—out in a cold gray fog somewhere north of the Farallon Islands on a 15-foot Boston Whaler into known big shark waters with no radio and no flares and only one good rod and a dinky little 18-inch gaff—after tracking me down (or up, actually) in the raw dirt and dead limbs of my Tiki bar.

And how we prevailed, on the sea—how we caught a fine fish—when all the others had gone south to Pacifica that day— and how we then came to the profoundly high decision to run straight through that maniac crease in the breakers and into Bolinas harbor—because we were thirsty and tired and we had our elegant 16-pound salmon—and because I knew a man with the whiff who lived in a small wooden house that we could almost see from a mile or so out on the ocean.

The Great Scorer will like that story—and when he adds it in with the others, he will know that he is dealing with a warrior.

HST at work in Rio de Janeiro
(Robert Bone)

Okay. I don't want to get mushy here. All I did in the beginning was invite you over to my weird new office at the Theatre—which I knew you'd enjoy, and also because I figured that part of my new job as Night Manager was to keep these two sleazy, baldheaded bastards out of jail by making them so suddenly hip and respectable in the public prints that no judge in SF—not even a Nazi—would feel comfortable about putting them on trial in the eye of a media circus.

That strategy worked nicely. If I'd billed the Mitchells for my work as a media-political consultant, the tab would have run at least $400K net. I did my work well, and I'm proud of it.

Indeed—and history is rife with these horrors—that the foul and notorious Mitchell Brothers should soon go free like friendly neighborhood raccoons, while I the Night Manager would eventually be jailed and pilloried and denounced in the public prints and 3,900 other newspapers all over the nation for running the company car up the tailpipe of a slow-moving, left-drifting Pontiac on the Bayshore Freeway while driving back from the airport after pimping their new movie in L.A. all afternoon with moguls from the Pussycat Theatre chain—

—No, none of this seemed possible when I first came down from the mountain to take a job in the city and live among allegedly civilized people. It frankly never occurred to me that I would have any dealings with the Law—much less be arrested six times in three months—outside of my admittedly strange new duties as Night Manager of the O'Farrell.

I have made three appearances in traffic court in 34 years of driving fast cars in wild conditions all over the world from Kentucky to Hong Kong—and two of them happened in the space of three days, in Leonard Louie's court.

*Teddible, teddible*—as Ralph would say—and the scars have not yet healed. The judge has somehow made himself a partner in my settlement with the whiplash boys, and if I make one mistake on the road in the next three years, I will be slapped in the SF County Jail for six months.

Bad business. If there is any way we can ease off the menace of that "probation," we should do it. Our lives will be easier, and so will Leonard Louie's. NOBODY needs me in that jail. I have learned my lesson: Drive carefully; there are people out there who really don't like me, and if I give them any handle at all, they will use it, and they will flog me . . . and we have better wars to fight and more honorable ways to spill our blood in public.

Anyway—for Joe/FYI—Jim Mitchell assumes that his insurance company is "first" re: the whiplash boys.

I agree. I took the rap and I spent all night in jail—alone; I didn't know you'd gone to Washington—with two Nazi cops who called me "big boy."

It happened in the course of "my duties"—for the O'Farrell and also for *Playboy*.

So let's try to settle this insurance claim and get me off of this queasy "restitution" spike. Jim Mitchell is not going to quarrel if his insurance pays off the whiplash boys. Fair is fair. I was the Night Manager—and I was driving them back from the airport in the official Night Manager's car. Both of our insurance rates are already fucked, anyway—so let's not haggle about it. What is it worth to Leonard to get the "restitution" matter settled by October 18? . . .

. . . Everybody in the world seems to be after me for money now, and this would not be a good time to go belly up in public for small debts.

HUNTER

# Where Were You When the Fun Stopped?

There was no laughter tonight, only the sounds of doom and death and failure—a relentless torrent of death signals: from the sheriff, in the mail, on the phone, in my kitchen, in the air, but mainly from Maria, who said she felt it very strongly and she understood exactly why I was feeling and thinking the way I did/do, but there was nothing she could do about it. She couldn't help herself. It was the death of fun, unreeling right in front of us, unraveling, withering, collapsing, draining away in the darkness like a handful of stolen mercury. Yep, the silver stuff goes suddenly, leaving only a glaze of poison on the skin.

## September 11, 2001

It was just after dawn in Woody Creek, Colorado, when the first plane hit the World Trade Center in New York City on Tuesday morning, and as usual I was writing about sports. But not for long. Football suddenly seemed irrelevant compared to the scenes of destruction and utter devastation coming out of New York on TV.

Even ESPN was broadcasting war news. It was the worst disaster in the history of the United States, including Pearl Harbor, the San Francisco earthquake, and the Battle of Antietam in 1862, when 23,000 were slaughtered in one day.

The Battle of the World Trade Center lasted about 99 minutes and cost 20,000 lives in two hours (according to unofficial estimates as of midnight Tuesday). The final numbers, including those from the supposedly impregnable Pentagon, across the Potomac River from Washington, likely will be higher. Anything that kills 300 trained firefighters in two hours is a world-class disaster.

And it was not even Bombs that caused this massive damage. No nuclear missiles were launched from any foreign soil, no enemy bombers flew over New York and Washington to rain death on innocent Americans. No. It was four commercial jetliners.

They were the first flights of the day from American and United Airlines, piloted by skilled and loyal U.S. citizens, and there was nothing suspicious about them when they took off from Newark, N.J., Dulles in D.C., and Logan in Boston on routine cross-country flights to the West Coast with fully loaded fuel tanks—which would soon explode on impact and utterly destroy the world-famous Twin Towers of downtown Manhattan's World Trade Center. Boom! Boom! Just like that.

The towers are gone now, reduced to bloody rubble, along with all hopes for Peace in Our Time, in the United States or any other country. Make no mistake about it: We are At War now—with somebody—and we will stay At War with that mysterious Enemy for the rest of our lives.

It will be a Religious War, a sort of Christian Jihad, fueled by religious hatred and led by merciless fanatics on both sides. It will be guerilla warfare on a global scale, with no front lines and no identifiable enemy. Osama bin Laden may be a primitive "figurehead"—or even dead, for all we know—but whoever put those All-American jet planes loaded with All-American fuel into the Twin Towers and the Pentagon did it with chilling precision and accuracy. The second one was a dead-on bull's-eye. Straight into the middle of the skyscraper.

Nothing—not even George Bush's $350 billion "Star Wars" missile defense system—could have prevented Tuesday's attack, and it cost next to nothing to pull off. Fewer than 20 unarmed Suicide soldiers from some apparently primitive country somewhere on the other side of the world took out the World Trade Center and half the Pentagon with three quick and costless strikes on one day. The efficiency of it was terrifying.

We are going to punish somebody for this attack, but just who or what will be blown to smithereens for it is hard to say. Maybe Afghanistan, maybe Pakistan or Iraq, or possibly all three at once. Who knows? Not even the Generals in what remains of the Pentagon or the New York papers calling for WAR seem to know who did it or where to look for them.

This is going to be a very expensive war, and Victory is not guaranteed—for anyone, and certainly not for anyone as baffled as George W. Bush. All he knows is that his father started the war a long time ago, and that he, the goofy child-President, has been chosen by Fate and the global Oil industry to finish it Now. He will declare a National Security Emergency and clamp down Hard on Everybody, no matter where they live or why. If the guilty won't hold up their hands and confess, he and the Generals will ferret them out by force.

Good luck. He is in for a profoundly difficult job—armed as he is with no credible Military Intelligence, no witnesses, and only the ghost of bin Laden to blame for the tragedy.

OK. It is 24 hours later now, and we are not getting much information about the Five Ws of this thing.

The numbers out of the Pentagon are baffling, as if Military Censorship has already been imposed on the media. It is ominous. The only news on TV comes from weeping victims and ignorant speculators.

The lid is on. Loose Lips Sink Ships. Don't say anything that might give aid to The Enemy.

*September 12, 2001*

r. Thompson and Col. Depp take delivery of a matched set of rare .454 Casull
Magnums—at a gun store somewhere in the Rocky Mountains, Summer 1997
(Deborah Fuller)

. . .

Johnny Depp called me from France on Sunday night and asked what I knew about Osama bin Laden.

"Nothing," I said. "Nothing at all. He is a ghost, for all I know. Why do you ask?"

"Because I'm terrified of him," he said. "All of France is terrified. . . . I freaked out and rushed to the airport, but when I got there my flight was canceled. All flights to the U.S. were canceled. People went crazy with fear."

"Join the club," I told him. "Almost everybody went crazy over here."

"Never mind that," he said. "Who won the Jets–Colts game?"

"There *was* no game," I said. "All sports were canceled in this country—even *Monday Night Football.*"

"No!" he said. "That's impossible! I've never known a Monday night without a game on TV. What is the stock market doing?"

"Nothing yet," I said. "It's been closed for six days."

"Ye gods," he muttered. "No stock market, no football—this is Serious."

Just then I heard the lock on my gas tank rattling, so I rushed outside with a shotgun and fired both barrels into the darkness. Poachers! I thought. Blow their heads off! This is War! So I fired another blast in the general direction of the gas pump, then I went inside to reload.

"Why are you shooting?" my assistant Anita screamed at me. "What are you shooting at?"

"The enemy," I said gruffly. "He is down there stealing our gasoline."

"Nonsense," she said. "That tank has been empty since June. You probably killed a peacock."

At dawn I went down to the tank and found the gas hose shredded by birdshot and two peacocks dead.

So what? I thought. What is more important right now—my precious gasoline or the lives of some silly birds?

Indeed, but the New York Stock Exchange opened Monday morning, so I have to get a grip on something solid. The Other Shoe is about to drop, and it might be extremely heavy. The time has come to be strong. The fat is in the fire. Who knows what will happen now?

Not me, buster. That's why I live out here in the mountains with a flag on my porch and loud Wagner music blaring out of my speakers. I feel lucky, and I have plenty of ammunition. That is God's will, they say, and that is also why I shoot into the darkness at anything that moves. Sooner or later, I will hit something Evil and feel no Guilt. It might be Osama bin Laden. Who knows? And where is Adolf Hitler, now that we finally need him? It is bad business to go into War without a target.

In times like these, when the War drums roll and the bugles howl for blood, I think of Vince Lombardi, and I wonder how he would handle it. . . . Good old Vince. He was a zealot for Victory at all costs, and his hunger for it was pure—or that's what he said and what his legend tells us, but it is worth noting that he is not even in the top 20 in career victories.

We are At War now, according to President Bush, and I take him at his word. He also says this War might last for "a very long time."

Generals and military scholars will tell you that 8 or 10 years is actually not such a long time in the span of human history—which is no doubt true—but history also tells us that 10 years of martial law and a wartime economy are going to feel like a Lifetime to people who are in their twenties today. The poor bastards of what will forever be known as Generation Z are doomed to be the first generation of Americans who will grow up with a lower standard of living than their parents enjoyed.

That is extremely heavy news, and it will take a while for it to sink in. The 22 babies born in New York City while the World Trade Center burned will never know what they missed. The last half of the 20th Century will seem like a wild party for rich kids, compared to what's coming now. The party's over, folks. The time has come for loyal Americans to Sacrifice . . . Sacrifice . . . Sacrifice. That is the new buzzword in Washington. But what it means is not entirely clear.

Winston Churchill said, "The first casualty of War is always Truth." Churchill also said, "In wartime, Truth is so precious that she should always be attended by a bodyguard of Lies."

That wisdom will not be much comfort to babies born last week. The first news they get in this world will be News subjected to Military Censorship. That is a given in wartime, along with massive campaigns of deliberately planted "Dis-information." That is routine behavior in Wartime—for all countries and all combatants—and it makes life difficult for people who value real news. Count on it. That is what Churchill meant when he talked about Truth being the first casualty of War.

In this case, however, the next casualty was Football. All games were canceled last week. And that has Never happened to the NFL. Never. That gives us a hint about the Magnitude of this War. Terrorists don't wear uniforms, and they play by inscrutable rules—The Rules of World War III, which has already begun.

So get ready for it, folks. Buckle up and watch your backs at all times. That is why they call it "Terrorism."

*September 19, 2001*

Big Sur, editorial conference, 1971
(Annie Leibovitz)

# Speedism

*"Hi, Mr. Thompson. My name is Wendy _____ from Suzuki, and I want more than anything else in the world to give you a brand-new Suzuki _____, which has a top speed of 200 mph [chuckle]. Yeah, I thought that would interest you [giggle]. Call me anytime at _____."*

*How long, O Lord, how long? Some people wait all their lives for a telephone call like that. But not me. I get them constantly, and on some nights I ask myself, Why?*

## Rules for Driving Fast

Speedism is the most recently identified Disease that curses modern Man. Yesterday's murdering speed freak is today's helpless victim of "Speedism." This is a Big Leap that has taken a long time to achieve. It is a milestone in medical history & many unsung heroes have sacrificed themselves for it, including Sid Vicious and the actor Richard Pryor, who set himself on fire while researching the Speedism virus.

This is wonderful news. A whole generation of coke fiends can rest easy now: They were not common addicts & criminals. No. They were helpless Victims of a highly contagious Virus, *Speedata Viruuseum*. The Disease is Debilitating, Demoralizing & Incurable, leaving the victim wracked with pain & utterly helpless for 6–9 months at a time.

Speedism can be Fatal when mixed with high-speed automobiles &
whiskey. It is wrong & I condemn it, but some dingbats will do it anyway. . . . And not All will survive, but so what?

For the others, the Living, here are some basic rules.

*No. 1*—Make sure yr. car is Functioning on all Mechanical &
Electrical levels. Do not go out on *any* road to drive Fast unless
all yr. exterior lights are working perfectly.

There is only failure & jail very soon for anybody who tries to
drive fast with one headlight or a broken red taillight. This is
automatic, unarguable *Probable Cause* for a cop to pull you over
& check everything in yr. car. You do not want to give them
Probable Cause. Check yr. lights, gas gauge, & tire pressure
before you drive Anywhere.

*No. 2*—Get familiar with the Brake pressures on yr. machine
before you drive any faster than 10 mph. A brake drum that
locks up the instant you touch the pedal will throw you sideways
off the road & put you into a fatal eggbeater, which means you
will Go To Trial if it happens. Be *very* aware of yr. brakes.

*No. 3*—Have no *small* wrecks. If you are going to loop out & hit
something, *hit it hard.* Never mind that old-school Physics bullshit about the Irresistible Force & the Immoveable Object. The
main rule of the Highway is that Some Objects are More Move-
able than Others. This occurs, for instance, when a speeding car
goes straight through a plywood billboard, but not when one
goes through a concrete wall. In most cases, the car going fastest
sustains less damage than the slower-moving vehicle.

A Small Wreck is almost always both Costly and Embarrassing. I
talked to a man tonight who said he had been demoted from Head-
waiter to Salad Boy when he had a small wreck in the restaurant's parking lot and lost all respect from his fellow workers. "They laughed at
me & called me an Ass," he said. "I should have hit the fucker at
seventy-five, instead of just five," he whined. "It cost me $6,800 any-
way. I would have been maître d' by now if I'd screwed it on & just
Mashed the bastard. These turds have made me an outcast."

*No. 4*—(This is one of the more Advanced rules, but let's pop it in here while we still have space.) Avoid, at all costs, the use of Any drug or drink or Hubris or even Boredom that might cause you to Steal a car & crash it into a concrete wall just to get the Rush of the airbags exploding on you. This new fad among rich teenagers in L.A. is an extremely Advanced Technique that only pure Amateurs should try, and it should *never* be done Twice. Take my word for it.

*No. 5*—The eating schedule should be as follows: Hot fresh spinach, Wellfleet Oysters, and thick slabs of Sourdough garlic toast with salt & black pepper. Eat this two hours before departure, in quantities as needed. The drink should be Grolsch green beer, a dry oaken-flavored white wine & a tall glass full of ice cubes & Royal Salute scotch whiskey, for the supercharge factor.

Strong black coffee should also be sipped while eating, with dark chocolate cake soaked in Grand Marnier for dessert. The smoking of oily hashish is optional, and in truth Not Recommended for use *before* driving at speeds up to 150 mph in residential districts. The smoking of powerful hashish should be saved until after yr. *return* from the drive, when nerve-ends are crazy & raw.

Road testing the Ducati 900, 1995
(Paul Chesley)

## Song of the Sausage Creature

There are some things nobody needs in this world, and a bright-red, hunch-back, warp-speed 900cc café-racer is one of them—but I want one anyway, and on some days I actually believe I need one. That is why they are dangerous.

Everybody has fast motorcycles these days. Some people go 150 miles an hour on two-lane blacktop roads, but not often. There are too many oncoming trucks and too many radar cops and too many stupid animals in the way. You have to be a little crazy to ride these super-torque high-speed crotch rockets anywhere except a racetrack—and even there, they will scare the whimpering shit out of you. . . . There is, after all, not a pig's eye worth of difference between going head-on into a Peterbilt or sideways into the bleachers. On some days you get what you want, and on others, you get what you need.

When *Cycle World* called me to ask if I would road-test the new Harley Road King, I got uppity and said I'd rather have a Ducati superbike. It seemed like a chic decision at the time, and my friends on the superbike circuit got very excited. "Hot damn," they said. "We will take it to the track and blow the bastards away."

"Balls," I said. "Never mind the track. The track is for punks. We are Road People. We are Café Racers."

The Café Racer is a different breed, and we have our own situations. Pure speed in sixth gear on a 5,000-foot straightaway is one thing, but pure speed in third gear on a gravel-strewn downhill ess-turn is quite another.

But we like it. A thoroughbred Café Racer will ride all night through a fog storm in freeway traffic to put himself into what somebody told him was the ugliest and tightest diminishing-radius loop turn since Genghis Khan invented the corkscrew.

Café Racing is mainly a matter of taste. It is an atavistic mentality, a peculiar mix of low style, high speed, pure dumbness, and over-weening commitment to the *Café Life* and all its dangerous pleasures. . . . I am a Café Racer myself, on some days—and many nights for that matter—and it is one of my finest addictions. . . .

I am not without scars on my brain and my body, but I can live with them. I still feel a shudder in my spine every time I see a picture of a Vincent Black Shadow, or when I walk into a public restroom and hear crippled men whispering about the terrifying Kawasaki Triple. . . . I have visions of compound femur-fractures and large black men in white hospital suits holding me down on a gurney while a nurse called "Bess" sews the flaps of my scalp together with a stitching drill.

Ho, ho. Thank God for these flashbacks. The brain is such a wonderful instrument (until God sinks his teeth into it). Some people hear Tiny Tim singing when they go under, and others hear the song of the Sausage Creature.

When the Ducati turned up in my driveway, nobody knew what to do with it. I was in New York, covering a polo tournament, and people had threatened my life. My lawyer said I should give myself up and enroll in the Federal Witness Protection Program. Other people said it had something to do with the polo crowd, or maybe Ron Ziegler.

The motorcycle business was the last straw. It had to be the work of my enemies or people who wanted to hurt me. It was the vilest kind of bait, and they knew I would go for it.

Of course. You want to cripple the bastard? Send him a 160-mph café-racer. And include some license plates, so he'll think it's a street-bike. He's queer for anything fast.

Which is true. I have been a connoisseur of fast motorcycles all my life. I bought a brand-new 650 BSA Lightning when it was billed as "the fastest motorcycle ever tested by *Hot Rod* magazine." I have ridden a 500-pound Vincent through traffic on the Ventura Freeway with burning oil on my legs and run the Kawa 750 Triple through Beverly Hills at night with a head full of acid. . . . I have ridden with Sonny Barger and smoked weed in biker bars with Jack Nicholson, Grace Slick, and my infamous old friend Ken Kesey, a legendary Café Racer.

Some people will tell you that slow is good—and it may be, on some days—but I am here to tell you that fast is better. I've always believed this, in spite of the trouble it's caused me. Being shot out of a cannon will always be better than being squeezed out of a tube. That is why God made fast motorcycles, Bubba. . . .

So when I got back from the U.S. Open Polo Championship in New York and found a fiery red rocket-style bike in my garage, I realized I was back in the road-testing business.

The brand-new Ducati 900 *Campione del Mundo Desmodue* Supersport double-barreled magnum Café Racer filled me with feelings of lust every time I looked at it. Others felt the same way. My garage quickly became a magnet for drooling superbike groupies. They quarreled and bitched at each other about who would be first to help me evaluate my new toy. . . . And I did, of course, need a certain spectrum of opinions, besides my own, to properly judge this motorcycle. The Woody Creek Perverse Environmental Testing Facility is a long way from Daytona or even top-fuel challenge sprints on the Pacific Coast Highway, where teams of big-bore Kawasakis and Yamahas are said to race head-on against each other in death-defying games of "chicken" at 100 miles an hour. . . .

No. Not everybody who buys a high-dollar torque-brute yearns to go out in a ball of fire on a public street in L.A. Some of us are decent people who want to stay out of the emergency room but still blast through neo-gridlock traffic in residential districts whenever we feel like it. . . . For that we need fine Machinery.

Which we had—no doubt about that. The Ducati people in New Jersey had opted, for reasons of their own, to send me the 900SP for testing—rather than their 916 crazy-fast, state-of-the-art superbike track-racer. It was far too fast, they said—and prohibitively expensive—to farm out for testing to a gang of half-mad Colorado cowboys who think they're world-class Café Racers.

The Ducati 900 *is* a finely engineered machine. My neighbors called it beautiful and admired its racing lines. The nasty little bugger looked like it was going 90 miles an hour when it was standing still in my garage.

Taking it on the road, though, was a genuinely terrifying experience. I had no sense of speed until I was going 90 and coming up fast on a bunch of pickup trucks going into a wet curve along the river. I went for both brakes, but only the front one worked, and I almost went end over end. I was out of control staring at the tailpipe of a U.S. Mail truck, still stabbing frantically at my rear brake pedal, which I just couldn't find. . . . I am too tall for these new-age roadracers; they are not built for any rider taller than five-nine, and the rearset brake pedal was not where I thought it would be. Midsize Italian pimps who like to race from one café to another on the boulevards of Rome in a flat-line prone position might like this, but I do not.

I was hunched over the tank like a person diving into a pool that got emptied yesterday. Whacko! Bashed on the concrete bottom, flesh ripped off, a Sausage Creature with no teeth, fucked up for the rest of its life.

We all love Torque, and some of us have taken it straight over the high side from time to time—and there is always pain in that. . . . But there is also Fun, the deadly element, and Fun is what you get when you screw this monster on. BOOM! Instant take-off, no screeching or squawking around like a fool with your teeth clamping down on your tongue and your mind completely empty of everything but fear.

No. This bugger digs right in and shoots you straight down the pipe, for good or ill.

On my first take-off, I hit second gear and went through the speed limit on a two-lane blacktop highway full of ranch traffic. By the time I went up to third, I was going 75 and the tach was barely above 4,000 rpm. . . .

And that's when it got its second wind. From 4,000 to 6,000 in third will take you from 75 mph to 95 in two seconds—and after that, Bubba, you still have fourth, fifth, and sixth. Ho, ho.

I never got to sixth gear, and I didn't get deep into fifth. This is a shameful admission for a full-bore Café Racer, but let me tell you something, old sport: This motorcycle is simply too goddamn fast to ride at speed in any kind of normal road traffic unless you're ready to go straight down the centerline with your nuts on fire and a silent scream in your throat.

When aimed in the right direction at high speed, though, it has unnatural capabilities. This I unwittingly discovered as I made my approach to a sharp turn across some railroad tracks, and saw that I was going way too fast and that my only chance was to veer right and screw it on totally, in a desperate attempt to leapfrog the curve by going airborne.

It was a bold and reckless move, but it was necessary. And it worked: I felt like Evel Knievel as I soared across the tracks with the rain in my eyes and my jaws clamped together in fear. I tried to spit down on the tracks as I passed them, but my mouth was too dry. . . . I landed hard on the edge of the road and lost my grip for a moment as the Ducati began fishtailing crazily into oncoming traffic. For two or three seconds I came face to face with the Sausage Creature. . . .

But somehow the brute straightened out. I passed a schoolbus on the right and then got the bike under control long enough to gear down and pull off into an abandoned gravel driveway, where I stopped and turned off the engine. My hands had seized up like claws and the rest of my body was numb. I went into a trance for 30 or 40 seconds until I was finally able to light a cigarette and calm down enough to ride home. I was too hysterical to shift gears, so I went the whole way in first at 40 miles an hour.

Whoops! What am I saying? Tall stories, ho, ho. . . . We are motorcycle people; we walk tall and we laugh at whatever's funny. We shit on the chests of the Weird. . . .

But when we ride very fast motorcycles, we ride with immaculate sanity. We might abuse a substance here and there, but only when it's right. The final measure of any rider's skill is the inverse ratio of his preferred Traveling Speed to the number of bad scars on his body. It is that simple: If you ride fast and crash, you are a bad rider. If you go slow and crash, you are a bad rider. And if you are a bad rider, you should not ride motorcycles.

The emergence of the superbike has heightened this equation drastically. Motorcycle technology has made such a great leap forward. Take the Ducati. You want optimum cruising speed on this bugger? Try 90 mph in fifth at 5,500 rpm—and just then, you see a bull moose in the middle of the road. WHACKO. Meet the Sausage Creature.

Or maybe not: The Ducati 900 is so finely engineered and balanced and torqued that you *can* do 90 mph in fifth through a 35-mph zone and get away with it. The bike is not just fast—it is *extremely* quick and responsive, and it *will* do amazing things. . . . It is a little like riding the original Vincent Black Shadow, which would outrun an F-86 jet fighter on the take-off runway, but at the end, the F-86 would go airborne and the Vincent would not, and there was no point in trying to turn it. WHAMMO! The Sausage Creature strikes again.

There is a fundamental difference, however, between the old Vincents and the new breed of superbikes. If you rode the Black Shadow at top speed for any length of time, you would almost certainly die. That is why there are not many life members of the Vincent Black Shadow Society. The Vincent was like a bullet that went straight; the Ducati is like the magic bullet in Dallas that went sideways and hit JFK and the Governor of Texas at the same time.

It was impossible. But so was my terrifying sideways leap across railroad tracks on the 900SP. The bike did it easily with the grace of a fleeing tomcat. The landing was so easy I remember thinking, Goddamnit, if I had screwed it on a little more I could have gone a lot farther.

Maybe this is the new Café Racer macho. My bike is so much faster than yours that I dare you to ride it, you lame little turd. Do you have the balls to ride this BOTTOMLESS PIT OF TORQUE?

That is the attitude of the new-age superbike freak, and I am one of them. On some days they are about the most fun you can have with your clothes on. The Vincent just killed you a lot faster than a superbike will. A fool couldn't ride the Vincent Black Shadow more than once, but a fool can ride a Ducati 900 many times, and it will always be a bloodcurdling kind of fun. That is the Curse of Speed which has plagued me all my life. I am a slave to it. On my tombstone they will carve, IT NEVER GOT FAST ENOUGH FOR ME.

## The Lion and the Cadillac

Fear? I know not fear. There are only moments of confusion. Some of them are deeply stamped on my memory and a few will haunt me forever.

One of my ugliest and most confused moments, I think, was when I was driving a junk Cadillac down the Coast Highway to Big Sur and a large mountain lion jumped into the moving car.

I had stopped for a moment beside the road to put out a newspaper fire in the backseat when this huge cat either jumped or fell off a cliff and landed on its back in the gravel right beside me. I was leaning over the side and pouring beer on the fire when it happened.

It was late in the day, and I was alone. When the beast hit the ground I had a moment of total confusion. And so did the lion. Then I jumped back in the car and took off down the hill in low gear, thinking to escape certain death or at least mutilation.

The beast had tried to pounce on me from above, but missed. . . . And now, as I shifted the junker into second, I heard a terrible snarling and realized that the cat was running right behind me and gaining . . . (I was, in fact, Terrified at that moment.) . . . And I think I must have gone temporarily insane when the goddamn thing came up beside me and jumped right into the car through the passenger-side window like a bomb.

It bounced against the dashboard and somehow turned the radio volume all the way up. Then it clawed me badly on my arm and one leg. That is why I shudder every time I hear a Chuck Berry tune.

I can still smell the beast. I heard myself screaming as I tried to steer. There was blood all over the seat. The music was deafening and the cat was still snarling and clawing at me. Then it scrambled over the seat and into the back, right into the pile of still-burning newspapers. I heard a screech of pain and saw the cat trying to hurl itself through the back window.

We were still rolling along at about thirty miles per hour when I noticed my ball-peen hammer sticking out of the mangled glove compartment.

I grabbed the hammer with my right hand, steering with my left, and swung it wildly over my shoulder at the mountain lion.

*Whack!* I felt it hit something that felt vaguely like a carton of eggs, and then there was silence. No resistance in the backseat. Nothing.

I hit the brakes and pulled over. My hand was still on the hammer when I looked back and saw that I had somehow hit the animal squarely on top of its head and driven the iron ball right through its skull and into its brain. It was dead. Hunched on its back and filling the whole rear of the car, which was filling up with blood.

I was no longer confused.

Backstage at the O'Farrell
(Michael Nichols / Magnum Photos)

## Geerlings & the War Minister's Son

Avenida Copacabana is always crowded at night, in the style of Miami Beach, which it physically resembles, and spiritually dwarfs. . . . Copacabana is the *beach city* for Rio de Janeiro, capital city of Brazil, where I happened to be living at the time of the horrible "Cuban Missile Crisis" in 1962, when expatriate Americans all over the world glanced around them in places like Warsaw and Kowloon or Tripoli and realized that life was going to be very different from now on: All countries north of the Equator were going to be destroyed forever by nuclear bombs before Sunday. WHACKO! The long-dreaded "nuclear trigger" was going to be pulled somewhere west of Bermuda when two enemy naval fleets collided on the sea lane to Cuba, around two in the afternoon—and that collision would signal the end of the world as we knew it. This was not a drill.

Please accept my apologies if this little foreign adventure story seems overwrought or maudlin—at the time that I told it, maybe it was, and so what? Those were extremely violent times, as I recall; I had spent a long year on a very savage road, mainly along the spine of the South American *cordillera,* working undercover in utterly foreign countries in the grip of bloody revolutions and counterrevolutions that made up the news of the day from the Panama Canal all the way down to the lonely frozen pampas of Argentina. . . . South America in the early 1960s was the most routinely murderous place in the world to find yourself doomed to be living when the World was destroyed by bombs.

And for me, that one fateful place in the world was Rio de Janeiro, Brazil, where I was living extremely well, under the circumstances. All things considered, Rio was pretty close to the best place in the world to be lost and stranded forever when the World finally shut down.

. . .

Geerlings was a Dutchman about thirty-three years old, built like some monster on Muscle Beach but without steroids—beyond an athlete, a dangerous brute with the temper of a wolverine, a handsome guy. His cheap shirts were always bulging, like his brain. He was the inventor of a radical coloring process for glass walls the size of swimming pools.

He fled Holland on a murder warrant—he'd killed Nazis with a Colt .45 that he stole from a dead American; he had grown up in Holland during the Second World War, and his hatred for the Germans was immense. He would go out at night looking for Krauts to beat up.

One night in Rio, we saw some stylish teenagers torturing a dog. They were both holding the dog, pulling its legs, and it was screeching. We came out of the nightclub across the street in a dull, bored mood, and here were these creeps strangling a dog in a well-lit public place; they were about 200 yards from Avenida Copacabana, a big busy street, and we smashed into them at a dead run, full speed and flailing. I remember saying, "Let's get those evil fuckers." He was like Oscar— Geerlings had that killer mentality, like a professional assassin.

It was the South Beach part of town, with wide granite sidewalks. They dropped the dog when we hit them, then they bounced along the sidewalk like rubber dolls. I was screaming, "You want to torture a dog, you fucks! We'll torture you!" No doubt it was excessive behavior— under the circumstances—and as usual in moments of public violence, people went all to pieces. Perhaps we were Feverish. Rio can do that to people, especially on Copacabana Beach: drastic dehumanizing halluci- nations, personality inversions at high speed, spontaneous out-of-body experiences that come with no warning at awkward moments.

. . .

They twisted away and ran desperately toward Avenida Copacabana, like, "If I can just get to Fifth Avenue there will be lights there, and people will see what's happening." And instead of letting them go— they fought briefly, a little bit of a swing—we pounded them as they took off, two young Brazilians about twenty-five or thirty, healthy boys, arrogant fucking punks.

I could see we were probably going to catch them. I saw the avenue up ahead, and knew what they were going to do. They were desper- ately trying to flag a passing Lotocao bus—like an open-air school bus that runs twenty-four hours a day. They were running desperately, spastic with fear and screaming for help, and I didn't want them to escape.

So here we come, charging out of the darkness, our Converse sneak- ers slapping the concrete, and they're running, these two native boys, screaming desperately for the bus to stop. It would be like two people running running down Forty-second Street through the crowd, trying to call for a taxi as if it were the last act of their lives. And instead of letting them go then, I caught up with what turned out to be the War Minister's son just as he reached the bus. It was a drama before it happened. All this screaming: "Please stop! Oh God! Help!" The one I was after was almost within a step of getting his foot on the lowest rung of the bus.

I had no choice—I was going faster than he was, and as he slowed down to get on the bus I hit him, running from behind, and blasted him against the bus with my hands out. I wasn't sure what to do. He *really* bounced off. Imagine that: thinking, Oh, Thank God—hands reaching down from the bus to help him escape. It was bad. We were brutish foreigners chasing two local boys for no apparent reason and attacking them.

The poor bastard was smashed—CLANG—against the side of the Lotocao, and I fell on top of him. Everything stopped when this terrible crash came—people ran out of stores and begged for police intervention. Maybe I got ahold of him and seized him; somehow he ended up sitting on the street, leaning against the back wheel of the bus, which didn't have any hubcaps. There must have been some deep confusion there. I remember his head bouncing off of the lug nuts on the axle; I remember telling myself, *Watch out, you fool—keep your knuckles away from those goddamn lug nuts.*

Meanwhile, Geerlings was brutalizing the other guy—it was a shameful outburst. Geerlings had the guy's feet bent back toward his neck, like a pretzel, trying to twist him the wrong way. A huge crowd had gathered. We were beating on both of them and screaming in English. The bus driver had stopped in the middle of the cross street; this was a bad fight, whatever it meant. And I was wearing shorts. So was Geerlings—a horrible Dutchman wanted for murder, an international criminal. I immediately pulled back.

After they got on the bus, we stopped for a *cafezinho* at the corner bar and waited for the mob to gather. I remember the two kids and the other people on the bus as it took off and rounded in first gear, the old cranky engines, these victims screaming through the windows and shaking their fists: "You dirty bastards! We kill you! You Fuck!"—in Brazilian . . . and we just laughed it off.

I don't know why we went and stood at the counter there in the coffee place—a *boutequim*, it had an open front facing the street, two cents for a cup of coffee—to try and explain it. "Well, those guys were bad! They beat the dog." It was hard to explain. Then, all of a sudden, the street began to fill up, people shouting, and I thought, What the hell. Is there a riot someplace? Something else is happening. There were maybe ten people in the *boutequim*, but we were facing the street. And this mob of people—it sounded like they were at a political protest. I said to Geerlings, "What the fuck is this?" There were people yelling and pointing at us, and then there were cops in the mob. I realized, Oh Fuck. It's Us. Those monsters had gotten off at the next stop and grabbed the nearest cop.

. . .

I had seen a jaguar outside a bar on Avenida Copacabana the night before. There are bars in Rio that look like delis, the kind in New York with a long counter and seats, except there's beer and food. While Geerlings was fucking with Germans, I went back to the bathroom. We're talking about a wooden shack—Avenida Copacabana is backed up to *favelas*, the hills. These gigantic mountains come straight down, four or five hundred feet; it's a jungle behind every building. Here I was, taking this routine piss in a ramshackle South American men's room, which had a window—the garbage area was outside this window in the middle of bushes and trees. I wasn't thinking about much of anything except what Geerlings might be doing to the Germans. I didn't try to do anything to prevent him from beating these people. I just wanted him to be careful. I didn't want to get busted for it.

I was looking out the window: blank darkness, garbage cans, and right in front of me, no more than three feet away, was a gigantic yellow- and black-spotted jaguar *tigre*, five, possibly six feet long, maybe five without the tail. A big cat.

I thought, What the fuck is this? I've never seen anything like this in my life. Ye gods! I had to go to Marigoso to confront cats at arm's length. I was stunned. I just watched it. It fucked around. It didn't make much noise. I don't know what would have happened if one of the boys had come out and thrown some more garbage into the can. This thing was huge. I didn't know what the hell to do, but I went back through the bar and the first thing I saw was Geerlings: He had hooked a Nazi in the nuts, and had him up against a phone booth with his cheek half pulled off. He wasn't kidding; we had to get out of there.

I said, "Goddamn. You won't believe this. While you were sitting out here fucking with Germans, I went back to the bathroom and there was a jaguar tiger, right in front of me. Right outside the window."

"Oh no. Come on," said Geerlings.

. . .

So the following night I took the little auto that I'd brought with me to Rio, a cheap .25 automatic. I carried it all over South America, usually loaded. Why carry one that's not? I tied it around my neck with a string—it was too hot to carry it anywhere else.

"All right, Geerlings," I said. "I'll show you. We're going to go back down here and get ourselves a *tigre.*"

I loaded up and we went back down to the bar and sat in the same place. Geerlings fucked with more Germans. The *tigre* never came back. How many times can you go to the men's room? None of it makes a lot of sense. We gave up on the tiger. Then we started wandering around to the various nightclubs—after the one disappointment, we were ripe for a dog incident. It was action. We had no action and it built up. That's really what it was—it was the explosion. If the cat had come, those guys wouldn't have been hit.

It seemed incidental really to both of us. But, holy shit—the mob and the police and being arrested to chanting and shouting was bad enough, but to have a loaded .25 automatic.

I guess my beating the guy against the lug nuts got their attention—he was the son of the War Minister, so I understood that we were in trouble. But they left Geerlings alone; I saw him in the front of the crowd asking questions of the police: "I'm here to help."

"Who are you?" the police asked Geerlings.

He was saying, "Well, it's a friend. A countryman. What's the trouble here? Don't ask me. I'm nobody."

Geerlings was trying to help in some way, but it was a mob scene, and I was trying to get the attention of the Embassy press officer. I was under arrest, and I was being led through a tunnel of chanting Cariokas: "String him up! Fuck him! U.S. out! Fuck U.S.A.! *Abajo!*"

There was going to be trouble when the gun was found—luckily, I had put it in my pocket. I saw Geerlings as I was being led down this corridor of people. It wasn't like he was on the fringes of the crowd: He was like Ruby in the Oswald thing. He was on the front line, but he was acting like he was just an interested bystander—very smart, and he was getting away with it. I was being interviewed, but I could see him there; he was still talking to another cop, asking questions and being very officious. The first chance I got, I stepped out of the line as I was being led somewhere else. I had my hand on the .25—in the middle of three hundred people.

As I approached him—this is really quick thinking—I pulled the gun out. When they weren't looking at me, I put the gun in his hand and said, "Run!"

There was a frozen moment, and he took off through the crowd like a bull. No more gun.

(Daniel E. Dibble)

## Yesterday's Weirdness Is Tomorrow's Reason Why

WILLIAM McKEEN: *Your use of drugs is one of the more controversial things about you and your writing. Do you think the use of drugs has been exaggerated by the media? How have drugs affected your perception of the world and/or your writing? Does the media portrayal of you as a "crazy" amuse, inflame, or bore you?*

HUNTER S. THOMPSON: Obviously, my drug use is exaggerated or I would be long since dead. I've already outlived the most brutal abuser of our time—Neal Cassady. Me and William Burroughs are the only other ones left. We're the last unrepentant public dope fiends, and he's seventy years old and claiming to be clean. But he hasn't turned on drugs, like that lying, treacherous, sold-out punk Timothy Leary.

Drugs usually enhance or strengthen my perceptions and reactions, for good or ill. They've given me the resilience to withstand repeated shocks to my innocence gland. The brutal reality of politics alone would probably be intolerable without drugs. They've given me the strength to deal with those shocking realities guaranteed to shatter *anyone's* beliefs in the higher idealistic shibboleths of our time and the "American Century." Anyone who covers his beat for twenty years—and my beat is "The Death of the American Dream"—needs every goddamned crutch he can find.

Besides, I *enjoy* drugs. The only trouble they've given me is the people who try to keep me from using them. *Res Ipsa Loquitur.* I was, after all, a Literary Lion last year.

The media perception of me has always been pretty broad. As broad as the media itself. As a journalist, I somehow managed to break most of the rules and still succeed. It's a hard thing for most of today's journeyman journalists to understand, but only because they can't do it. The smart ones understood immediately. The best people in journalism I've never had any quarrel with. I *am* a journalist and I've never met, as a group, any tribe I'd rather be a part of or that are more fun to be with—despite the various punks and sycophants of the press.

It hasn't helped a lot to be a savage comic-book character for the last fifteen years—a drunken screwball who should've been castrated a long time ago. The smart people in the media knew it was a weird exaggeration. The dumb ones took it seriously and warned their children to stay away from me at all costs. The *really* smart ones understood it was only a censored, kind of toned-down, children's-book version of the real thing.

Now we are being herded into the nineties, which looks like it is going to be a *true* generation of swine, a decade run by cops with no humor, with dead heroes, and diminished expectations, a decade that will go down in history as The Gray Area. At the end of the decade, no one will be sure of anything except that you *must* obey the rules, sex will kill you, politicians lie, rain is poison, and the world is run by whores. These are terrible things to have to know in your life, even if you're rich.

Since it's become the mode, that sort of thinking has taken over the media, as it has business and politics: "I'm going to turn you in, son—not just for your own good but because you were the bastard who turned *me* in last year."

This vilification by Nazi elements within the media has not only given me a fierce joy to continue my work—more and more alone out here, as darkness falls on the barricades—but has also made me profoundly orgasmic, mysteriously rich, and constantly at war with those vengeful retro-fascist elements of the Establishment that have hounded me all my life. It has also made me wise, shrewd, and crazy on a level that can only be known by those who have been there.

WM: *Some libraries classify* Fear and Loathing in Las Vegas *as a travelogue, some classify it as nonfiction, and some classify it as a novel. How much of this book is true? How would you characterize this book (beyond the jacket copy info in* The Great Shark Hunt*)? You refer to it as a failed experiment in Gonzo journalism, yet many critics consider it a masterwork. How would you rate it?*

HST: *Fear and Loathing in Las Vegas* is a masterwork. However, true Gonzo journalism as I conceive it shouldn't be rewritten.

I would classify it, in Truman Capote's words, as a nonfiction novel in that almost all of it was true or *did* happen. I warped a few things, but it was a pretty accurate picture. It was an incredible feat of balance more than literature. That's why I called it *Fear and Loathing*. It was a pretty pure experience that turned into a very pure piece of writing. It's as good as *The Great Gatsby* and better than *The Sun Also Rises*.

WM: *For years your readers have heard about* The Rum Diary. *Are you working on it, or on any other novel? Do you have an ambition to write fiction? Your stint as a newspaper columnist was successful, but do you have further ambitions within journalism?*

HST: I've always had and still do have an ambition to write fiction. I've never had any real ambition within journalism, but events and fate and my own sense of fun keep taking me back for money, political reasons, and because I am a warrior. I haven't found a drug yet that can get you anywhere near as high as sitting at a desk writing, trying to imagine a story no matter how bizarre it is, as much as going out and getting into the weirdness of reality and doing a little time on The Proud Highway.

*March 1990*

## Letter to John Walsh

To: John Walsh / ESPN
*June 21, 2002*

JOHN.

Things are savage here, but I think of you constantly & thanx for yr. elegant assessment of Jann & the hideous world as we know it.

But I fear no evil, for the Lord is with me. Yea though I walk in the shadow of death, I fear no Evil, for the Lord is with me. . . .

You bet. He is our ace in the hole . . . Or maybe not. Maybe John Ashcroft is greater than God. Who knows? Ashcroft is the new point man for Bush Inc., yet he is dumb as a rock. He is like some Atavistic endeavor on speed—just another stupid monster as Attorney General of the U.S.A., a vengeful jackass with an IQ of 66.

How long, O Lord, how long? These Pigs just keep coming, like meat oozing over a counter . . . And they keep getting Meaner and Dumber.

Yeah. Trust me on this, Bubba. I knew *Ed Meese* in his prime, and I repeatedly cursed him as the murderous pig that he was—a low form of life that hung on the neck of this nation like a crust of poison algae. He was scum. Ed Meese was a Monster.

But he was *nothing* compared to John Mitchell, the anal-compulsive drunkard who was Nixon's Attorney General in the terrible time of Watergate. He was the weirdest act in town.

John Mitchell was a big-time corporate lawyer and his wife was a serious drinker from Arkansas who squealed on him by accident and brought down the whole structure of the U.S. federal government. . . . It was wonderful. Those animals were forced into the tunnel, one by one, and destroyed like offal.

That is the nature of professional politics. Many are called, but few survive the nut-cutting hour—which appears to be coming down on our goofy Child President these days. . . . Ah, but it was ever thus, eh? Vicious thieves have always ruled the world. It is our *wa*. We are like pigs in the wilderness.

                                                            HUNTER

# PART THREE

Gambling on a football game with Ed Bradley
(HST archives)

# The Foreign Correspondent

*My opposition to war is not based upon pacifist or non-resistant principles. It may be that the present state of civilization is such that certain international questions cannot be discussed; it may be that they have to be fought out. We ought not to forget that wars are a purely manufactured evil and are made according to a definite technique. A campaign for war is made upon as definite lines as a campaign for any other purpose. First, the people are worked upon. By clever tales the people's suspicions are aroused toward the nation against whom war is desired. Make the nation suspicious; make the other nation suspicious. All you need for this is a few agents with some cleverness and no conscious and a press whose interest is locked up with the interests that will be benefited by war. Then the "overt act" will soon appear. It is no trick at all to get an "overt act" once you work the hatred of two nations up to the proper pitch.*

—Henry Ford

## May You Live in Interesting Times

There is an ancient Chinese curse that says, "May you live in interesting times," which was told to me by an elderly dope fiend on a rainy night in Hong Kong near the end of the War in Vietnam. He was a giddy old man, on the surface, but I knew—and he knew that I knew—of the fear and respect he commanded all over Southeast Asia as a legendary Wizard in the far-flung Kingdom of Opium. I had stopped by his shop in Kowloon to get some advice and a chunk of black medicine for my friends who were trapped in the NVA noose that was inexorably closing in on Saigon. They refused to leave, they said, but in order to stay alive in the doomed and dysfunctional city, they needed only two things—cash money and fine opium.

I was no stranger to either one of these things, at the time—and I was, after all, in Hong Kong. All I had to do to get a satchel of green money and pure opium delivered to the *Newsweek* bureau was make a few phone calls. My friends trapped in Saigon were Journalists. We have a strong sense, people of my own breed and tribe, and we are linked—especially in war zones—by strong bonds of tribal loyalty. . . .

## Last Days of Saigon

*So bye bye, Miss American Pie,*
*Drove my Chevy to the levee, but the levee was dry,*
*Them good ole boys were drinkin' whiskey and rye,*
*Singin' this'll be the day that I die,*
*This'll be the day that I die . . .*

I had never paid much attention to that song until I heard it on the Muzak one Saturday afternoon in the rooftop restaurant of the new Palace Hotel, looking down on the orange-tile rooftops of the over-crowded volcano that used to be known as Saigon and discussing military strategy over gin and lime with London Sunday *Times* correspondent Murray Sayle. We had just come back in a Harley Davidson–powered rickshaw from the Viet Cong's weekly press conference in their barbed-wire enclosed compound at Saigon's Tan Son Nhut airport, and Sayle had a big geophysical map of Indochina spread out on the table between us, using a red felt-tipped pen as a pointer to show me how and why the South Vietnamese government of then-President Nguyen Van Thieu had managed to lose half the country and a billion dollars' worth of U.S. weaponry in less than three weeks.

I was trying to concentrate on his explanation—which made perfect sense, on the map—but the strange mix of realities on that afternoon of what would soon prove to be the next to last Saturday of the Vietnam War made concentration difficult. For one thing, I had never been west of San Francisco until I'd arrived in Saigon about ten days earlier—just after the South Vietnamese Army (ARVN) had been routed on worldwide TV in the "battles" for Hué and Da Nang.

This was a widely advertised "massive Hanoi offensive" that had suddenly narrowed the whole war down to a nervous ring around Saigon, less than fifty miles in diameter . . . and during the past few days, as a million or more refugees fled into Saigon from the panic zones up north around Hué and Da Nang, it had become painfully and ominously clear that Hanoi had never really launched any "massive offensive" at all—but that the flower of the finely *U.S.-trained* and heavily U.S.-equipped South Vietnamese Army had simply panicked and run amok. The films of whole ARVN divisions fleeing desperately through the streets of Da Nang had apparently surprised the NVA generals in Hanoi almost as badly as they jolted that bonehead ward heeler that Nixon put in the White House in exchange for the pardon that kept him out of prison.

Gerald Ford still denies this, but what the hell? It hardly matters anymore, because not even a criminal geek like Nixon would have been stupid enough to hold a nationally televised press conference in the wake of a disaster like Da Nang and compound the horror of what millions of U.S. viewers had been seeing on TV all week by refusing to deny, on camera, that the 58,000 Americans who died in Vietnam had died in vain. Even arch-establishment commentators like James Reston and Eric Sevareid were horrified by Ford's inept and almost cruelly stupid performance at that press conference. In addition to the wives, parents, sons, daughters, and other relatives and friends of the 58,000 American dead, he was also talking to more than 150,000 veterans who were wounded, maimed, and crippled in Vietnam . . . and the net effect of what he said might just as well have been to quote Ernest Hemingway's description of men who had died in another war, many years ago—men who were "shot down and killed like dogs, for no good reason at all."

My memories of that day are very acute, because it was the first time since I'd arrived in Saigon that I suddenly understood how close we were to the *end,* and how ugly it was likely to be . . . and as that eerie chorus about "Bye bye, Miss American Pie" kept howling around my ears while we picked at our Crab St. Jacques, I stared balefully out across the muddy Saigon River to where the earth was trembling and the rice paddies were exploding in long clean patterns like stitches down the sleeve of a shirt. . . . Carpet bombing, massive ordnance, the last doomed snarling of the white man's empire in Asia.

"Well, Murray," I asked him. "What the fuck do we do *now?*"

He drained the last of a tall bottle of fine French Riesling into our crystalline flutes and languidly called for another. It was somewhere around lunchtime, but the penthouse dining room was empty of cash customers, except us, and we were not in a hurry. "We are surrounded by sixteen NVA divisions," he said with a smile. "The enemy is right out there in that smoke across the river, and he wants vengeance. We are doomed."

I nodded calmly and sucked on a corncob pipe full of steamy Khymer Rouge blossoms, then I leaned over the map and made a wet red circle around our position in downtown Saigon.

He looked at it. "So what," he said. "Those people are *cannibals,*" he snapped. "They will hunt us down and *eat* us."

"Nonsense," I said. "I am a personal friend of Colonel Vo Don Giang. We will be put in cages for a while, then set free."

# One Hand Clapping

I knew a Buddhist once, and I've hated myself ever since. The whole thing was a failure.

He was a priest of some kind, and he was also extremely rich. They called him a monk and he wore the saffron robes and I hated him because of his arrogance. He thought he knew everything.

One day I was trying to rent a large downtown property from him, and he mocked me. "You are dumb," he said. "You are doomed if you stay in this business. The stupid are gobbled up quickly."

"I understand," I said. "I am stupid. I am doomed. But I think I know something you don't."

He laughed. "Nonsense," he said. "You are a fool. You know nothing."

I nodded respectfully and leaned closer to him, as if to whisper a secret. "I know the answer to the greatest riddle of all," I said.

He chuckled. "And what is that?" he said. "And you'd better be Right, or I'll kill you."

"I know the sound of one hand clapping," I said. "I have finally discovered the answer."

Several other Buddhists in the room laughed out loud, at this point. I knew they wanted to humiliate me, and now they had me trapped—because there *is* no answer to that question. These saffron bastards have been teasing us with it forever. They are amused at our failure to grasp it.

Ho ho. I went into a drastic crouch and hung my left hand low, behind my knee. "Lean closer," I said to him. "I want to answer your high and unanswerable question."

As he leaned his bright bald head a little closer into my orbit, I suddenly leaped up and bashed him flat on the ear with the palm of my left hand. It was slightly cupped, so as to deliver maximum energy on impact. An isolated package of air is suddenly driven through the Eustachian tube and into the middle brain at quantum speed, causing pain, fear, and extreme insult to the tissue.

The monk staggered sideways and screamed, grasping his head in agony. Then he fell to the floor and cursed me. "You swine!" he croaked. "Why did you hit me and burst my eardrum?"

"Because *that*," I said, "is the sound of one hand clapping. That is the answer to your question. I have the answer now, and you are deaf."

"Indeed," he said. "I am deaf, but I am smarter. I am wise in a different way." He grinned vacantly and reached out to shake my hand.

"You're welcome," I said. "I am, after all, a doctor."

Zorro at work, Woody Creek, 2002
(Anita Bejmuk)

# The Invasion of Grenada

TRIAL RUN FOR PANAMA AND AFGHANISTAN
. . . SPRINGBOARD FOR IRAQ AND KOREA—
SEE THE NEW WORLD ORDER IN ACTION . . .
WHY NOT? HITLER HAD SPAIN, WE HAVE
GRENADA . . .

*I believe the government has not only a right but an obligation to lie to the people.*
—Jody Powell, *Nightline* (ABC News),
October 26, 1983

There are some interesting attitudes on the street these days, and not all of them come from strangers. Old friends call me late at night from places like Nassau and New York and Bangkok, raving angrily about suicide bombers in Lebanon. They call me from the Blue Lagoon Yacht Club on the south side of St. Vincent, offering big boats for hire to run the blockade around the war zone in Grenada, only 100 miles away. I get collect calls from Miami and from federal prison camps asking me who to vote for. The janitor at the Woody Creek Tavern wants to join the U.S. Marines and kill foreigners for a living.

"They have a buddy system," he said. "We could join together and go to the Caribbean."

"Or Lebanon," I said. "Any place with a beach."

He shrugged. The difference between Lebanon and Grenada was not clear in his mind. All he wanted was some action. He was a dope fiend, and he was bored.

Five years in a trailer court on the fringe of the jet-set life had not agreed with him. His teeth were greasy and his eyes were wet and he was too old to join the Marines. But there was excitement in his voice. In late afternoons at the Tavern, he would stand at the bar with the cowboys and watch the war news on network TV, weeping openly and cracking his knuckles as Dan Rather described combat scenes from Grenada, leathernecks hitting the beach, palm trees exploding, natives running for cover, helicopters crashing into jagged mountainsides.

. . .

I called the Blue Lagoon Yacht Club on the south side of St. Vincent the other day and asked for the manager, Mr. Kidd. Another man came on the line and said Mr. Kidd was gone to Barbados for a while, with some people from the CIA. Well, I thought, why not? We will all work for them sooner or later.

"So what?" I said. "I need a boat. Who's in charge there?"

"I am," he replied. "There are no boats, and Mr. Kidd is gone."

"I need a boat tomorrow," I said. "For seven days, to Grenada."

"To Grenada?" he said. "To the war?"

"That's right," I said. "I need something fast, around forty feet, with radar and triple sidebands. I have plenty of money. Mr. Kidd knows me well."

"It doesn't matter," he said. "Mr. Kidd's gone."

"When do you expect him back?" I asked.

"Maybe never," he replied.

"What?" I said. "What's happened to him?"

"I don't know," he replied. "He went to the war. Maybe he got killed." He paused, waiting for me to say something, but I was thinking.

"All hell broke loose around here," he said finally. "You know that, don't you?"

"Yeah," I said. "I know that."

"It's big business," he said. "Mr. Kidd even sold his own boat. They had seabags full of hundred-dollar bills. I've never seen so much money."

"Okay," I said. "Do you have any planes for hire?"

There was another pause, then he laughed.

"Okay," he said. "Give me a number and I'll get back to you."

Indeed, I thought, you treacherous sot. There was something odd in the man's voice. I said I was between planes in the Dallas airport and would call him back later.

"Who is this?" he asked. "Maybe I'll hear from Mr. Kidd."

"Tell him Dr. Wilson called," I said, "from Texas."

He laughed again. "Good luck," he said.

I hung up, feeling vaguely uneasy, and called a travel agent.

. . .

Forty hours later, I was on a plane from Barbados to Pearls Airport in Grenada. There was no need for a boat after all. LIAT Airlines was flying again, running four flights a day into the war zone, and every seat was taken. There was no such thing as a secure reservation on the Liberation Shuttle once the blockade was lifted. It was an ugly ride with a long sweaty stop in St. Vincent, and most of the passengers were edgy.

News reports from Grenada said the invasion was over and the Cuban swine had surrendered. But there were still snipers in the hills around the airport and along the road to St. George's. The Marines, still reeling from the shock of 289 dead from a single bomb in Beirut a week earlier, were not getting much sleep on this island.

## THE WRONG IS ALWAYS WRONG
*—Grenadian Voice*, November 26, 1983

The pros and cons of bombing the insane—even by accident—was only one of the volatile questions raised by the invasion of Grenada. It was a massive show of force by the U.S. Military, but the chain of events leading up to it was not easy to follow. Some people said it was a heartwarming "rescue mission," 2,000 Marines and paratroopers hitting the beach to pluck 400 or so American medical students out of the jaws of death and degradation by bloodthirsty Cubans. Others said it happened because Castro had loaned his friend Maurice Bishop $9 million to build a new airport on the island, with a runway 10,000 feet long and capable of serving as a Cuban military base on the edge of strategic sea-lanes in the south Caribbean. And still others called it a shrewd and finely planned military move, a thing that had to be done once the neighboring islands asked formally for American help. "We did the right thing for the wrong reasons," a ranking Democratic Party official told me on the telephone just before I left for Grenada. "You know I hate to agree with Reagan on anything at all, but in this case I have to go along with him."

Well, I thought. Maybe so. But it was hard to be sure, from a distance of 4,000 miles, so I decided to have a look at it. The trip from Woody Creek to Grand Junction to Denver to Atlanta to Miami to Barbados to Pearls Airport on the north shore of Grenada took two days, and by the time I got there I had read enough newspapers in airports along the way to have a vague grip on the story, at least on the American side of it.

A crowd of local Stalinists had run amok in Grenada, killing everybody who stood in their way and plunging the whole island into terrorism, looting, and anarchy. The murdering swine had even killed Maurice Bishop, Grenada's answer to JFK, and after that they'd planned to kill, capture, or at least maim hundreds of innocent American medical students who were trapped like rats on the island. A battalion of U.S. Marines, en route to Lebanon in response to the disaster two days earlier at the Beirut airport, was instead diverted to Grenada, along with a U.S. Navy battle fleet and the 82nd Airborne, to crush Communist mutiny and rescue American citizens.

This task had been quickly accomplished, without the burden of any civilian press coverage, and Defense Department film of the actual invasion showed U.S. troops in heroic postures, engaging the enemy at close quarters and taking 600 Cuban prisoners. It was a fitting response to the massacre at the U.S. Marine compound in Lebanon, except that it happened 7,000 miles away and the Arabs called it a bad joke. "It was just another cowboy movie," a Syrian diplomat told me several weeks later in the lounge of the United Nations Plaza Hotel. "All it proved was that Americans would rather shoot than think."

There was no shortage of conflicting opinions on the invasion of Grenada. It was called everything from "hysterical gunboat diplomacy" to a long-overdue assertion of the Monroe Doctrine, a swift and powerful warning to any other so-called revolutionaries who might try to seize turf in the American Hemisphere. "We taught those bastards a lesson," said a businessman at the Ionosphere Club in Miami International Airport. "Fidel Castro will think twice before he tries a trick like this again, and so will the Sandinistas."

In Grenada with Loren Jenkins, 1984
(Laura G. Thorne)

. . .

Wisdom is cheap in airport bars and expensive Third World hotels. You can hear almost anything you want, if you hang around these places long enough—but the closer you get to a war zone, the harder it is to speak with strangers about anything except the weather. By the time I got to Barbados, only an hour away from Grenada, not even my fellow passengers in the standby line at LIAT Airlines had anything to say about the invasion or what they were doing there. I did the last leg of the trip without saying a word to anybody. About half the people on the plane, a hellishly hot DC-4 that stopped for a while in St. Vincent's, were white men of indeterminate origin. Some, carrying locked attaché cases of expensive camera equipment, wore faded T-shirts from long-lost hotels in the Orient. I recognized Al Rakov, from Saigon, but he pretended not to know me and I quickly understood.

Things got worse when the plane touched down in Grenada. The seedy little airport was a madhouse of noise and confusion, jammed with sweating immigrants and American troops carrying M16s. People with odd passports were being jerked out of line and searched thoroughly. Cobra helicopters roared overhead, coming and going like drone bees, and the whole place was surrounded by rolls of sharp concertina wire. It was very much a war zone, a bad place to break any rules. A typewritten "notice to journalists" was tacked on a plywood wall by the immigration desk, advising all those with proper credentials to check in and sign the roster at the military press center in St. George's, on the other side of the island.

It was dark by the time I cleared Customs. A man named Randolph helped me load my bags into the back of his old Chevrolet taxi, and we took off for the St. George's Hotel. The road went straight uphill, a series of blind S-turns with a steep drop-off on one side and wet black cliffs on the other.

It was an hour's drive, at least, and the road was scarred every six or eight feet with deep, teeth-rattling potholes. There was no way to relax, so I thought I might as well ask Randolph how he felt about the invasion. He had not said much since we left the airport, but since we were going to be together for a while and I wanted to stop somewhere along the way for a cold beer, a bit of conversation seemed in order. I did it more out of old journalistic habit than anything else, not expecting any real information, but Randolph surprised me.

"You are asking the right person," he said sharply. "You are talking to a man who lost his wife to the Revolution."

Whoops, I thought. There was something in the tone of his voice that caused me to reach into my satchel for a small tape recorder. Randolph was eager to talk, and he had a story to tell. All I had to do was ask a question now and then, to keep pace with him, as we drove in low gear through the darkness.

It was a narrow country road, the main highway across the island, past Grenville and Great Bay and over the steep volcanic humps of Mt. Lebanon and Mt. Sinai, through the Grand Etang Forest. There were small houses along the way, like a back road in New England, and I settled back to listen as Randolph told his tale. At first I took him for a CIA plant; just another eloquent native taxicab driver who happened to be picking up journalists at the airport when they finally emerged from the Customs shed and looked around them to see nothing more than a cluster of wooden shacks in a palm grove on the edge of the sea. Pearls Airport looks like something that was slapped together about fifty years ago in the Philippines, with a dirt road bordering the airstrip and a few dozen native functionaries hanging around the one-room Bar & Grocery.

The population of the whole island is 110,000, about the size of Lexington, Kentucky, and population density is roughly one person per square mile—compared to one person per square foot in Hong Kong. This is clearly an undeveloped island, nothing at all like Barbados or Jamaica or Trinidad, and it is hard to imagine anything happening here that could make headlines all over the world and cause an invasion by the U.S. Marines.

But Randolph explained that things were different on the other side of the island, where the recent violence had happened. He welcomed the U.S. invasion, he said. It had freed him, at last, from the grip of a cruel situation that had been on his neck like an albatross ever since he and his wife had decided to join the Revolution, almost five years ago.

Neither one of them had been Communists, at the time, and Marxist was just another word he'd picked up in school, along with Maurice Bishop and Bernard Coard and the other neighborhood kids. All they knew about the U.S.A., back then, was that it was a big and powerful country where cowboys and soldiers killed Indians. They knew nothing at all about Russia, Cuba, or guns.

But things changed when Grenada became independent. Some of the boys went off to school in England, and they came back feeling ambitious. The new government was corrupt, they said; the prime minister was crazy, and the world was passing them by. Bishop and a few of his friends decided to start a political party of their own, which they called the New Jewel Movement. It was The People's Party, they said; mainly young people, with a hazy socialist platform and reggae music at rallies. Hundreds of people joined, creating a nucleus of grassroots enthusiasm that forced Eric Gairy out of office and replaced him with Maurice Bishop.

Randolph went along with it, he explained, because he believed the New Jewel Movement was going to make a better life for all the Grenadian people. He knew most of the leadership personally, and he was, after all, a businessman. While Bishop had gone off to the London School of Economics and Coard was at the University of Dublin, Randolph was climbing the ladder of commerce as an independent trucker and saving money to buy his own home. When the New Jewel came to power, he was not without friends in high places. Among them were Hendrick Radix, the new attorney general, and Hudson Austin, soon to be appointed commanding general of The People's Revolutionary Army. It was a heady time, for Randolph, the year of life in the fast lane. He had a home on a hill in St. George's, a commercial trucking license, and enough personal influence to get his new wife a job at party headquarters.

That was when the trouble started. First it was General Austin, who cheated him out of some money; then it was Phyllis Coard, wife of the deputy prime minister, who lured his wife off to Cuba. After that it was all downhill for him.

. . .

My tape recorder was running from the time we left Pearls Airport until we pulled into the small parking lot of the St. George's Hotel. We made a few stops in dimly lit huts along the way for cold beer, which Randolph graciously paid for, because I had no Grenadian money. "Don't mention it," he said. "It's my pleasure."

Which was true. He was having a good time, and so was I. There are worse ways to enter a war zone than by stopping at every back country pub along the road and mingling with friendly people. In one place I got edgy when a huge negro wearing a hospital shirt called me a "stupid fucking Russian," but Randolph waved him off. "That man is totally crackers," he whispered. "He is one of those who ran away from the insane asylum when the bombs hit."

. . .

From my room in the St. George's Hotel, high on a steep green hill overlooking the harbor in downtown St. George's, I can see the whole town coming awake on a hot Sunday morning. The roosters begin crowing around six, the church bells begin a joyous tolling at around seven, and when I wake up at nine, there is a half-eaten pile of blue grapes on the floor between my bed and the shower stall in my bathroom. It is the sign of the fruit bat. I have never seen the beast, but the grapes are there every morning. The fruit bat brings his midnight meal into my room every night, through the window, and gnaws on his grapes while hanging upside down from the ceiling. It is his regular eating place, and neither war nor revolution nor invasion by U.S. Marines and a horde of international newsmongers will change his dinner hour.

The fruit bat is a big one. I can hear him flapping around sometimes in the darkness, and by the sound of the wings, he seems about the size of a crow. Some of them carry paralytic rabies, but it is hard to know which ones.

. . .

The lobby of the St. George's is usually empty on Sunday morning. The locals along with a handful of British subjects have gone to church, and the war correspondents are sleeping. Even Maitland—the young bartender with the high black forehead and the quick brown eyes of a boy who should be in law school somewhere—is not at his post today. The bar, attached to the dining room off a flight of steep stairs, is empty.

Even the dining room is empty. The only people in sight are a few taxi drivers sitting sleepily on the concrete wall looking down on the harbor and the big freighters tied up at the pier along the Carenage.

There is a press briefing scheduled for 10 A.M. at the Maryshaw

House, recently converted into an international press center, and some of the correspondents will want to wake up in time to be there.

My room is number 15 and there is only one key. No master at the desk, no passkey with the maid, no locksmith on the premises or anywhere closer than Bridgetown. When I locked myself out of the room yesterday, the entire infrastructure of the hotel broke down. Maitland had to abandon the bar and spend the next 45 minutes outside in the rain on a broken, rotten-wood ladder that we managed to brace up against the wall beneath my window. I held the ladder while he pulled the glass slats out of the louvered window and crawled inside to open the door.

The St. George's is a world-class hotel. It has always been one of my favorites, ranking up there with the Hotel Continental Palace in Saigon and the infamous Lane-Xang in Laos. Just after the invasion, there were six hundred reporters headquartered here and only nineteen rooms, nine with hot water. No women on the premises, no ice in the drinks, no credit cards honored, no phones, no TV, hot sauce and stale ham for breakfast . . . but the management was gracious, three elderly women who remained determinedly neutral in a situation that would have destroyed the best minds behind any desk at any Hilton or Holiday Inn.

After four weeks in the frantic heat of an utterly baffling war zone, there were no more surprises at the St. George's. When I came back to my room the other night, I found two huge wooden crosses leaning against the wall outside my door. One was about nine feet long, made of four-by-fours bolted together, and the other was six feet long, constructed in the same way. Maitland told me they belonged to the people who had checked into number 16, right next door to me—an American evangelist and his teenage son, who had carried the crosses through sixty-eight countries in six years. Nobody asked why.

> *The invasion of Grenada would not have happened if other island states in the area had not been frightened into overreacting. It takes only twelve men in a boat to put some of these governments out of business.*

—Commonwealth Secretary-General Sir Shridath Ramphal, Barbados, November 29, 1983

. . .

There is a lot of loose talk in the waterfront bars on the Carenage these days. People are talking about vengeance and violence and perhaps another invasion. Psy-Ops, the U.S. military's unit for winning, whipping, and terrifying the hearts and minds of the population, has been spreading the word that Fidel Castro is promising the people of Grenada "a surprise present for Christmas."

They are still reeling from the shock of the last invasion, a full-bore assault by the U.S. Marines, Rangers, Seals, Navy jets, warships, the 82nd Airborne; thousands of parachutes, terrible explosions at all hours of the day and night, their prime minister murdered and their women carried off by wild Cubans. Their cars were stolen and all their doors were kicked in and some of their closest friends and relatives were chopped in half by machine gun fire, set on fire by rockets, drilled full of holes like something out of a Fearless Fosdick nightmare. We hit this place like it was Iwo Jima. The invasion of Grenada was one of those low-risk, high-gain, cost-plus operations that every West Point graduate dreams of. Unleash the whole weight of the U.S. military arsenal on a small island in the Caribbean and call it a great victory. Bash the buggers silly; bomb the insane; walk heavy, talk wild, and kick ass in every direction. That's how it went in Grenada.

Nobody knows why quite yet, but it will all come out in the wash. The word in the St. George's lobby today was that Tony Rushford, the new attorney general and legal representative of the British Crown, was going to put Bernard Coard on trial for murder as soon as possible.

"Those bastards are going to wish they'd never heard the word *revolution* before we get finished with this place," said a CIA plotter working for the U.S. embassy, disguised as a Caribbean scholar. "All this bullshit about Nazis and wargames and Negro target practice is going to come to a screeching halt. All you hear around this place is people saying we've got to put these bastards on trial. Okay, we're going to give you a goddamn trial. We'll have Bernie Coard and we'll hang Hudson Austin and we'll hang Liam James and Abdullah and Redhead and every other one of those Communist sons of bitches. Their mouths will run like jelly. The myth of the New Jewel Movement will be utterly destroyed. We won't even need Maurice Bishop's body. There are plenty of witnesses, and we have every one of them by the balls."

I was shocked by the tone of his voice.

He was talking about the entire leadership of the so-called military coup that overthrew Maurice Bishop's neo-Marxist, limbo-style revolutionary government that had ruled Grenada for four and a half years until an orgy of shocking violence in the last days of October turned the island into something like Uganda in the blackest days of Idi Amin . . . Bernard Coard was the deputy prime minister, a once-respected Marxist theoretician and personal friend of Bishop's. Hudson Austin was the general in charge of The People's Revolutionary Army. Abdullah, James, and Sgt. Lester "Goat" Redhead were the soldiers accused of the killings. Not just Bishop, but four of his ministers and his mistress and dozens, perhaps hundreds, of innocent civilians had been gunned down by the army when a mass rally attempted to restore Maurice Bishop to power.

There was no question of guilt, but there were some legal niceties to be observed. The bodies had been burned, and, under British Commonwealth law, it is awkward to hold a murder trial without a corpse. Treason was another possibility, but the only witnesses were dead or in Richmond Hill Prison locked up by the CIA. The first phase of the trial was scheduled for February, but without bodies or witnesses it was going to be what Tony Rushford called "a sticky wicket."

"Our mistake was not killing them instantly," said a colonel from the U.S. Army. "Summary execution—shot while attempting to escape." He laughed bitterly, sipping his beer at the Red Crab, a chic roadhouse on the outskirts of town. The mayor of Ft. Lauderdale was at the other end of the bar, whooping it up with a businessman from New Jersey who was gnawing on the throat of a black woman.

"You people are shameless," I said to the colonel.

"We are warriors," he replied, stuffing the bowl of his pipe full of Mixture 79.

"The thousand-year Reich lasted twelve years and eight months," I said.

"That's plenty of time," he replied. "Two years from today, I'll be retired and drawing a full pension."

The Yanqui press in Grenada with U.S. Army censors, Winter 1984
(HST archives)

. . .

*There is some art you don't have to sign.*

—Psy-Ops

Saturday night was quiet in Grenada. For the first time in three weeks there were no soldiers on the road to Grand Anse. No 82nd Airborne patrols, no roadblocks bristling with M16s and dim red flashlights, no roaring of big Cobra helicopters overhead; a man in the right mood could move along the road in a quick little topless Mini Moke and be menaced by nothing at all except wild dogs and potholes.

It was a night like any other night 300 years ago in Grenada. That is about how long it has been since the people who live here have had any peace from drunken foreigners. First it was boatloads of vicious Caribbean Indians coming over the horizon in war canoes, then it was pirates and Spaniards and Moors—all of them crazed on grog—and then came the French, who built prisons, and 200-odd years of sodden, sweating Englishmen. Finally, in 1974, came independence and a voodoo-crazed prime minister who spoke of flying saucers at the UN. Sir Eric Gairy, weirder than Papa Doc, lasted five years. He was overthrown in 1979 by a cabal of homegrown Marxists and international Trotskyites. Four years after that came the U.S. Marines.

It is a war story, but it is not like Vietnam. This is not Indochina, and the U.S. is not losing.

The people who run the White House, along with the Pentagon and the CIA, have finally done what we pay them to do, and they have done it pretty well. If the business of America is business—as Mr. Coolidge said—then a lot of people are going to get big Christmas bonuses for what was done here in the savage year of our lord 1984. We have seen America's interests threatened in the Caribbean basin, and we have crushed that threat like a roach. The Pentagon has finally won a war, in public, and the victors are enjoying the spoils.

As well they should. These are warriors, and some of them fought and died here, Cubans and Grenadians as well as eighteen American soldiers. It was not altogether a toy war. The action was swift and hazy, the truth remains unknown, and the future is decidedly cloudy.

But never mind these things. They are fey. They are only side effects compared to the wave we are riding on the south coast of Grenada these days.

Earlier in the night we had a series of crude and unstable discussions with people from the 21st Military Police Company on the lawn of what used to be the Calabash Hotel, far out on the beach past Grand Anse. They have turned the whole place into a war zone, with sandbags and machine-gun nests and trip flares strung between palm trees. And they stretched rolls of concertina wire across the lawn in front of the *Time* magazine photographer's cabana, which caused a serious argument. This was the work of the infamous "Captain Calabash," a wild-eyed MP commander who kept his troops in a sleepless frenzy of bogus security drills around the perimeters of the hotel grounds, seizing turf like a homeless mad dog for reasons that were never made clear. When his troops weren't patrolling the moonlit beach with night-vision scopes and enough weaponry to kill every fish between Grenada and the south side of Barbados, they were doing discipline drills with commando knives and twenty-five-pound steel balls and digging up the beach to fill sandbags that the Captain ordered to be stacked in huge piles across the driveways and walkways, all the way out to the sea. . . . Even the CIA spooks were embarrassed.

## DINNERTIME IN GRENADA . . . MORGAN PLAYS THE PIANO AT THE RED CRAB . . . THE BOMBING OF THE INSANE ASYLUM, THE TRIAL OF BERNARD COARD, RAISING SERIOUS QUESTIONS . . . WHAT TO DO WITH BERNIE?

Some people will tell you that the army has become sophisticated, and they will have evidence to bear it out. They will have T-shirts from the war zone and they will have color slides from the beach on Prickly Bay where the naked girl danced with Captain Henegan's sentries. Or they may have videotapes of Navy F-14s dive-bombing an insane asylum overlooking St. George's harbor across from the St. George's Hotel.

Morgan was his name, they said. He played late-night piano at the Red Crab, a Caribbean roadhouse set back in the palm trees not far from the Calabash Hotel. He showed up one night not long after the invasion, and after he played a few tunes like "Fandago" and "Way Down upon the Swanee River" people liked him, and when the place was crowded, he would play for as long as they wanted, doing singa-long gigs with the State Department people and the Military Police.

They would gather around his piano and raise their beer mugs and croak hoarsely at one another, like young lions. On some nights, Colonel Ridgeway, from the State Department, would come in with a carload of women and then go out back with the waiters and smoke huge spliffs on the ledge behind the garbage cans.

V. S. Naipaul was there, along with Hodding Carter and General Jack "Promotable" Farris and a girl who was posing for a centerfold spread for *Australian Playboy*. Farris wouldn't come inside, for military image reasons; he would sit outside in his Jeep and watch the merri-ment from afar, feeling Joy in his heart and safe at last from all fears of botch and embarrassment. And never seeing his main man, Jim Ridge-way, back there on the ledge with the Rastas.

It was our kind of war. And when somebody finally asked Morgan where he came from and he said he'd spent the past year or so in the insane asylum up there on the hill near Fort Frederick, people laughed and called for another round. "Good old Morgan," they said, "he's crazy as a loon."

Which was true, or at least certifiable. This is not one of those situa-tions where you want to start delving into questions like who's crazy and who's not. Nobody needs that down here. This thing was weird from the start. People fought and died on this island, for reasons that were never ex-plained—and probably never will be until Bernard Coard comes to trial.

That should happen sometime around the spring of 1988, when the press is busy elsewhere. His lawyer will be Ramsey Clark, former attorney general of the U.S.; the prosecution will represent the Queen of England, and among those subpoenaed will be Fidel Castro, the director of the CIA, the Russian ambassador in Grenada at the time, several members of the Vigoreese Family from Marseilles, and a whole raft of armed dingbats ranging from international Trotskyites to wild whores from Trinidad and Mini Moke salesmen from Paris and vicious thugs wearing uniforms and pearl-handled .45s.

The trial of Bernard Coard—the man who killed the revolution in order to save it—will not be ignored in some circles.

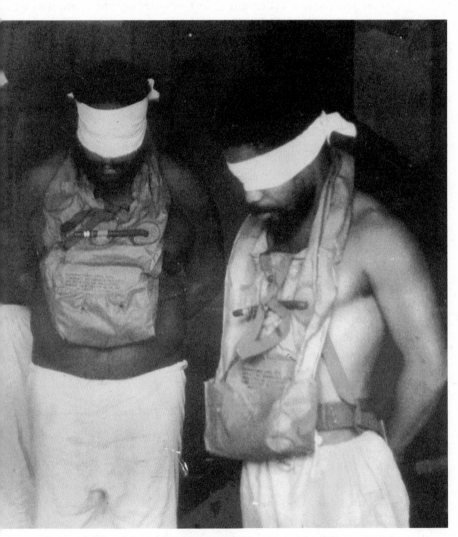

Bernard Coard faces the firing squad in Grenada, Winter 1984
(United Press)

There are no charges, as yet, but speculation ranges from murder and treason to unlawful conspiracy and crimes against the Crown. All we know for sure is that Bernard Coard—ex–deputy prime minister of Grenada in the last days of the Maurice Bishop regime—holds the key to the cruel mystery of whatever happened here in the autumn of '83.

It was a strange time, a profoundly weird chain of events. The U.S. Marines invaded; a gentle and widely popular sort of Caribbean Marxist revolution destroyed itself in a fit of insane violence; a place that could just as easily have been invaded and conquered by a gang of Hell's Angels got jumped on by the Rangers and the U.S. Marines and the 82nd Airborne and the Military Police and the U.S. Navy and Blackhawk helicopters and Psy-Ops and Night Vision scopes and concertina wire and huge explosions at all hours of the day and night and naked women brandishing machine guns.

We conquered Grenada. Even Morgan understood that. He had been in a cell on Row B when the first bombs hit. He is a mulatto, who appears to be about 40 with long blondish hair and a red headband. There is a touch of Woodstock in his bearing. Morgan looks like he was born, once again, on the corner of Haight and Ashbury in the summer of '67. He was sitting peacefully in his cell, listening to other inmates howling and jabbering frantically at the sound of low-flying jets overhead, when "suddenly the whole place exploded," he said. And after that, he fled.

. . .

I wanted to stay in Grenada for the funeral of Maurice Bishop, which was scheduled for Saturday, but when they still hadn't found the body by Wednesday, I changed my mind and decided to get out of town.

It was raining hard in the morning when we drove over the mountain to Pearls Airport on the other side of the island. There are no speed limit signs along the roads in Grenada. You can drive as fast as you want to, or as fast as your car can stand it. The potholes are square now, since the Army moved in, but some of them are still six feet deep and even the small ones are axle breakers.

There are three ways to drive on these roads, and the first two usually depend on whether you own the car or rent it. A new Mitsubishi will run about $22K in Grenada, and people who own them tend to spend a lot of time in second gear, creeping through the potholes like snails in a minefield.

The renters like to get into third gear, ignoring the damage, and bash ahead like dumb brutes, at least until the kidneys start bleeding— and when the car breaks in half, turn it in for another one. The roads are littered with wrecks, ranging from Datsun sedans to Soviet military trucks, all of them stripped to the skeleton. The radio goes first, then the jack and the wheels and all the engine parts, and finally the engine block itself, which makes a fine dead-head anchor for an offshore fishing boat. Rearview mirrors can be mounted on the bathroom wall for shaving purposes, and the seats from a new Toyota will make a stylish set of porch furniture for the whole family.

> *I recognize when power moves.*
> —Richard J. Daley, Mayor of Chicago, 1968

The invasion of Grenada was one of those stories with an essentially Midwestern heart. It was a fine mix of show business and leverage and big-time political treachery, and even Abe Lincoln would have admired the move for its swiftness, if nothing else. This is, after all, an election year, and the President is not the only one who is running for re-election. The whole Congress is up, along with a third of the Senate, and it is bad business in an election year to go back home to the district and question the wisdom of an incumbent President who has pulled off the first successful U.S. military invasion since the Inchon Landing in 1950.

On my last night in the St. George's Hotel I took a long-distance call in the lobby from a man who works on the floor of the Chicago Board of Trade. "Don't come back here with any of your liberal bullshit about oppressing the Third World," he said. "You drunken bastards have had your way long enough. It's about time you told the truth for a change."

## Ambassador to Cuba

I have just received an invitation to visit Havana, from the head of the Cuban Film Commission, and my heart is full of fear. At first I was happy, but then I did some research and a feeling of queasiness came over me. I was more & more paralyzed by *Angst en Walging,* as the Dutch say. The more questions I asked, the more heinous became the answers. What had once seemed like a token of idyllic good fortune suddenly transmogrified itself, right in front of my eyes, into a guaranteed horrible experience in the dark underbelly of life in the tropics. Everything I learned convinced me that I was about to be fleeced, busted, and put in prison for treason.

MEMO FROM THE CUBA DESK:
HST / MARCH 30, 1999

Dear Jann:

Liftoff for Cuba is at 0930 & I am very excited. You will be happy to know that I am sparing no expense in moving The Desk to Cuba for the next two weeks. We are finely organized. The job is well in hand & all the key signs are perfect. The moon is in Venus & Mescalito is rising. The nights are becoming almost perfectly dark, for our purposes. No moon at all, only starlight, and no light at all when it rains.

(THIS IS AN URGENT REMINDER TO SEND A FEW SMALL LITHIUM BATTERY–POWERED *FLASHLIGHTS* IN THE *ROLLING STONE* PACKAGE TO ME AT THE NACIONAL. TELL MIKE GUY.)

The weather forecast for Cuba calls for bright mornings, rain showers in late afternoon, and extremely dark nights with strange winds. That is good news for those of us who see by starlight or have single-cell Lithium spot/floods that can illuminate a naked figure running on a beach 1,000 feet away. Not many people have those advantages, and those who do will prevail. . . . *Sic semper Tyrannus,* eh? You bet. That is the simple secret of the Winning Tradition we have established & maintained (with a few spectacular exceptions) for almost 30 years.

Wow! Who else in Journalism can make that claim? Think about it. We should establish an annual award, with lavish ceremony, for the National Affairs Desk selection for Finest Journalism of the Year, as chosen by a dazzling jury of experts like Tom & Halberstam & me & Ed Bradley—

OK. You get the idea. So let's get back to Cuba. I am leaving in a few hours and I still have to pack my Portable Ozone equipment, which is legal but very delicate. . . . That's right. I forgot to tell you that I am getting into the Ozone Business, which is a sleeping giant in Cuba. Yes, and more on that later.

I have also learned that Hemingway was into voodoo & that Castro will live for another 50 years because of Ozone . . . Also enc. find my Journal notes, to date.


TO: BOB LOVE / *ROLLING STONE*
JANUARY 29, 1999
FROM: HST


Bobby:
I have just been advised by recent travelers that having a *Journalist Visa* is, in fact, a very important & professionally desirable thing to have in Cuba. It confers a sort of VIP status & political access, as well as immunity to prosecution under the goddamn Helms-Burton Act.

The same immunity is provided, I'm told, to those who "bring medicine" into Cuba under the auspices of the U.S.–Latin American Medical Aid Foundation. (members.aol.com.uslamaf/)

A Journalist Visa also makes it "legal" (and thus easier) to conduct money transactions in Cuba. It also entitles you to drive a car with a Black license plate, which is important. Or maybe it's Yellow plates that get you through roadblocks & cause thieves & pimps & traffic cops to give your car a wide berth.

In any case, I think I might need some help from You/RS in re: securing whatever documents, visas, letters of transit, etc., that are necessary or even helpful for me to do my job down there. As Michael says, people in Cuba are very wary of talking to people who might get them in trouble. . . . And that is why so many citizens turn strangers who don't act right in to the police whenever they get pissed off.

Whoops. Never mind that. But all the same I trust you will investigate this matter and let me know ASAP. We are, after all, professionals.

Thanx,
Hunter

MEMO FROM THE NATIONAL AFFAIRS DESK
/ / / JANUARY 30, 1999
*FROM HUNTER S. THOMPSON:*
*HOTEL NACIONAL #6: HAVANA, CUBA 60606*
*TO JANN / RS / NYC*

Okay. I guess that will be my forwarding address for a while. Either that (above) or the Swiss Embassy, or maybe that horrible Isle of Pines Prison where Castro put those poor bastards from the Bay of Pigs. Who knows? We seem to be heading into a void of some kind, a political Time Warp full of whores & devils & cops, where, for all practical purposes, there is no Law at all & everything you do is half-illegal.

Sounds like Washington, eh? Yessir. Mr. Bill is very big in Cuba, these days. Many people are counting on him to deliver the bacon. He is Dollar Bill, Mr. Moneybags, and he is about to make a lot of people rich.

But we'll get to that later. Right now I want to tell you a few little things about my assignment in Havana & the relentless high-risk weirdness I am being forced to deal with. (Whoops, strike that. It is dangerous to use words like "force" and "deal" in Cuba. Almost everybody will turn you in to the police if you talk like that.)

"Bomb" is another politically unacceptable word, like "whores" & "guns" & "dope."

SUNDAY NIGHT / AFTER THE SUPER BOWL
JANUARY 31, 1999 / OWL FARM

The Cuban situation is deteriorating faster than it is coming together. There is a constant sense of angst about it, a sense of being bushwacked. Some people would call it paranoid, but they would be the dumb ones, the *Incognocenti*. Smart people understand that there is no such thing as paranoia. It is just another mask for ignorance. The Truth, when you finally chase it down, is almost always far worse than your darkest visions and fears.

But I am, after all, a suave gringo. I understand that many assignments are fraught with risk, personal danger & even treachery. Greed and human Weakness are ever present.

There is nothing funny, for instance, about having your passport & all your money stolen while traveling illegally in a foreign country.

Okay for that. The time has come to talk about Fun, about Victory and Victimization—about who has a sense of humor and who doesn't.

TO: COL. DEPP / LONDON / FEBRUARY 2, 1999
FROM: DR. THOMPSON / WOODY CREEK
SUBJECT: PUBLIC FLOGGINGS I HAVE KNOWN

Okay, Colonel—Good work on your brutal publicity. Kick the shit out of five or six more of those rotters & you'll make the cover of *Time*.

Or maybe you want to come to CUBA this weekend & help me write my new honky-tonk song: "Jesus Hated Bald Pussy."

Anyway, this act with the *Plank* might have legs. Let's give it a whirl in HAVANA. We could both load up on Absinth & trash a nice suite in the *Hotel Nacional*. Invite 50 or 60 Beautiful People to a party/celebration in honor of Che Guevara, which then "got out of hand." DEPP JAILED AFTER ORGY IN CUBA, PROSTITUTES SEIZED AFTER MELEE IN PENTHOUSE, ACTOR DENIES TREASON CHARGES.

Why not? And I do, in fact, have a balcony suite at the Hotel Nacional a/o February 4–14, and I could use a suave Road Manager. Shit, feed the tabloids a rumor that you have Fled to Cuba to avoid British justice. Yeah, crank that one up for a few days while you drop out of sight—and then we hit them with the ORGY IN CUBA story, along with a bunch of lewd black-and-white photos, taken by me. Shocking Proof.

Yessir. This one is definitely do-able, & it will also give me *a story*. You bet. And *Sleepy Hollow* will open in the Top Three. Trust me. I understand these things.

Meanwhile, you should be getting your finished album & 6,666 *pounds* (less my 10%) *in coin* from EMI very shortly. And I am going off to Cuba, for good or ill, on Thursday. Send word soonest.

DOC

MEMO ON WHY I AM GOING TO CUBA: WRITE THIS MESSAGE DOWN & REPEAT IT EVERY DAY . . .

I AM GOING TO CUBA TO PAY MY RESPECTS TO THE CUBAN PEOPLE & TO THANK FIDEL CASTRO FOR THE COURAGE OF HIS STRUGGLE & THE BEAUTY OF HIS DREAM. But I am mainly going for *Fun*. First, the Diary, then the Meaning . . . Remember that.

SATURDAY NIGHT, MARCH 27, 1999
NOTES

Today is not a good day for traveling to Cuba.

Hot damn, the White House is getting aggressive again.

(I understand it now. Clinton's current behavior correlates with The Advanced Syphilis Syndrome.)

Maybe this is not the time for me to travel to Cuba & denounce my own country as Nazis & be quoted on the AP wire as saying "The President is entering the final stages of Terminal Syphilis. Nothing else can explain it." (Note: Call my old friend Sandy Berger & ask *him* why we are bombing Yugoslavia.)

Ten thousand Serbs rioted in Grand Central Station yesterday, carrying signs that said NATO = NAZIS. U.S. embassies all over the world are on Red Alert & the president of Yugoslavia is on TV urging people all to strike *now* against American interests everywhere.

(5:33 A.M. Sunday morning): Jesus! Now CNN has a bulletin about a grenade attack on the U.S. embassy in Moscow: 2

grenade launchers & a Kalashnikov machine gun. Then the man fled in a white car. Who was it? Who knows? Police are rounding up the usual suspects . . . Stealth bombers blasted out of the sky over Belgrade, brave pilot flees in white car, Troops massed for invasion, WWIII looms . . . Yes sir, now is the time to go abroad & pass through many foreign airports. No problem. . . .

In the Hemingway Boat Marina, Havana, 1999
(Heidi Opheim)

. . .

Holy shit. This is insane. Now the official spokesman for NATO comes onstage & launches into a bleeding rave about War Crimes & Atrocities & a blizzard of bombs on all Warmongers who think they can get away with butchering innocent people as a way of life.

"Let me say, however, that if Yugoslavia had a democratic government, none of this would ever have happened."

What? Who are we talking about here? Who is flying those planes that are carpet bombing civilian targets 6,000 miles away from home?

Don't tell me, Bubba—let me guess. It must be the Hole in the Wall gang. No?

Well, his name ain't *Milosovich,* Bubba. And Adolf Hitler has been dead for 50 years.

There is something happening here, Mr. Jones—and you don't know what it is, do you? It sounds like a blizzard of Syphilis. Madness. Clinton, etc. . . .

> *These people are different from the others, Jack—they went
> to Yale, they play bridge, they fuck each other.*
>
> —CIA gossip, Havana

Right. That's what they were saying about the CIA 40 years ago, back in the good old days when they were feeding LSD-25 to each other for experimental purposes in the name of National Security. The Agency was planning to drop LSD bombs on Moscow & other enemy cities when WWIII got going. That is where the phrase "bomb their brains loose" comes from. It was CIA jargon, top secret.

But the experiments got out of hand & WWIII never happened—at least not the way they were planning it—so the phrase was dropped from the secret agency codebook.

Until now. Now it is back in style. Spooks laugh when they say it to each other at lunch. "Yes sir, we are bombing their brains loose in Belgrade. They can run, but they can't hide." That is the way CIA men talk.

We were listening to three of them flirt with one another like brutalized Yalies do.

We ran into them in a lounge at Miami International Airport when the plane was delayed for three hours by a bomb scare. There was panic for a while, but the spooks paid no attention & kept drinking, so I figured I'd do the same. Why worry? I thought. The safest place to be in a bomb panic is close to police. Keep smiling & act like a deaf person. If you accidentally drop money on the floor, count to three before you reach down to grab it. They are trained to shoot anything that moves suddenly or starts talking to the bartender about Bombs.

. . .

I was killing some time in the smoking lounge at the Miami International Airport when I noticed a man waving to me from the other side of the room. I came alert instantly. It is not a good omen, in my business, to see a strange man pointing his finger at you in a crowd at the Miami airport. For many people it is the last thing they see before they are seized by police & dragged off to jail in a choke hold. Suspicion of Criminal Activity is all they need here to lock you up & do serious damage to your travel plans. . . . Being arrested in any airport is bad, but being arrested in the Miami airport is terrifying.

I tried to ignore the man as I saw him approaching my table. Stay calm, I thought, maybe it's only an autograph seeker. . . . Then I felt his hand on my arm and he hoarsely shouted my name. I recognized the voice.

It was my old friend Rube, a rich cop from Oakland. He was on his way to Cuba, he said, to do some business and look for a woman to marry. "I have been in love with her for a long time," he said. Now he was finally free to get married. His wife back in Oakland had frozen all his assets.

I knew at once that he was on the lam. There was a fugitive look about him, despite his appearance of wealth & confident suaveness.

. . .

Cuba is not a new story for me. I have been on it for 40 years, and at times I have been very close to it—too close, on some days, and I have never pretended to be neutral or dispassionate about it. When I was 20 years old I harangued the editors of the *Louisville Courier-Journal* to send me to Cuba so I could join Fidel Castro in the Sierra Maestra mountains and send back dispatches about the triumph of the revolution. I was a Believer—not a Marxist or a Communist or some kind of agrarian Stalinist dilettante—but I was also a working journalist, and editors were not eager to pay my expenses to go to Cuba to fight with Castro in the mountains.

> *HAVANA* (CNN): FEBRUARY 15, 1999—
> *Cuba unveiled a two-pronged crackdown Monday, proposing harsh new penalties for common criminals and political opponents who "collaborate" with the U.S. government. The planned legislation, which would expand the use of the death penalty and introduce life imprisonment, follows a speech last month by President Fidel Castro in which he pledged to get tough on the growing crime problem on the Communist-ruled island.*
>
> *"There are even irresponsible families who sell their daughters' bodies and insensitive neighbors who think this is the most natural thing in the world. . . . There will be no escape for those who want to live like parasites at any price, at any cost, outside the law."*
> —Fidel Castro, January 5, 1999

It is a straight shot from Cancun to Havana, sixty-six minutes by jet plane across the Gulf of Mexico with a Soviet-blonde stewardess serving free rum and synthetic ham and cheese sandwiches. It is an easy trip on most nights, and innocent people have nothing to worry about. As our plane approached Havana our mood was almost festive. Heidi filled out the visa forms while I jabbered in broken Spanish to the man sitting next to me, asking how much money I should pay for the food.

He nodded sympathetically and stared down at his hands while I fumbled with my wallet, then he turned to face me and spoke calmly. "I speak no English," he said. "I want no United States dollars." Then he signaled for the stewardess and spoke rapidly to her in Spanish while I listened nervously. Flying into Cuba is not a good time to start arguing with passengers about money.

Finally she looked over at me and smiled. "No problem," she said. "We cannot accept your dollars. All service on this flight is free of charge."

Other passengers were staring at us now, but she laughed and shrugged them off. "Don't worry," she said. "He misunderstood you. He thought you were trying to give him money."

"Oh no," I said quickly. "Of course not. I was talking about the sandwich. Money is not a problem for me. I have no money. I am a cultural ambassador."

That seemed to satisfy her, and she went away. I had received detailed instructions about how to identify myself in Cuba, and I was well armed with credentials. "You are very famous down here," the ambassador had told me on the telephone. "Your movie about Las Vegas was well received at the Cuban film festival recently, so you will enjoy a diplomatic status that will be very helpful, as long as you don't bring any drugs."

"Don't worry," I assured him. "That movie was Hollywood propaganda. I am no longer a dope fiend. I gave that stuff up a long time ago."

"That's good," he said. "A cultural ambassador enjoys many privileges in Cuba these days, but dope fiends are being rounded up and put in prison—sometimes for life, and we won't be able to help you at all."

I was thinking about this conversation as our plane approached the coast of Cuba, but I was not apprehensive. I was traveling officially this time and I knew I had nothing to fear. My nerves were calm and I leaned back. I was looking forward to some serious grappling with booze, which is still a very acceptable vice in Cuba. I was even considering an offer to become a distributor of Absinth on the island, but that was still in the planning stages and I was not in any hurry.

Cuba was going to be busy. My schedule was already thick with cultural obligations: dinner with the ambassador, lunch with the minister of culture, book signings at the Film Institute, judging the Water Ballet at the Hotel Nacional, marlin fishing with the Old Man of the Sea . . . The list was long, and I was already looking for ways to pare it down and make time for my nonofficial business, which was equally important and would probably involve meeting with people who had recently fallen out of favor with the government in the wake of the Crackdown that followed Castro's ruthless denunciation of pimps and pederasts and collaborators at the beginning of '99.

There was also the matter of Johnny Depp's arrival in three days, which I knew would attract some attention in cultural circles, and I understood that we would have to be suave and well liked in public.

We needed government approval to shoot our movie in Havana. It was definitely not the time to be getting any criminal publicity.

As the lights of the city came into view up ahead and the stewardess said it was time to buckle our seat belts, I began to feel nervous and I decided to go up to the lavatory for a shave and a lash of the toothbrush before we landed. There was muttering when I stood up, but I felt it was necessary. An ambassador should always be clean-shaven and never have booze on his breath. That is a cardinal rule of the business.

I was fumbling around for a razor when I discovered the ball of hashish in my dopp kit. It was snuggled into a corner behind a bar of soap from the Four Seasons in New York, and I tried to ignore it. No doubt it had been there for many months or even years, unnoticed by anybody until now. The sight of it made me dizzy and weak. The razor fell from my fingers and I sagged against the tin wall as the stewardess hammered on the door and I felt the plane descending. For an instant I was paralyzed by panic, then my criminal instincts took over and I fired a blast of Foamy into my shaving kit, making a nasty mess on the bottom, but it was no use. The ball of hash still loomed up like a black iceberg, so I grabbed it and tried to flatten it out, then I dropped it in my coat pocket and tried to forget about it.

When I got back to my seat I said nothing to Heidi about the hashish, for fear she would go all to pieces. (I had sworn to be clean and she had trusted me . . .) Nor did I say anything to Michael Halsband, our tour guide and confidential photographer from New York, who had been assigned to this visit at the last moment.

He was a total stranger, in fact, and I was leery of him from the start, but he met us in Cancun anyway and attached himself like a leech. . . . I didn't know it at the time, but he would be with me for the rest of the trip. He was a swarthy little man wearing a seersucker coat and a goofy grin of a surfer on his face.

He introduced himself as a famous rock and roll photographer and almost immediately tried to sell me a used Rolleiflex camera. He was paying his own expenses, he said, and he had our letters of passage from the Cuban government and the prestigious Ludwig Institute—we would quickly become dependent on these people.

As our plane approached Havana, however, I saw no reason to

upset him with my story about mysteriously finding contraband in my kit at the last moment. A lot of people have gone to prison in Cuba for telling stories like that to cops. So I fastened my seat belt and prepared for the ordeal of wading through a cordon of military police.

They were all around the jetway when the door opened, with Soviet submachine guns and angry dogs on leashes. "We have nothing to worry about," I said to Heidi. "We are coming into a war zone. Pay no attention to these freaks. They will not bother us. We are innocent. Just follow Halsband and do what he does."

Our fellow passengers fell silent as we were herded out the door and into a long white-tiled hallway with no exits. Finally we arrived at the Immigración gate and I noticed people being jerked out of line by men in black suits . . . Halsband was one of those. The sight of it put me into a panic, but I tried to stay calm and grin vacantly into the air and pretend like nothing was happening. Other passengers in line behaved the same way; nobody wanted to see anything weird, so they ignored it. What the hell? People are jerked out of line by police every day in airports all over the world—and we were, after all, coming into one of the few remaining Communist-ruled nations on Earth.

Heidi was next in line, and she too was seized for questioning. I could see Halsband emptying his pockets and babbling at cops while they searched him.

We found ourselves separated and taken off in different directions. Cuban security techniques are very sophisticated, they say. We were individually searched and questioned, then released in a maze of confused passengers.

It was at that point that I decided to break ranks and flee, but there was nowhere to run. All the escape routes were sealed off by cops with dogs, and our luggage was nowhere in sight. I looked around quickly and saw that the only place where a sick man could sit down was an ominous-looking enclosure where cops were interrogating suspects, including the man who'd been sitting next to us on the plane.

So that is where I went. It is a firm rule of behavior in times of emergency in airports: When you are guilty always move toward the police, never run away from them.

The cops eyed me warily as I sat down among them, but they said nothing. Well, I thought, this is it for me. I took off my hat and removed the huge black widow spider from it, then I lit a cigarette.

The Ludwig people were waiting outside, but we couldn't communicate with them. All the other passengers had left the airport, but not us. We were conspicuously detained like people on Devil's Island while soldiers rummaged through my Kevlar luggage, one item at a time, and Heidi was taken away to the X-ray booth.

My first sense of real trouble came when I heard the sound of shattering glass from the search and seizure area. It was a rubber ball-peen hammer that exploded with the sound of shattering glass whenever you whacked something with it. It was not the kind of humor you normally want to bring to a Communist war zone.

I could see them over my shoulder, but I tried not to notice. The soldiers were demonstrating the hammer to each other, and finally one of them laughed. Thank God, I thought, at least these people have a morbid sense of humor. . . . They also laughed at the Retractable Stabbing Knife, which Heidi explained by jamming it into her chest.

I was rattled by the scene at the airport, and so was our welcoming committee. They were cultural-exchange people, ranking officials of the prestigious Ludwig Institute, a German art foundation that runs many of Cuba's foreign-exchange programs. The Ludwig people walk tall in Havana and they are not accustomed to having their guests detained and ransacked at the airport. By the time our luggage was finally released, there was nobody else in the Arrivals terminal except cops, and I had already met most of them. They eyed us sullenly as we drove away in the darkness toward Havana. I had a queasy feeling that we had not seen the last of them.

Our host, a jovial man called Helmo, was eager to dismiss what he called "the unpleasantness at the airport" and to "refresh ourselves with laughter." Halsband was mildly hysterical about his own ordeal with the Aduana police and Heidi was still crying. I tried to shake it off by drinking heavily from a bottle of rum.

I was feeling a little better about life when we finally arrived and pulled into the long, palm-lined driveway of the Hotel Nacional. There was something familiar about it, from a distance, and I had a weird sense of coming home, but I knew it was impossible. I had never been to Havana, never even dreamed about it—but I was extremely familiar with The Breakers hotel in Palm Beach, and the Nacional looks exactly like it.

From a distance—but once you get inside, it is different, very different, and it takes a while to grasp this. We were met at the door by the same sharp-looking baggage handlers that you see at The Breakers. The air when you step out of the car is the same balmy breeze that you feel in Palm Beach, the same heady mix of salt air and romance and mystery. Even the vast lobby and the elevators and the hallways are exact replicas of The Breakers. The only real difference, at first, was that we were taken immediately to a special elevator and ushered straight up to the super-exclusive sanctuary of the Sixth Floor, where our oceanfront suites were prepared.

I have always hated The Breakers, in truth, and I will always hate the Hotel Nacional—but I hate a lot of places that look nice in the tourist brochures; I go to hotels for business reasons, not to relax and have fun. Sometimes it ends up that way, but you can't count on it. The way I look at it, business is business, and the only things that really matter in hotels are privacy, fresh oysters, and good telephones.

The terrace bar at the Hotel Nacional was almost empty when we arrived. A lone bartender stared at us but said nothing. The walls were covered with signed photos of American celebrities from the forties and fifties: black-and-white glossies of people like Frank Sinatra, Errol Flynn, and Ava Gardner, along with political heroes like Winston Churchill and Meyer Lansky. It is a strange mix of people to run into at that hour.

It was in the deserted terrace bar of the Hotel Nacional that I first heard the story of Artie Diamond, the vicious convict from Sing Sing who intimidated the whole prison by biting off the ear of a con boss who called him a sissy. It was a Mike Tyson story, being told in slow motion by a hard-bitten man from New York who once fought for the middleweight championship of the world on an undercard with Tyson before he started carrying his Artie Diamond act too far.

We were all sitting outside in the darkness, huddled around a lumpy wicker table with a glass top that went sideways and spilled the drinks every time a breeze came up. A lone waiter scurried back and forth with trays of rum daiquiris and black Cuban coffee balanced crazily in the wind.

. . .

You can learn a lot of things just by hanging out in front of the Hotel Nacional in Havana. There is a heavy mix of criminals and foreigners and beautiful women with special agendas. Nobody is exactly what they seem to be in Havana, and that is especially true at the Hotel Nacional, which enjoys a worldwide reputation for the finest hospitality in Cuba.

The Malecon is the long, wide boulevard that runs along the waterfront in Havana. The harbor is badly polluted, but a mile offshore, where the Gulf Stream runs, the water is pure and fast. No islands dot the horizon. There is nothing between here and Key West except ninety miles of deep water and six million sharks. Some people go out there for fun, but not many. The Gulf of Mexico at night is strictly for business—commercial freighters, commercial fishermen, floating wreckage, and the occasional human skeleton.

The Malecon is different. There is life along the boulevard, strolling lovers and pedicabs and knots of police-affiliated hoodlums gathered here and there under streetlights, hooting at cars and tossing fish heads to crocodiles, which can surface like lightning and jump five feet straight up in the air when they think they see fresh meat. Cuban crocodiles are a special breed of beasts, famous for their athleticism and their cruelty. A croc in a fit of temper can swallow a small boy and two six-packs of beer in one gulp.

. . .

Bill Clinton has a long and ugly history involving Cuba. It goes back to the 1980 Mariel boatlift, when Castro emptied his country of "dissidents" by sending 125,000 "refugees" to Key West in a matter of weeks, many of them criminally insane. They were taken off the boats and shipped up U.S.A. 1A to detention camps in Miami, where many found work and refuge in the city's vast and thriving anti-Castro Cuban community, but not all. About 50,000 of them were screened and found to be so vicious, violent, and incorrigible that they could never be assimilated into any culture, anywhere, and they could not go back to Cuba because of their status as "political refugees." So they were sent off in chains to various prisons around the country, to maximum-security cages like Danbury, Lompoc, and Marion—where they immediately terrorized the existing prison population and even the guards and wardens. They were extremely bad people, the meanest of the mean, and also Criminally Insane. They were dangerous and utterly uncontrollable.

Some 18,000 of these savage incorrigibles wound up at a U.S. military prison in Fort Chaffee, Arkansas, despite the vehement objections of the politically ambitious young governor, William Jefferson Clinton, then running for re-election. His Republican opponent, along with every newspaper in the state, denounced Clinton for allowing this dangerous scum to be funneled into central Arkansas, but Bill blamed it on Jimmy Carter, who had blatantly "double-crossed" him by sending those brutes to Fort Chaffee without his prior knowledge or consent.

Shortly before the gubernatorial election, a massive jailbreak sent 7,000 of the most violent "refugees" into the streets of one of our permanent army bases at Fort Chaffee, where they ran amok with machetes until the National Guard finally quelled the uprising after three days of tear gas and bloody hand-to-hand fighting.

The voters were not amused. Clinton was mauled on Election Day and moved ignominiously out of the Governor's Mansion. It was the only election Bill Clinton ever lost. He waited two years, then ran again and won, and the rest is history. But he never forgot the nightmare inflicted on him by Jimmy Carter and the Cubans.

. . .

Skaggs was a free thinker and he had an active mind. He owned three boats in the Marina Hemingway and didn't mind saying that he had come to Cuba to have fun and he had plenty of dollars to spend. That is a dangerous mix in Havana these days, with the government suddenly enforcing a crackdown on everything he stood for, but he said it didn't bother him. "I have all my papers in order," he explained as we careened along the Malecon at top speed in a new silver Z28 convertible with the Rolling Stones booming out of the speakers. "The police here are all Communists," he added. "You have to remember that. They are Primitive people, but they are very sophisticated on a military level. You can't put anything over on them. I was arrested three times on my way over to your hotel today."

"What?" I said. "Three times? In one day? Jesus Christ, Skaggs. That's frightening. Maybe this is the wrong night for us to be out on the streets."

"Don't worry," he said. "They know I have all my paperwork in order. I think they're just queer for this car. They like to pull me over and fondle it while they check me out."

Skaggs is a gentleman of leisure from Arkansas, a man of the sporting life who is also a good friend of Bill Clinton's. I have known him for many years and consider him a good and honorable man, essentially, but he has a deep streak of the Arky and the boomer and the wild boy in him that is likely to go sideways on you and reach for a shotgun at any moment. He is a handsome man with suave manners and a relentless appetite for profitable business investments.

Cuba was one of these, he admitted, but his enviable position as a friend of the president was becoming an awkward burden on his sense of possibility. "I've had three or four federal grand juries on my ass for five years," he said. "First they tapped all my phones, then they started following me everywhere I went. People I'd known all my life were afraid to be seen with me. I moved out of town to the duck lodge, but it was no use. Finally I said, 'Fuck this, I'm getting too old for it,' so I bought a goddamn boat and went to Cuba."

. . .

The yacht harbor at Marina Hemingway on the outskirts of Havana was one of the first Enemy enclaves to be shut down completely. There were no more parties on the party boats tied up along the seedy-looking canals. Cuban girls were no longer allowed in the marina, and the only Cuban men in sight wore official police uniforms. It was like the Nazis had suddenly clamped down on the waterfront in Casablanca. Ernest Hemingway would have been shocked.

We spent a lot of time in the maze of dim gravel streets that wind through Marina Hemingway. Only a few big boats remained from the decadent good old days before the War and the fearful crackdown on prostitution that so crippled the Party spirit in Havana, and the few people still living onboard were treated like perverts and spies. My friend Skaggs from Little Rock was arrested four times on the first day we met with him, and his boat was visited three times by police one night when we were trying to relax and watch the War news on his clandestine TV set in the galley.

We were sitting around a teakwood map table in the cabin of his

Grand Banks trawler in the Hemingway Marina when the TV news
came alive with a flurry of live photos of American prisoners of war just
captured in Yugoslavia. It was one of those scenes that you know will be
clearly imprinted in your memory for the rest of your life—people weeping and shouting in Texas with horror in their eyes and neighbors tying
yellow ribbons around telephone poles in one another's front yards under the watchful eyes of many TV cameras and dogs howling off-camera.

Skaggs slammed his fist on the table and cried out: "GOD-
DAMNIT, THIS IS TOO DEPRESSING. THEY SHOULD TAKE
THOSE BASTARDS OUT AND EXECUTE THEM TOMOR-
ROW MORNING."

"What?" I said. "Get a grip on yourself, Skaggs. Those people can't
be executed. They are prisoners of war."

"Bullshit," he said. "They are spies. They should be EXECUTED.
That's the only way to get the president's attention."

I was shocked. Skaggs is a died-in-the-wool Clinton backer, and his
wife is strongly opposed to the death penalty under any circumstances.
She makes two or three trips to Washington every year to lobby against
Police Brutality. It was weird to hear him calling for the execution of
U.S. POWs.

But she was not with us on the boat in Cuba that night, so he felt
free to vent. "The bastard has gone too far this time," he explained.
"He thinks he can drop a 2,000-pound bomb on anybody who won't
salute him." He shook his head angrily and chopped off another few
chunks of ice with his fishing tool. "The president is not crazy. He's
just plain stupid. I learned that a long time ago, back when I was still
raising money for his goddamn never-ending campaigns."

The boat rocked gently beneath our feet as he jumped down into
the darkened hold where he kept his music equipment. "Hot damn!"
he exclaimed. "Let's hear some Sonny Boy Williamson!"

I felt a shudder go through me as the amp kicked in. Everybody
jumped and Heidi tried to stand up, but the music was too powerful.
It turned every beam and strut and bench on the boat into a wooden
tuning fork; it was like a shock through the colon every time Sonny
Boy hit a G string. Glasses rattled on the table.

The music was so loud and the War news so terrifying that it took
us a while to realize that somebody was pounding on the back door. It

was a cop complaining about the noise, but Skaggs took him outside and we went back to sucking heavily on our Cohibas.

We were not degenerates, and neither was Skaggs, to my knowledge, and we were doing nothing illegal. But cops were watching us anyway, and that is a nervous feeling when you're sitting on a boat in a foreign harbor.

. . .

We were waiting for Ray (a.k.a. Colonel Depp)—my personal bodyguard and international road manager from London—in the airport lounge when I heard the unmistakable whine of an electric drill from behind a closed door near the baggage carousel. It was penetrating something that was too soft to offer much resistance, and I thought I knew what it was. My own Kevlar suitcase had been drilled five times when we came through the airport two nights earlier—five neat little holes going into the bag from five different directions—and now I knew it was Ray's turn. I knew we were in for a long wait.

Halsband slumped on his stool and ordered four more Mojitos while Heidi paced crazily back and forth on the slick tile floor. Ray was nowhere in sight, and we could only guess at his fate. Once they start drilling your luggage in this country, the next few hours are going to be very edgy. First your bag will be marked with an ominous red XXX, then it will be thoroughly searched and examined. You will be questioned repeatedly about the same things: "Why do you have all these red cigarettes? Are you wearing false teeth? Will you come with me to the X-ray machine on the other side of that wall? Why are you here? What are you carrying in that toothbrush? Was your mother born in Algiers? Who is your personal dentist? Why are you acting so nervous?"

The correct answer to all of these questions is "No"—over and over, "No"—and the price of inconsistency can be ten years in a Cuban prison. Never be inconsistent. If the Customs cop thinks he heard you say that your mother is a dentist in Algiers the first time he asks, your answer must be exactly the same when he asks the same question five minutes later. Do not change your story in even the smallest detail. That way lies trouble.

I knew Ray was carrying a mixed bag of personal presents, including bottles of Absinth and night-vision binoculars and frozen shirts and Nazi SS jewelry. He also had rare medicines from Europe and oriental hand fans and many thousands of dollars and perfumes and cameras and pornography and sophisticated tattoo paraphernalia. He looked like an international Pimp with no respect for the law. If his luggage was searched he was doomed.

A Cuban band was singing "Guantanamera" on TV in the airport bar, but we were all too nervous to enjoy the music. "We may have to make a run for the car," I whispered to Halsband. "Somebody is about to get busted here."

He looked startled and quickly drank off his Mojito. "Stop worrying about cops," he said. "Everybody's a cop in this country. Ray will have no trouble," he said. "He is bulletproof."

Just then the lights went dim in the airport and people stopped talking. I felt a hand clutch my arm in the darkness and heard Heidi moaning, "O my god, O my god . . ."

It was Ray. He had slipped unnoticed through the gate when the lights went dim and the mob of paranoid tourists began to panic. We paid the bill quickly and rushed out to our waiting white "limousine," saying nothing. Terror is never very far away in Cuba, and smart people flee like rats at the first sign of it. The first thing to do when a panic starts is get a grip on your wallet and walk, not run, toward the nearest exit. Women always clutch their purses and try not to show signs of fear in these moments, but suave behavior is difficult when the lights go out in a foreign airport full of perverts and thieves and spies and Communist police all around you.

Yes sir, and that is when the last thing you need for a goddamn fail-safe escape vehicle is a broken-down 49-year-old Cadillac sedan with a secondhand Yugo engine under the hood.

. . .

Whenever I think of Cuba now I see the Malecon at night and Tall Cops on shiny, black motorcycles circling around on the boulevard far down below my balcony at the Hotel Nacional, controlling the traffic and scanning the seawall for pimps and accused collaborators . . . I remember the War news on TV and the constant babble of Christiane Amanpour somewhere in Albania and Dan Rather waiting to be bombed in Belgrade and U.S. prisoners of war exhibited on worldwide

TV with lumps on their heads and bleeding black eyes and their cheek muscles rigid with fear. I remember the War news raving twenty-four hours a day on both TV sets in our suite and people of all persuasions rushing in and out with crazy news and rumors. We went through thirty or forty weird meat sandwiches and forty-eight silver buckets of rare ice every twenty-four hours. The phones rang sporadically, often for no reason at all, and the few phone messages that got through were garbled and frightening: Havana was about to be bombed and/or destroyed by U.S. nukes full of napalm and nerve gas and vermin eggs. A man from Houston called and said a bomb blew the gates off the U.S. embassy last night. A lawyer from Sweden on a decadent-looking yacht called *White Power* said he'd heard on his shortwave radio that Clinton had officially declared a state of war against Cuba.

It turned out not to be true—but real news travels slowly in Cuba and the military police went on Invasion Alert status anyway, and the streets were swept clean of degenerates and other usual suspects who might be trying to swim naked in the harbor.

. . .

We were under close and constant surveillance the whole time. We were treated like rich prisoners of war. Our rooms were bugged, our baggage was drilled, cops roamed the hallways and had a key to every safe in the hotel.

There is a serious *crackdown* in Cuba on Drugs, Prostitution, and Bombs. You want to grin and do the Salsa any time you have to stand in line for anything, even waiting for a cab. The urge to dance and spend dollars is an acceptable vice on this island, but anything else can be dangerous.

Degenerates are no longer fashionable in Cuba, and anybody suspected of "collaborating" with the U.S. Embassy is a degenerate. That is the long and the short of it. War zones are always difficult, especially for the Enemy—and the Enemy, as we quickly discovered in Cuba, is us. You bet. You want to see the bogeyman, Bubba? Just look in the mirror. People in Cuba do not see the American Century the same way we do. If sheep go to heaven and goats go to hell, we are definitely the goats of this story.

HST and James Carville, Little Rock, 1992
(Stacey Hadash)

# Witness III

## Statement by Dr. Hunter S. Thompson, March 13, 1990

BE ANGRY AT THE SUN

That public men publish falsehoods
Is nothing new. That America must accept
Like the historical republics corruption and empire
Has been known for years.

Be angry at the sun for setting
If these things anger you. Watch the wheel slope and turn,
They are all bound on the wheel, these people,
    those warriors.
This republic, Europe, Asia.

Observe them gesticulating,
Observe them going down. The gang serves lies,
    the passionate
Man plays his part; the cold passion for truth
Hunts in no pack.

You are not Catullus, you know,
To lampoon these crude sketches of Caesar. You
   are far
From Dante's feet, but even farther from his dirty
Political hatreds.

Let boys want pleasure, and men
Struggle for power, and women perhaps for fame,
And the servile to serve a Leader and the dupes
   to be duped.
Yours is not theirs.

                        —Robinson Jeffers

## From the *Aspen Times Daily,* Monday, June 18, 1990

KNOCK, KNOCK—WHO'S THERE?

Editor:

And so it's done
Who lost,
Who won—
Each and every
One and all
Both sides—
Losers
Winners—
None
Justice done
A dis-service
Did she—
Deserve this
Mockery?
Did we?
I think not

In the end
All we've got
Are the rules
We choose to play by
Fair and square
Even Steven
Even though
Who's got the dough
'S better chance
To finish even
The good doctor
Fought the law
To a draw
Called their bluff
Had the stuff
The courage and conviction
To risk it all
Bet his freedom—
On a pair of deuces—
Right and privacy,
'Gainst a black king—
Of—hypocrisy
And so—
Now we know
Tho' the Hunter prevailed
On this occasion,
Chased the fox
From his doors—
Is that someone
Knockin' on yours?

—Edward T. Cross

(HST archives)

· · ·

Why is it, Lord, that tonight I find myself writing feverishly on a 30-year-old IBM Selectric typewriter . . . It is sure as hell *not* a matter of convenience. This thing is slow and heavy and primitive. It is a sort of dark *institutional* red color that makes it appear to be twice as large as it is. Some people fear it—especially when they can see three or four brand-new customized *Super Electrics* laying idle around the house still wrapped in cellophane while the slow labored *THUNK* of these ancient keys slapping into the ribbon is the only sound in the room.

To me it sounds like hardened steel ball-bearing tumblers dropping into place. Indeed, I know that sound well. It is a sound you never hear except in quasi-desperate situations where the Fate of NEARBY people depends entirely on yr. ability to solve a particularly stubborn vault combination lock when you are trying to flee for yr. life before a horde of boozed-up cannibal Nazis swarms in through the windows and butchers your whole family, only to find that all yr. guns and money and helicopter keys are hopelessly locked up in this goddamn dysfunctional safe that refuses to open.

Ho ho. That is when you want to hear those beautiful little tumblers fall. *Click click click,* just like in Hollywood . . . These are the sounds that really matter in yr. life.

Yes sir, and that is about all we need to know about atavistic typewriters and amateur safecrackers for today. Let us return now at once to the more violent days of yesteryear and my fight to the death with vicious crooked cops in that incredibly violent winter of 1990 when they tried to take me into the system.

### D.A. SNAGS THOMPSON IN SEX CASE
#### By David Matthews-Price,
#### *Times Daily* Staff Writer
#### February 28, 1990

Hunter S. Thompson, in an episode reminiscent of some of his books, has been charged with sexually assaulting a woman writer who came to his house ostensibly to interview him last week.

Thompson, 52, surrendered at the District Attorney's office on Monday and is free on $2,500 bond.

Thompson told the *Times Daily* he's innocent and believes the alleged victim isn't so much a writer as she is a business woman who wants publicity for her new venture, which is selling sexual aids and lingerie.

"She's a business person in the sex business," Thompson said.

He said he's also suspicious of the motives of the District Attorney, who had six officers search his Woody Creek house on Monday for drugs. Officers said they found a small quantity of suspected cocaine and marijuana.

Thompson offered his own headline for the case: "Lifestyle-police raid home of 'crazed' gonzo journalist; 11-hour search by six trained investigators yields nothing but crumbs."

## Lab Results Pending

District Attorney Milt Blakey said he's waiting for the results of lab tests before deciding whether to bring drug charges.

Thompson is already facing charges of third-degree sexual assault for allegedly grabbing the woman's left breast and third-degree simple assault for supposedly punching her during an argument about whether the interview should take place in a hot tub. Both misdemeanors carry a maximum two-year sentence in the county jail.

The woman making the allegations is a 35-year-old self-employed writer from St. Clair, Mich., who said she was visiting Snowmass Village with her husband last week.

The *Times Daily* was unable to contact the
alleged victim on Tuesday. However, her story
about the Feb. 21 incident was detailed in an affidavit for an arrest warrant written by district
attorney investigator Michael Kelly.

## Affidavit Tells Story

The woman said she had written Thompson before
arriving in Snowmass to request an interview. Such
interviews are the fascination of out-of-town
journalists. Just last week *Time* magazine published a first-person account of another writer's
attempt to interview Thompson, a columnist for the
*San Francisco Examiner* and national editor of
*Rolling Stone* magazine.

The woman said she arrived at Thompson's house
in a taxicab, on Woody Creek Road, and was greeted
by a woman named Kat who introduced her to Thompson and two of his friends, identified only in the
affidavit as Semmes and Tim.

## Drug Suspicions

Within a few minutes, the woman suspected the
group had been using drugs, the affidavit stated.

"She suspected some members of the group might
be using drugs because from time to time they
would get up (and) go into the other room and then
return in a minute or so," the affidavit stated.

Then, about three hours after arriving at the
house, the alleged victim said she saw Thompson
carrying a green grinder that produced a white
powder substance, according to the affidavit.

"This substance, which she believed to be
cocaine, was then passed around to the group and
that with the exception of Tim and herself each

ingested (snorted) some of it into their noses by means of a straw," the affidavit said.

## Paranoid Group

"She observed the group becoming increasingly suspicious and paranoid," the affidavit said.

The woman writer said she got up and called her husband, a move which made the group suspicious that she might be an undercover agent.

She assured them that she wasn't an agent, she explained. Then Semmes and Tim left the house and Thompson gave her a tour of the residence.

She said Thompson showed her his favorite room, which contained a hot tub, and he supposedly suggested that she join him for a dip in the water.

Next, she claimed that Kat attempted to persuade her to join Hunter in the hot tub by telling her things such as "He's a harmless guy," "(He's) a little crazy at times, but he will never hurt you," "He'd really like you to get into the hot tub with him," etc., according to the arrest warrant affidavit. "She told Kat she had no intention of getting into the tub and that it was her intention to conduct a professional interview," the affidavit stated.

Soon the argument began and the woman said Thompson lost control and threw a glass of cranberry juice and vodka in her direction. She said she ducked.

Then, she claims Thompson grabbed her left breast, "squeezing and twisting it very hard. He then punched her in her left side with his right fist, and finally pushed her backwards with the palms of [his] . . . hands," the arrest warrant affidavit stated.

She said that Thompson then went to the room

where he keeps some of his guns and that she ran out of the house and sat on the porch. A cab took her away about 15 minutes later.

Thompson, in an interview with the *Times Daily,* said the woman was "real drunk, sloppy drunk."

Thompson said the woman wanted sex with him.

"I pushed her away from me. She went backwards and one hand brushed her breast," Thompson said.

## Conflict of Interest

A day later, the woman called the sheriff's department. Sheriff Bob Braudis said that because of his 20-year friendship with Thompson, he felt he would have a conflict of interest handling the case. Braudis gave the investigation to the District Attorney's office, which has its own investigators.

Thompson said officers took 11 hours to search his house because they were frustrated they couldn't find much evidence of drug usage or wrongdoing.

"I don't know if that (11-hour search) helps my reputation or hurts it," he said.

District Attorney Blakey said officers found possible drug paraphernalia and a small quantity of suspected marijuana and possible cocaine. The suspected drugs have not been weighed, Blakey said. All of the possible drug-related items have been sent to the Colorado Bureau of Investigation lab in Montrose, the prosecutor added.

## Overzealous Cops?

Blakey bristled Tuesday at suggestions that Thompson—who has made fun of cops in his books—was set up by overzealous law officers.

"That's absolutely not true," Blakey said. "If

there was overzealous law enforcement here, he
wouldn't have been called and asked to come to the
D.A.'s office (to be arrested).

"Hunter Thompson is just like anyone else; he's
going to get fair treatment under the law, no better or worse," Blakey promised.

*"For my part, I had lived about 10 miles out of
town for two years, doing everything possible to
avoid Aspen's feverish reality. My lifestyle, I
felt, was not entirely suited for doing battle with
any small town political establishment. They had
left me alone, not hassled my friends (with two un-
avoidable exceptions—both lawyers), and consis-
tently ignored all rumors of madness and violence in
my area. In return, I had consciously avoided writing about Aspen . . . in my very limited congress
with the local authorities I was treated like some
kind of half-mad cross between a hermit and a
wolverine; a thing best left alone as long as possible."*

Hunter S. Thompson
Rolling Stone *magazine*
Oct. 1, 1970

. . .

The Witness case turned on the day they decided to search the
house, the day I got arrested. I got in such a rage that it was war.
From then on I was in a kill-or-be-killed scenario; until then I hadn't
really paid that much attention to it. It was a bag of shit. But my own
lawyer got me busted. He invited me down to the courthouse to be
taken and fingerprinted. I knew I was in trouble. So from then on it
was just that rage. I don't know if that's good or bad. It's focus and
concentration. It was a little bit like the Mailbox—when I made that
decision to ask, "What Witnesses?" That eerie soliloquy . . . "It's a
matter of taste." It always boils down to a question of taste.
The Mailbox incident was a confidence builder, I think, but it

didn't teach me that I was smarter than they were. It taught me that they were not as smart as they thought they were. I did not plead guilty on that one, and I got in the habit of that. It is a red thread in this book. I have been looking for one, and that is what it is.

## GONZO'S LAST STAND?

Sometime on the night of February 21, Dr. Charles Slater called the Sheriff's Office to complain that Thompson had assaulted his wife—the precise time of his call is very much at issue, for the *Aspen Times Daily* has reported that the tape which automatically records all incoming calls is missing Dr. Slater's. Later on that night (sometime between 2 A.M. and 5 A.M. on February 23, actually), Palmer's former boyfriend and business partner Marco DiMercurio also called. Saying that he was speaking from Los Angeles, DiMercurio claimed that Thompson had in the course of the evening held a gun to Palmer's head. He insisted that there be an investigation, but warned that Palmer couldn't be interviewed until after 2 P.M.

By then, Sheriff Braudis had withdrawn from the case: A close friend of Thompson's, he'd been criticized for not being sufficiently aggressive in investigating the dispute between Thompson and Floyd Watkins. Seeking to ensure the appearance of fairness, Braudis transferred the complaint to Chip McCrory, the deputy district attorney for Aspen. McCrory, formerly a prosecutor from a Denver suburb, was appointed to the Aspen office in 1985, becoming chief deputy after his predecessor resigned in 1988.

Though McCrory is neither well liked nor regarded as politically ambitious, the conservative down-valley Republican named Milton Blakey is af-

fectionately called "Judge Blakey" by those who
like him well enough to tease him about his much
desired judicial appointment. . . .

With Blakey's encouragement, McCrory has moved
sharply away from the path marked out by his prede-
cessors who'd tempered the prosecutorial urge with
a healthy dose of what the Supreme Court has called
"community standards." McCrory, for instance, recently brought—and lost, after less than an hour of
jury deliberation—a felony case for the alleged
sale of some $25 worth of cocaine. Even more prob-
lematic was his decision to seek a felony conviction
against a well-regarded young woman who, while being booked for a DUI, pushed a recovered-alcoholic
jailer who was pressuring her about the virtues of
AA. Even members of the jury that had just convicted
her were horrified to discover that the law that Mc-
Crory chose to invoke—which was designed to dis-
courage incarcerated prisoners from assaulting
their guards during riots—carried an inescapable
mandatory prison sentence. ("Old Aspen," including
the mayor, has contributed generously to her appeal
fund.) For the zealous McCrory, who'd been prominent among those criticizing the sheriff's allegedly laissez-faire attitude toward Thompson,
Palmer's tale of sex, violence, drugs, and weaponry
must have seemed a dream come true.

Whatever the cause, McCrory seems to have reacted
to Palmer's complaint with more speed than pru-
dence. Without interviewing any of the other people
who'd been at Thompson's, McCrory drew up charges
for assault and sexual assault, and then—after a
local judge had passed on signing a search warrant—
had it signed by a judge some 60 miles downvalley.
The Village Voice, *May 15, 1990, Vol. XXXV, No. 20*

. . .

There are a lot of jackasses in the world who think they are smarter than I am. There are a lot of smart cops. But most of them don't get into this kind of chickenshit case.

## D.A. MAY FILE CASE AGAINST ASPEN WRITER
### By Eve O'Brien
### Special to *The Denver Post*

The district attorney of Pitkin County said yesterday he has enough evidence to file felony drug charges against journalist Hunter S. Thompson after a raid on Thompson's home last month. . . .

At a county court hearing yesterday, filing of formal charges was scheduled in district court April 9. Deputy District Attorney Chip McCrory, who is handling the case, said the assault charges, both misdemeanors, and any felony charges will be lodged at that time.

Thompson didn't make an appearance at the hearing yesterday, much to the chagrin of television crews outside the Pitkin County Courthouse. . . .

*March 14, 1990*

. . .

The whole case turned, in the beginning, on a hearing that I didn't go to, in court. It was the first official thing that happened and I thought by not going I would lessen the effect of the case by not kicking up such a noise over the stupid thing. It was a misdemeanor at that time. Ho ho. I sent Michael Solheim as an observer to see what happened in the courtroom, and I didn't expect much of anything, just an "Okay, you're arrested." It was a very pro forma kind of thing. Nothing was expected to happen. It was late afternoon when Solheim got back here and said, "It started out as a misdemeanor, but . . ." After a huddle in front of the judge, where the attorneys approach the bench— my attorney and the D.A. and the prosecutor—the judge announced that the charges had been changed to felonies. And that he was getting rid of the case—out of his court—and it would be turned over to the district court, as felonies. I recognized at once when I heard the news that my own lawyer had participated. His record as a lawyer and as a human being is real weak: I can't believe that fucking lawyer. I wish I could tell you his name, but let's just call him "Chickenshit."

From one little huddle, the case went from Magistrate Tam Scott's court to District Felony Court. Solheim came out here to report that, and I got extremely agitated, and that is when I decided to fire Chickenshit. I called him and asked him what happened—he jabbered some kind of talk about "Well, it was just necessary," or "It was obvious"—lawyer crap. He kept sending me bills for a year or two; I should have had him arrested for fraud.

It is a hard decision, to get rid of your lawyer. That's always bad. Prejudicial, really; the defendant fires one lawyer, and brings in an outsider . . . and Chickenshit was an insider. It was a difficult decision to BOOM, just kick him out the door. The longer the lawyer's on the case, the more information he has, but at that particular time, it was necessary.

I had a list of the top five criminal lawyers in Colorado, whose names had been suggested. Hal Haddon was on that list, and I called him first. I had known Hal for years, since the McGovern campaign. On the phone I found myself apologizing to him, saying, "Oh I'm sorry to do this, but . . . that fucking lawyer . . ." I was apologizing for everything. He said, "Christ, I thought you'd never ask." Hot damn, man. The next day, Hal drove over the Divide to take the case.

That was a huge morale booster; "Ah, finally, we rumble." After I got rid of Chickenshit—from then on it was fun. It was agony with that other lawyer; if you do not trust your lawyer and have good reason not to, that is very unpleasant and uncomfortable.

In the beginning, I didn't think I was going to need a huge criminal lawyer. But once Haddon came over here, and he told me how much trouble I could be in, as they always do: *You might die from this . . .* well, I just figured, if I was going to die, it was better to die fighting.

I remember Haddon said this only once in the case: "My theory as a lawyer is that: Lawyers will take you all the way up to the door of justice, and just say, Well, it's up to the jury now—justice will be done." Haddon said, "My theory is, I want to take the client through the door."

## THOMPSON HIT WITH 5 FELONIES
## JUDGE DISQUALIFIES HIMSELF
### By David Matthews-Price
#### TIMES DAILY STAFF WRITER

Hunter S. Thompson didn't act Monday like a man who had just learned he was facing a possible 16 years in prison.

Moments after the District Attorney hit the "gonzo" journalist with five felony charges and three misdemeanors, Thompson and his lawyers retired to a conference room in the Aspen courthouse. Somebody asked what they were doing in there. . . .

"We're just smoking crack," said Thompson with a grin.

Judge J. E. DeVilbiss announced that he was disqualifying himself from the case. He gave no reason in court for removing himself and he wouldn't comment outside the courtroom either. Ninth District Judicial District Chief Gavin Litwiler will decide who replaces DeVilbiss.

*April 10, 1990*

. . .

There were several judges; nobody really wanted this. DeVilbiss recused himself; we went through all the judges in the county—all three on the district level. Nobody would touch it. We had to go to Grand Junction to find a judge.

## NEW JUDGE NAMED IN THOMPSON CASE
### By David Matthews-Price
#### TIMES DAILY STAFF WRITER

A Grand Junction judge—who is regarded as a good listener, but unpredictable—was selected

Thursday to handle the drug, sex, and explosives case of author Hunter S. Thompson.

Mesa County District Judge Charles A. Buss will replace Aspen District Judge J. E. DeVilbiss, who withdrew from the case on April 9 without explanation. . . .

## Independent Judge

"From my experience, he takes every case on an individual basis and I don't think there is any way to predict how he will rule," said Grand Junction attorney Steve Laiche. Laiche, who is now in private practice, appeared almost daily before Judge Buss when he was a deputy district attorney.

"When you are before him, you don't know how you are going to do, but he is going to listen," Laiche told the *Times Daily* on Thursday.

Laiche said it's hard to generalize about how Buss rules on drug cases. But, the attorney noted, there are other judges in Grand Junction who would probably give drug defendants longer sentences than would Buss. . . .

*April 20, 1990*

. . .

It wouldn't have meant much to half-win a case on the right to smoke marijuana in the home.

Deciding it was a Fourth Amendment case and not a marijuana case was the right thing to do. Legally it wasn't. Legally it was risky. But politically it was right.

Almost everything I did was contrary to Haddon's wishes and habits. He said he never had a case where every time he went into court, he knew what he was going to say by reading the morning newspapers.

(CA Press Photo Service)

THOMPSON BOUND OVER FOR TRIAL
By David Matthews-Price
*Times Daily* Staff Writer

A judge Tuesday threw out one of the five felony charges pending against gonzo journalist Hunter S. Thompson because a witness who claimed to have seen him consume cocaine later admitted she wasn't sure what it was he put up his nose. . . .

*May 23, 1990*

. . .

I think Haddon was surprised to win the preliminary hearing: Not even God can win a preliminary hearing. I just got angry. It wouldn't have meant much to half-win a case on the right to smoke marijuana in the home. That wasn't an issue with me.

# BEWARE

# Today: the Doctor
# Tomorrow: You

**The Hunter S. Thompson Legal Defense Fund**
**Box 274, Woody Creek, Colorado 81656**

Paid for George Stranahan and Michael Solheim

(HST archives)

(*Aspen Daily News*)

TODAY: THE DOCTOR, TOMORROW *YOU.* That was the breakthrough. After that, the majority of people I knew in town were prepared to fight this to the end. I saw then that I had the support of the newspapers and my friends hadn't turned against me.

I had recognized a threat when it was announced to the press that it was a felony case. I recognized the lack of support I had then, mainly due to the charge that I'd put a gun to her head. Nobody knew what had actually happened that night, until I got on the trumpet—the coconut telegraph. I realized it was a threat; I understood it instantly, and my response was to take out a full-page ad in the *Aspen Times* and the *Daily News* to explain my case—point one, two, etc. I labored over it; dense, gray type, like a legal argument. Solheim and I struggled for days. And finally I said, "Fuck this. Never mind it." And I came up with that line: "Here's what we'll put in there—just white space and 'Today the Doctor, Tomorrow You,' underlined . . ." When the ad appeared . . . it was like magic. Maybe one of the best decisions of my life. Now, if I had come out with some legal gray page explaining *my* position, it would not have worked. It had to be "we."

I recognized that. I was trying to put the ad together—to be effective—and it wasn't. But that "Today the Doctor, Tomorrow You" just came to me in a moment of stress. And, shit, the tide turned immediately.

## GONZO'S LAST STAND? (CONTINUED)

" . . . I have more public support now than when I ran for sheriff," Thompson laughs, and he's almost certainly right: There are a lot of houses in Aspen where 66 hours of searching could produce something incriminating. As a supportive ad in the *Aspen Times* read, "Today the Doctor, Tomorrow You." But beyond that, there is something about the D.A.'s invasion of Thompson's house that seems to grate on the Western sensibility of even Aspen's conservatives. Finally, of course, there is the matter of the Fourth Amendment of the United States Constitution.

A few years ago, McCrory's warrant would have been worth as little legally as it is morally, but the Nixon/Reagan legacy on the Supreme Court means that it has a better than even chance of standing up against the challenge Thompson's lawyers plan to bring. And what that means is that on the basis of someone's unsupported word that you used drugs (burned the flag/plotted insurrection/planned a possibly illegal demonstration/committed sodomy/possessed pornography/arranged an abortion) in the privacy of your own home, the cops can break down your door. . . .
The Village Voice, *May 15, 1990, Vol XXXV, No. 20*

. . .

I had to mobilize the whole national and international network. would call the papers. I could get the *Times* in London . . . I could mobilize people. And Haddon recognized that suddenly we had a cause here. For Haddon it was like going into combat with somebody you know is good and think is right, you're a lawyer and he's not, and he—your client—starts making announcements to the press. Every move he makes is not with your counsel . . . I just left the legal stuff to him.

## THOMPSON REJECTS PLEA BARGAIN; TAKES DELIVERY OF CONVERTIBLE
### By David Matthews-Price,
### *Times Daily* Staff Writer
### May 22, 1990

On the eve of his preliminary hearing on drug charges, author Hunter S. Thompson rejected a plea bargain offer from prosecutors and received a red convertible from well-wishers who traveled here from San Francisco.

His supporters, led by porn theater owners Jim and Art Mitchell, left the Bay Area in a convoy of a half dozen vehicles at 3 A.M. Sunday—or "after work," as they put it. They arrived Monday morning at Thompson's cabin near Woody Creek.

As the convoy was arriving, Thompson was on the phone talking to his lawyer about the plea bargain offer from the District Attorney.

Thompson was adamant Monday about the importance of refusing the District Attorney's offer—even one allowing him to plead guilty to one misdemeanor and have a felony conviction purged from his record if he completes two years of probation.

"First, I'm innocent," Thompson said. "And, second, if I plead guilty, that means their search was right, that they got away with it."

He said defendants across the country who are innocent are forced to accept plea bargains in drug cases because they can't afford to fight the system. He said he won't do that.

"This is getting worse because people are caving into this. Somebody has to say, 'enough,'" Thompson said.

Echoing that position were the Mitchell Brothers, owners of the O'Farrell Theatre in San Francisco and longtime friends of Thompson. They said they came to Aspen to support Thompson, who wrote about the government's unsuccessful 11-year battle to shut down their establishment, which features nude dancing. "Somebody has to stand up to this," Art Mitchell said.

"Yeah," said Roxy, a dancer who works for the Mitchells who only wanted to give her first name. "The search of Hunter Thompson's is like being raped by the police."

"I sure wouldn't appreciate a search like that," added Gigi, another Mitchell Brothers employee who arrived in Aspen wearing a scanty shirt and a mini-skirt.

"But, Gigi, you would answer the door differently than Hunter," interjected a smiling Alex Benton, a member of the convoy.

Benton said the only problem during the road trip was on Interstate 80 near Truckee when a California state patrolman stopped the convertible that was later given to Thompson. In the backseat was a 3-foot-tall stuffed buffalo head that was also given to Thompson on Monday in memory of the movie and book "Where the Buffalo Roam."

"He wanted to see the papers on the buffalo," said Benton. The patrolman let the convoy continue without seeing the papers, but said he doubted the group would make it through Utah, according to Benton.

The patrolman also gave them a speeding ticket.

The buffalo head and convertible are to be displayed in a rally that's supposed to take place this morning before Thompson's preliminary hearing begins at 10 A.M. at the Pitkin County Courthouse.

"We just hope the judge has a sense of humor," said Thompson.

## The Alleged Crime

Thompson is charged with four drug felonies, a fifth for possession of explosives, and three misdemeanors including sexual assault. If Thompson, who is free on bond, is bound over on the charges today, his trial is set to begin Sept. 4.

The charges stem from a complaint from former porn filmmaker Gail Palmer-Slater, 35, of St. Clair, Mich. She claims that while visiting Thompson's home on Feb. 21, she was punched and her breast was twisted by the famed gonzo journalist, who she said had been using cocaine.

Six investigators searched Thompson's house for 11 hours for evidence of the alleged assault; they found LSD, four Valium pills and trace amounts of cocaine.

Deputy District Attorney Chip McCrory offered to drop charges—and avoid a trial—if Thompson were to plead guilty to one misdemeanor charge and accept a deferred judgment and sentence on a felony count of LSD possession.

The offer expires at 10 o'clock this morning, when the hearing begins.

If Thompson were to complete two years of probation—that is, pass two years of random drug tests—he could have the felony conviction removed from his record. If he were to flunk any drug tests, or were arrested for any other reason during the two-year period, he would automatically be convicted of the LSD charge and face a maximum four-year prison sentence.

Thompson, author of a half-dozen bestsellers, has written frequently about his use of drugs.

## A Counter Offer

In rejecting the offer, Thompson's attorney made a counter offer: drop all of the charges and Thompson will plead no contest to a charge of improper storage of explosives.

Thompson said the blasting caps found in the search were left on his property by an employee of the Salvation Ditch Co, who had been using them for construction.

Thompson's attorney, Hal Haddon of Denver, said he isn't expecting any sort of victory at today's preliminary hearing. At a preliminary hearing, a judge is supposed to look at the evidence "in the light most favorable" to the prosecution, according to state statutes.

"Even the deity can't win at a preliminary hearing," Haddon quipped.

But the hearing will give Haddon the opportunity to question government witnesses and determine how to attack the District Attorney's case.


## THE SINISTER SEX AND DRUGS CASE OF
## HUNTER S. THOMPSON
### By Richard Stratton

Some theorize that the Thompson persona is theater. No one, they argue, could be this crazy and live to write about it. But what Dr. Thompson is really up to is Life as Art.

"The only thing necessary for the triumph of evil is for good men to do nothing," Thompson quotes Bobby Kennedy in *Songs of the Doomed*. He lives and writes with the sensibilities of an outlaw, a man who refuses to kowtow to unenlightened authority. He is as rigorous in the demands he places on his integrity as he is about his art. *Songs of the Doomed: More Notes on the Death of the American Dream; Gonzo Papers, Vol. 3,* published soon after the Colorado sex-and-drugs case, contains some of his most vivid and visionary writing since *Fear and Loathing in Las Vegas*.

It took 99 days, but Dr. Thompson got his share of Justice. The government lost faith in their case.

"Comes now Milton K. Blakey, District Attorney in and for the Ninth Judicial District of the State of Colorado, and moves this Honorable Court to dismiss this case and as grounds therefore states that:

"The People would be unable to establish guilt beyond a reasonable doubt.

"Dated this 30th day of May 1990," read the

D.A.'s Motion to Dismiss. Judge Charles Buss granted the motion and dismissed the charges with prejudice, meaning that they cannot be brought again at a later date.

"Why couldn't you have made this decision before you filed?" the judge asked Chief Deputy Attorney Chip McCrory. The D.A. responded that he was having witness problems and that the new findings made it clear just how difficult it would have been for the state to get a conviction.

Dr. Thompson was vindicated, but hardly pacified. "We've grown accustomed to letting anyone with a badge walk over us," he said at the time. "Fuck that!" he wrote in a press release issued from Owl Farm the next day. He denounced the Dismissal as "pure cowardice" and said he would "appeal at once" to the Colorado Supreme Court.

Thompson described the District Attorney's "whole goddamn staff" as "thugs, liars, crooks, and lazy human scum. . . . These stupid brutes tried to destroy my life," he said, "and now they tell me to just forget it.

"They are guilty! They should all be hung by their heels from iron telephone poles on the road to Woody Creek!"

Instead of hunkering down to lick his wounds, Dr. Thompson has rallied a new offensive. He has established a Fourth Amendment Foundation "to promote public awareness of the erosion of the Fourth Amendment to the United States Constitution and the consequent threat to the privacy, peace, and security of citizens in their own homes, and to provide legal assistance to citizens whose right to privacy has been infringed."

For, as he fully understands, the truly sinister aspect of the Doctor's case is that government forces, all in the name of some shadowy War on

Drugs, are in fact turning this nation into a police state.

In August of 1990, Dr. Thompson was back in court. This time he was there to file a Notice of Intent to sue the District Attorney's office, collectively and individually, with a $22 million civil lawsuit for Malicious Prosecution, Gross Negligence and Criminal Malfeasance with Harmful Intent.

"The worm has turned," writes Dr. Thompson. "They are doomed. They will soon be in prison. Those bastards have no more respect for the law than any screwhead thief in Washington. They will meet the same fate as Charles Manson and Neil Bush."

Lunch has been served. It is now four o'clock in the morning. Earlier in the day—actually, the previous day—as I purchased a disposable camera, the man in the shop asked me whose picture I intended to take.

"Ah, some old freak over in Woody Creek," I told him.

"Which one?" he wanted to know. "There are a lot of them over there."

"The main one," I told him. "The last outlaw. I'm doing a story on his case for *High Times*."

"Listen, do me a favor," the man said. "Ask him the one question that is on everyone's mind: How does he do it? How does he continue to live the way we did back then and survive?"

It is the most perplexing aspect of this baffling character. How does he do it? We've been drinking heavily all night. He's got a head full of THC. Every so often, like an anteater, he buries his nose and comes up gasping. The Dunhills are consumed incessantly. He keeps the hours of a vampire who's been sucking blood from speed freaks. And yet . . . yet, he makes sense. To me he makes more sense than anyone else who is writing today, because he UNDERSTANDS WHAT IS HAPPENING.

I spent the '80s in prison. When I got out it seemed to me the country had changed drastically for the worse. I worried that only those hundreds of thousands of us locked up during this despicable decade had a decent perspective on just how bad things have become. Then I read *Songs of the Doomed.*

So I asked the Doctor, "How do you do it?" We are out in his backyard, a combination one-hole golf course and target-shooting range. Dr. Thompson is demonstrating an infrared nightscope he has attached to a high-powered rifle. He even looks well. In his fringed Indian apron, and wearing some kind of wooly dive-bomber's cap, traces of chocolate cake from lunch on his lips, he looks remarkably healthy for a man who, by his own admission, has never just said no.

"I made my choice a long time ago," the Doctor says as he peers through the scope. "Some say I'm a lizard with no pulse. The truth is—Jesus, who knows? I never thought I'd make it past 27. Every day I'm just as astounded as everyone else to realize I'm still alive."

Possibly he doesn't understand, but I doubt this. I realize through the fog in my own brain that Dr. Thompson is in a kind of psychophysiological state of grace, because he has for all these years remained true to himself.

High Times, *August 1991*

. . .

Well well well . . . it is twelve years later now, and the Police Problem in this country is even worse today than it was then. The American Century is over, we are still beating up on pygmy nations on the other side of the world, and our once-proud quality of life in the good old U.S.A. has gone up in smoke for all but 1 percent of the population.

And our President is still named Bush—just like it was in 1990, when that gang of doomed pigs attacked my house and tried to put me in prison. They were stupid, and they got what they deserved. They were disgraced, humiliated, and beaten like three-legged mules on the filthy road to Hell. *Res Ipsa Loquitur.*

I was never especially proud of that squalid episode in my life, but I really had no choice. It was *Root hog or die,* in the vernacular of the Chinese hog farm, and apparently it was not in my nature to simply roll over and die.

Marlon Brando explained this to me about 40 years ago when we were both bogged down in some kind of Indian Fishing Rights protest on a riverbank near Olympia, Washington. "Okay," he said to me at a violent press conference for the Indian cause, when the Native American gentlemen were expressing their hatred of being lumped together with "all those niggers" under the collective rubric of Civil Rights. I was disgusted by those rude alcoholic fascists, but Marlon was trying to stay neutral. It was touching.

"Okay," he said. "Why don't we have another look at this situation. So you're a nasty counter-puncher, eh? We're all impressed, but so what?" Marlon could get a little edgy on you, with no warning at all in those days. He had a scary way of *leaning* on people who got in his way. I admired him for it, even when I was the leanee.

But he was wrong about me. I was a working journalist, just trying to understand what was happening, so I could write a true story about it, and I am not much different today. I liked Marlon, but at that moment in time he was getting in *my* way, so I popped him. That is my nature.

Maybe that is why I could understand the Hell's Angels so naturally. They were essentially desperate men who had banded together in what they told one another was self-defense. They were the proud and crazy *elite* of social outlaws, and they insisted on being left alone to do their thing in peace, or else.

Ho ho. And a central ethic of Total Retaliation whenever they were crossed, which scared the shit out of normal people who had no appetite for being chain-whipped in public or gang-raped in their own homes.

"Are you talkin' to *me*, pervert? I hate it when perverts get rude with me, you rotten little bastard."

. . .

Which gets us back, I guess, to my sleazy little morality tale about 99 days of being in the grip of the provably corrupt American Law Enforcement system at its worst with provably evil intentions.

They were bullies and cowards who had somehow been given a license to carry loaded weapons and put anybody who argued with them in prison. That half-bright punk of a District Attorney had campaigned *un-opposed* for re-election for *16 straight years,* doing anything and everything he *wanted* to do, in the name of public security and aggressive law enforcement by pistol-packing cowboys who got paid about a dollar an hour, plus perks, to whip the villagers into line.

Yes sir. And those perks were Huge, Bubba, huge. They ranged, and still do, from 50 cents a mile whenever they stepped into their taxpayer-funded fast new police cruisers to being the only one in the neighborhood with a license to kill.

. . .

Okay folks. The time has come to wrap this story up. I can't be spending all this space rambling on and on about the time I went to trial 12 years ago for Sex, Drugs, Dynamite, and Violence in a little cowboy town on the western slope of the Colorado Rockies because of stupid, vengeful police work. It was no big deal, as major criminal cases go—just another goofy example of dumb cops abusing their power in public and not getting away with it, for a change.

We busted them like shit-eating dogs. They were Punished, Mocked, and Humiliated with the whole world watching, just like they had schemed from the start—except in my case, their plans went horribly wrong, and when the deal finally went down, *they* were the ones on Trial.

It was wonderful, a stunning happy ending to what began as

just another tragic rock & roll story, as if Bob Dylan had been arrested in Miami for jacking off in a seedy little XXX theater while stroking the spine of a fat young boy.

Jesus! That is so horrible that I hate to see myself actually writing it. What is wrong with me? Why would I even *think* of a scene like that?

. . .

Well, shucks, folks. I guess I'm just lucky. It's just amazing, isn't it?

Right. And Ted Williams was lucky, too.

Whoops. And so much for hubris, eh? I was never able to swing a baseball bat like Ted Williams, and I will never be able to write a song like "Mr. Tambourine Man." But what the hell? Neither one of those Yo-yos could write *Fear and Loathing in Las Vegas,* either. . . . At the top of the mountain, we are all Snow Leopards. Anybody who can do one thing better than anyone else in the world is a natural friend of mine.

Even Criminal Lawyers will qualify for that thin-air club on some days, and my wildly publicized trial in the winter of 1990 was one of those. What had begun as just another routine case of a booze-maddened autograph seeker run amok very quickly mushroomed into a profoundly serious Life or Death situation for me in the middle of another goddamn Urgent book deadline, and I suddenly realized that I was going to need major-league criminal trial attorneys if I wanted to avoid the dismal fate of a wild beast caught in a net and headed for the Bronx Zoo forever.

There is not much difference between the death penalty and going to jail for the rest of your life to a snow leopard or any other wild beast. Even a fish will fight to the death, rather than be hooked and tortured by strangers who may or may not eat him alive. It's like they used to say in New Hampshire—LIVE FREE OR DIE.

That was before the state brazenly peddled its soul to the cruel and greasy BUSH family from Texas. Along with its bogus reputation for independence and freedom. Going to New Hampshire today is like going to a leafy greenish high-end boutique in Utah where they sell the skulls of famous bigamists who died in prison for fifteen dollars or a bottle of brown whiskey. . . .

Ah, but never mind Utah for now, eh? Only a freak would jabber like that about the two most god-fearing states in the union. And where did *that* come from, anyway? I must be going crazy. Why go out and pick fights in an election year? We are not what we seem to be.

In any case, that was when I hired Hal Haddon and began my long quixotic journey to becoming the Poet Laureate of the NATIONAL ASSOCIATION OF CRIMINAL DEFENSE LAWYERS, who rode in droves to my defense in my time of great and imminent peril. They slithered in like champions when the great Whistle blew—along with Ralph Steadman, the heroic Mitchell Brothers gang from San Francisco, Bob Dylan, the wild Sabonic sisters from Russia, and Jack, etc. . . . and we kicked the shit out of those Nazis who were trying to kill us. . . . Hallelujah! Fuck those people. OK, time to quit, I see. But not for long. We will RUMBLE, young man, RUMBLE!

Yes. Thank you. Don't mention it. . . . And now we will get back to normal. Why not?

I was talking about this with Bob Dylan last night, and there was not a hint of Violence as we got down to our discussions. "We may never be able to defeat these swine," he told me, "but we don't have to join them."

Yes sir, I thought. The too much fun club is back in business. Let us rumble.

Summit Conference with Bob Dylan, Aspen, Labor Day, 2002
(Anita Bejmuk)

. . .

DRAT! I wish I had more time and space for this story right now—but the publisher's armed narks from N.Y. are on my back like leeches, and I can barely hear myself think. Somewhere in the chaos I hear myself yelling, *"Please don't slit yourself, JoJo. Just get back in the truck. I'll give you whatever you want."*

Oh no, I thought quickly. That is definitely not *me*. I would never talk like that. It must be a music nightmare.

And it *was,* because I never heard those voices again, and those Screws in New York never bothered me again, once I got a chance to mix the big board for Mr. Bobby. Nobody fucked with me after that.

. . .

And that is why I secretly worship God, folks. He had the good judgment to leave me alone to write a few genuine black-on-white pages by myself, for a change. Only Anita is with me now, and that's how I want it. . . . Mahalo. *Res Ipsa Loquitur. Amor Vincit Omnia.*

Okay, and it's about it for now, people. It is 10:00 A.M. in Manhattan, and I can almost *feel* those bastards getting jittery in their cubicles.

Oh ye of little faith. We are, after all, professionals.

*HST/ wc/ September 3, 2002*

The Doctor speaks at a press conference on the steps of the Pitkin
County courthouse with Black Bill and lawyers Hal Haddon and
Gerry Goldstein, after all charges were dropped
(Nicholas Devore III)

# Letter from Lawyer Goldstein

*June 15, 2002*
Dr. Hunter S. Thompson
Owl Farm
Woody Creek, Colorado
Re: *It's Been an Interesting Ride*

Dear Doc:

As I headed out to deep East Texas, I was marveling at your huevos for standing up to our hometown police when they ran amok through your roost at Owl Farm. Your willingness, then and now, to take a stand against intolerance, wherever it rears its ugly head, is a testament to your tenacity. Your reputation may be that of the poet laureate of our generation, but you teach us by more than just word. Your example of political and social activism speaks volumes about good citizenship. As you reminded me recently:

> "The only thing necessary for the triumph of evil, is for good men to do nothing."[1]

A lot of water has passed under the bridge in the intervening decade since we stood on the steps of the Pitkin County Courthouse, basking in the celebrative sunshine of that victorious moment, and most of it has seen the erosion of Constitutional guarantees set in place by our Founding Fathers as a bulwark to protect the governed from their government. For example, the United States Supreme Court has since ruled that the police can:

• Search your home based upon the consent of someone who has absolutely no authority to give same,[2]
• Stop your car based upon an "anonymous tip" completely lacking any indicia of reliability,[3]

---

1. From an undated letter written by English political writer Edmund Burke (1729–1797) to Thomas Mercer.
2. *Illinois v. Rodriquez,* 497 U.S. 177 (1990).
3. *Alabama v. White,* 503 U.S. 953 (1990).

- Subject a motorist to mandatory sobriety tests without any indication they have been drinking or that their driving is impaired,[4] and
- Hold innocent citizens for up to two days without giving reason or recourse.

The tragic events of September 11, 2001, changed more than Manhattan's skyline; it profoundly altered our political and legal landscape as well. Anyone who witnessed the desecration of those buildings and the heart-wrenching loss of life, who didn't want to run out and rip someone a new asshole, doesn't deserve the freedoms we still enjoy. However, anybody who thinks for one moment that giving up our freedoms is any way to preserve or protect those freedoms, is even more foolhardy.

Yet barely one month later, on October 26, 2001, Congress overwhelmingly passed the USA Patriot Act. It rolled through the Senate on a vote of 99 to 1, and the lone holdout, Wisconsin Senator Russ Finegold, said he didn't really know whether he was opposed to the bill or not, he just wanted to read it before voting. There were only two copies of the 346-page document extant at the time, and the Senate had been run out of their building by the anthrax scare.

That single Congressional enactment authorizes the detention of non-citizens suspected of terrorist acts without filing of charges or resort to judicial authority, permits roving wiretaps, and extends to American citizens the secret proceedings, surveillance, and wiretaps of the Foreign Intelligence Surveillance Court, which sits in a vault atop the Department of Justice Building, and allows only Deputy Attorneys General of the United States to appear. Imagine an adversary process that allows only one side's advocate to appear. No wonder that in its 24-year history not a single request for surveillance was turned down. Not until last month, when the secret judge refused to apply these secret proceedings to citizens, cataloging 75 instances

---

4. Michigan Department of State Police v. Sitz, 496 U.S. 444 (1990).

where the FBI had lied to them. The Just Us Department has appealed that secret decision to a secret appeals court, presumably at some other secret location.

At the same time, the Bureau of Prisons, by executive fiat, has authorized monitoring of attorney-client communications by direction of the Attorney General, without any judicial authorization. Almost one hundred and fifty years ago, the Supreme Court reminded those in power:

> The Constitution of the United States is the law for rulers and people, equally in war and in peace, and covers with the shield of its protection all classes of men, at all times, and under all circumstances. No doctrine, involving more pernicious consequences, was ever invented by the whit of man than that any of [the Constitution's] provisions can be suspended during any of the great exigencies of Government.[5]

But this is not the first time civil liberties have been eroded in the face of national crises. Abraham Lincoln suspended the Great Writ of Habeas Corpus, Woodrow Wilson had his Palmer raids, and Franklin Roosevelt interred Asian-American citizens for no reason, other than their national origin. All of this is enough to make even the most ardent civil libertarian throw up their hands. But not you, Doc, no, you have refused to remain silent or to go quietly into the night. Your tireless defense of others, faced with official oppression, stands in the best tradition of true patriots.

You championed the cause of a displaced young Innuit woman,[6] who found herself in the grip of a draconian legal entanglement, calculated to imprison her for the crime of seeking the return of her purse from a thieving pack of rowdies. At your insistence, we gathered a team of legal eagles and launched a midday raid on the Leadville courthouse, nestled near the

5. *Ex Parte Milligan,* 71 U.S. 2 (1866).
6. Jesse Barron.

Continental Divide, in a King Air Beechraft, stuffed so full of partisan supporters that Brother Semmes Luckett was heard to exclaim: "King Farouk didn't require an entourage this large."

More recently, you sent out a clarion call to defend an incarcerated Colorado woman,[7] condemned to suffer a lifetime for the misdeeds of another she had barely met. The idea that a citizen could spend the rest of her life in prison for a crime she did not intend, want, nor desire should be foreign to any sense of justice and fairness. In response you brought the weight and legal prowess of the National Association of Criminal Defense Lawyers Amicus Committee to her defense, and rallied a Colorado Governor's wife, a Denver city councilperson, the Pitkin County Sheriff,[8] a Presidential Historian, and yours truly to the steps of our State Capital, all to the strains of Warren Zevon bellowing "Lawyers, Guns and Money."

In 1990 you founded the Fourth Amendment Foundation, a collection of legal titans willing to take a stand against our government's increasingly pervasive intrusions into its citizen's privacy. While our forefathers were concerned that King George's Red Coats were breaking down their doors and rummaging through their underwear drawers, today we are faced with more sophisticated means of invading our privacy. The new technology is not physical. You cannot see it. You cannot feel it. But in a way, it is more sinister and dangerous because of that. Stealth-like, it steals your thoughts. It steals your conversations. It invades the crossroads between the Fourth Amendment right to be free from unreasonable search and seizure and the First Amendment rights to free speech and association. It cuts to the quick the citizenries' right to protest and complain about their government. The Fourth Amendment protection of a citizen's privacy against his or her government's intrusion is the linchpin upon which all other civil liberties rest. Freedom of speech and association, so essential to a free society, would mean little if the citizens' activities and communications were not protected from

---

7. Lisl Auman.
8. Bob Braudis, by far the most enlightened and intelligent law enforcement officer I've ever met.

government interference and interception. George Orwell created his sterile environment and maintained control over the citizenry, not by imprisoning their bodies, but by exposing their thoughts and communications to government scrutiny.

With recent advances in electronic technology allowing Big Brother to spy upon the most intimate and confidential parts of our lives and communications, the citizen today is in need of greater, not lesser protection. Yet in the face of the dreaded drug scare and threat of international terrorism, courts continue to erode the citizens' zone of privacy by paternalistically balancing these perceived dangers against the public's willingness to acquiesce. While the majority does "rule" in our republican form of democracy, our Constitution was designed to protect certain rights and liberties from that majority, as well as for them. Recognizing that "[a]mong deprivations of rights, none is so effective in cowing a population, crushing the spirit of the individual and putting terror in every heart . . . [as] uncontrolled search and seizure,"[9] your Fourth Amendment Foundation vigilantly stands guard against further encroachments upon the citizens' diminishing expectation of privacy.

Doc, you are a fast take, and your comprehension and analysis of legal issues and theory are quite remarkable. You tenaciously cling to high principle, and expect no less from those around you. All of which probably accounts for why you are such a pain in the ass to have for a client. It takes a lot of love to represent you, Brother.

But the reason I'd do it again in a heartbeat, is that your selfless and indignant stand against injustice has served as a catalyst and stimulus for others, including myself. As Michael Stepanian reminded me at a recent gathering, "Hunter is necessary, now more than ever, Hunter is necessary."

Yours in the continuing fight,
(Signed) Gerald H. Goldstein
for Goldstein, Goldstein & Hilley

---

9. *Brinegar v. U.S.,* 338 U.S. 160, 180–181 (1949) (Jackson, J., dissenting)

# It Never Got Weird Enough for Me

*How can grownups tell [the kids of America] drugs are bad when they see what they've done for Thompson, a man who glided through the 1960s thinking acid was a health food?*
—Bernard Goldberg, *Bias*

Dear Dr. Thompson,

My name is Xania and I am very beautiful and my family is very rich. I am eight years old and I live in Turkey. We live by the sea, but I am bored here. They treat me like a child, but I am not. I am ready to escape. I want to leave. I want to get married and I want to marry *you*. That is why I write you today. I want you to suck my tits while I scream and dance in your lap and my mother watches. She is the one who says this. She loves you very much and so do I.

I am eight years old and my body is well advanced. My mother is twenty-six and, boy! You should see *her*. We are almost twins and so is my grandmother, who is only forty-two years old and looks the same as me. I think she is crazy like my mother. They are beautiful when they walk around naked, and so am I. We are always naked here. We are rich and the sea is so beautiful. If the sea had brains, I would suck them out of it. But I can't. The sea has no penis.

*Why* is that, Doc? If you are so smart, answer *that* one! Fuck you. I knew you wouldn't help us. Please send three plane tickets right *now*. I love you! We are *not* whores. Please help me. I know I will see you soon. We travel a lot. My father wants you to marry me. He is sixty-six years old and he owns the main banks of Turkey. All of them. We will have a beautiful, beautiful wedding when you show them us naked and I dance while you suck my tits and my father screams. O God I love you! Our dream is now. Yes.

Your baby,
Xania

(Billy Noonan)

# Fear and Loathing in Elko

<u>FEAR AND LOATHING IN ELKO: BAD CRAZI-
NESS IN SHEEP COUNTRY . . . SIDE ENTRANCE
ON QUEER STREET . . . O BLACK, O WILD, O
DARKNESS, ROLL OVER ME TONIGHT</u>

<u>MEMO FROM THE NATIONAL AFFAIRS DESK:
THE GHOST OF LONG DONG THOMAS AND
THE ROAD FULL OF FORKS</u>

January 1992

Dear Jann,

God*damn,* I wish you were here to enjoy this beautiful weather
with me. It is autumn, as you know, and things are beginning to
die. It is so wonderful to be out in the crisp fall air, with the leaves
turning gold and the grass turning brown, and the warmth going
out of the sunlight and big hot fires in the fireplace while Buddy
rakes the lawn. We see a lot of bombs on TV because we watch it
a lot more, now that the days get shorter and shorter, and darkness comes so soon, and all the flowers die from freezing.

Oh, God! You should have been with me yesterday when I
finished my ham and eggs and knocked back some whiskey and
picked up my Weatherby Mark V .300 Magnum and a ball of
black Opium for dessert and went outside with a fierce kind of
joy in my heart because I was Proud to be an American on a day
like this. It felt like a goddamn *Football Game,* Jann—it was like
*Paradise.* . . . You remember that *bliss* you felt when we powered
down to the farm and whipped Stanford? Well, it felt like That.

I digress. My fits of Joy are soiled by relentless flashbacks and
ghosts too foul to name. . . . Oh no, don't ask Why. You could have
been president, Jann, but your road was full of forks, and I think
of this when I see the forked horns of these wild animals who dash
back and forth on the hillsides while rifles crack in the distance and
fine swarthy young men with blood on their hands drive back and
forth in the dusk and mournfully call our names. . . .

O Ghost, O Lost, Lost and Gone, O Ghost, come back again.

Right. And so much for autumn. The trees are diseased and the Animals get in your way and the President is usually guilty and most days are too long, anyway. . . . So never mind my poem. It was wrong from the start. I plagiarized it from an early work of Coleridge and then tried to put my own crude stamp on it, but I failed.

So what? I didn't want to talk about fucking autumn, anyway. I was just sitting here at dawn on a crisp Sunday morning, waiting for the football games to start and taking a goddamn very brief break from this blizzard of Character Actors and Personal Biographers and sickly Paparazzi that hovers around me these days (they are sleeping now, thank Christ—some even in my own bed). I was sitting here all alone, thinking, for good or ill, about the Good Old Days.

We were Poor, Jann. But we were Happy. Because we knew Tricks. We were Smart. Not Crazy, like they said. (No. They never called us late for dinner, eh?)

Ho, ho. Laughs don't come cheap these days, do they? The only guy who seems to have any fun in public is Prince Cromwell, my shrewd and humorless neighbor—the one who steals sheep and beats up women, like Mike Tyson.

Who knows why, Jann. Some people are too weird to figure.

You have come a long way from the Bloodthirsty, Beady-eyed news Hawk that you were in days of yore. Maybe you should try reading something besides those goddamn motorcycle magazines—or one of these days you'll find hair growing in your palms.

Take my word for it. You can only spend so much time "on the throttle," as it were. . . . Then the Forces of Evil will take over. Beware. . . .

Ah, but that is a different question, for now. Who gives a fuck? We are, after all, Professionals. . . . But our Problem is not. No. It is the Problem of *Everyman*. It is *Everywhere*. The Ques-

tion is our *Wa;* the Answer is our Fate . . . and the story I am
about to tell you is horrible, Jann.

I came suddenly awake, weeping and jabbering and laughing
like a loon at the ghost on my TV set. Judge Clarence
Thomas . . . Yes, I knew him. But that was a long time ago.
Many years, in fact, but I still remember it vividly. . . . Indeed, it
has haunted me like a Golem, day and night, for many years.

It seemed normal enough, at the time, just another weird
rainy night out there on the high desert. . . . What the Hell? We
were younger, then. Me and *the Judge.* And all the others, for
that matter. . . . It was a Different Time. People were Friendly.
We *trusted* each other. Hell, you could *afford* to get mixed up
with wild strangers in those days—without fearing for your life,
or your eyes, or your organs, or all of your money or even getting
locked up in prison forever. There was a sense of *possibility.* People were not so afraid, as they are now. You could run around
naked without getting shot. You could check into a roadside
motel on the outskirts of Ely or Winnemucca or Elko when you
were lost in a midnight rainstorm—and nobody called the
police on you, just to check out your credit and your employ-
ment history and your medical records and how many parking
tickets you owed in California.

There were Laws, but they were not feared. There were Rules,
but they were not worshiped . . . like Laws and Rules and Cops
and Informants are feared and worshiped today.

Like I said: It was a different time. And I know the Judge
would tell you the same thing, tonight, if he wanted to tell you
the Truth, like I do.

The first time I actually met the Judge was a long time ago,
for strange reasons, on a dark and rainy night in Elko, Nevada,
when we both ended up in the same sleazy roadside Motel, for
no good reason at all. . . . Good God! What a night!

I almost forgot about it, until I saw him last week on TV . . .
and then I saw it *all over again.* The horror! The *horror*! That
night when the road washed out and we all got stuck out there—

somewhere near Elko in a place just off the highway, called Endicott's Motel—and we almost went *really* Crazy.

Yours,<br>HST

. . .

It was just after midnight when I first saw the sheep. I was running about eighty-eight or ninety miles an hour in a drenching, blinding rain on U.S. 40 between Winnemucca and Elko with one light out. I was soaking wet from the water that was pouring in through a hole in the front roof of the car, and my fingers were like rotten icicles on the steering wheel.

It was a moonless night and I knew I was hydroplaning, which is dangerous. . . . My front tires were no longer in touch with the asphalt or anything else. My center of gravity was too high. There was no visibility on the road, none at all. I could have tossed a flat rock a lot farther than I could see in front of me that night through the rain and the ground fog.

So what? I thought. I know this road—a straight lonely run across nowhere, with not many dots on the map except ghost towns and truck stops with names like Beowawe and Lovelock and Deeth and Winnemucca. . . .

Jesus! Who *made* this map? Only a lunatic could have come up with a list of places like this: Imlay, Valmy, Golconda, Nixon, Midas, Metropolis, Jiggs, Judasville—all of them *empty*, with no gas stations, withering away in the desert like a string of old Pony Express stations. The Federal Government owns ninety percent of this land, and most of it is useless for anything except weapons testing and poison-gas experiments.

My plan was to keep moving. Never slow down. Keep the car aimed straight ahead through the rain like a cruise missile. . . . I felt comfortable. There is a sense of calm and security that comes with driving a very fast car on an empty road at night. . . . Fuck this thunderstorm, I thought. There is safety in speed. Nothing can touch me as long as I keep moving fast, and never mind the cops: They are all hunkered down in a truck stop or jacking off by themselves in a culvert behind some dynamite shack in the wilderness beyond the highway. . . . Either way, they wanted no part of me, and I wanted no part of them. Only trouble could come of it. They were probably nice people, and so was I—but we were not meant for each other. History had long since determined that. There is a huge body of evidence to support the notion that me and the police were put on this earth to do extremely different things and never to mingle professionally with each other, except at official functions, when we all wear ties and drink heavily and whoop it up like the natural, good-humored wild boys that we know in our hearts that we are. . . . These occasions are rare, but they happen—despite the forked tongue of fate that has put us forever on different paths. . . . But what the hell? I can handle a wild birthday party with cops, now and then. Or some unexpected orgy at a gun show in Texas. Why not? Hell, I ran for Sheriff one time, and almost got elected. They understand this, and I get along fine with the smart ones.

. . .

But not tonight, I thought, as I sped along in the darkness. Not at 100 miles an hour at midnight on a rain-slicked road in Nevada. Nobody needs to get involved in a high-speed chase on a filthy night like this. It would be dumb and extremely dangerous. Nobody driving a red 454 V-8 Chevrolet convertible was likely to pull over and surrender peacefully at the first sight of a cop car behind him. All kinds of weird shit might happen, from a gunfight with dope fiends to permanent injury or death. . . . It was a good night to stay indoors and be warm, make a fresh pot of coffee, and catch up on important paperwork. Lay low and ignore these loonies. Anybody behind the wheel of a car tonight was far too crazy to fuck with, anyway.

Which was probably true. There was nobody on the road except me and a few big-rig Peterbilts running west to Reno and Sacramento by dawn. I could hear them on my nine-band Super-Scan short-wave/CB/Police radio, which erupted now and then with outbursts of brainless speed gibberish about Big Money and Hot Crank and teenage cunts with huge tits.

They were dangerous Speed Freaks, driving twenty-ton trucks that might cut loose and jackknife at any moment, utterly out of control. There is nothing more terrifying than suddenly meeting a jackknifed

Peterbilt with no brakes coming at you sideways at sixty or seventy miles per hour on a steep mountain road at three o'clock in the morning. There is a total understanding, all at once, of how the captain of the *Titanic* must have felt when he first saw the Iceberg.

And not much different from the hideous feeling that gripped me when the beam of my Long-Reach Super-Halogen headlights picked up what appeared to be a massive rock slide across the highway—right in front of me, blocking the road completely. Big white rocks and round boulders, looming up with no warning in a fog of rising steam or swamp gas . . .

The brakes were useless, the car was wandering. The rear end was coming around. I jammed it down into Low, but it made no difference, so I straightened it out and braced for a serious impact, a crash that would probably kill me. This is It, I thought. This is how it happens— slamming into a pile of rocks at 100 miles an hour, a sudden brutal death in a fast red car on a moonless night in a rainstorm somewhere on the sleazy outskirts of Elko. I felt vaguely embarrassed, in that long pure instant before I went into the rocks. I remembered Los Lobos and that I wanted to call Maria when I got to Elko. . . .

My heart was full of joy as I took the first hit, which was oddly soft and painless. No real shock at all. Just a sickening *thud,* like running over a body, a corpse—or, ye fucking gods, a crippled 200-pound *sheep* thrashing around in the road.

Yes. These huge white lumps were not boulders. They were *sheep.* Dead and dying sheep. More and more of them, impossible to miss at this speed, piled up on one another like bodies at the battle of Shiloh. It was like running over wet logs. Horrible, horrible. . . .

And then I saw the *man*—a leaping Human Figure in the glare of my bouncing headlights, waving his arms and yelling, trying to flag me down. I swerved to avoid hitting him, but he seemed not to see me, rushing straight into my headlights like a blind man . . . or a monster from Mars with no pulse, covered with blood and hysterical.

It looked like a small black gentleman in a London Fog raincoat, frantic to get my attention. It was so ugly that my brain refused to accept it. . . . Don't worry, I thought. This is only an Acid flashback. Be calm. This is not really happening.

I was down to about thirty-five or thirty when I zoomed past the man in the raincoat and bashed the brains out of a struggling sheep, which helped to reduce my speed, as the car went airborne again, then bounced to a shuddering stop just before I hit the smoking, overturned hulk of what looked like a white Cadillac limousine, with people still inside. It was a nightmare. Some fool had crashed into a herd of sheep at high speed and rolled into the desert like an eggbeater.

. . .

We were able to laugh about it later, but it took a while to calm down. What the hell? It was only an accident. The Judge had murdered some range animals.

So what? Only a racist *maniac* would run sheep on the highway in a thunderstorm at this hour of the night. "Fuck those people!" he snapped, as I took off toward Elko with him and his two female companions tucked safely into my car, which had suffered major cosmetic damage but nothing serious. "They'll never get away with this Negligence!" he said. "We'll eat them alive in court. Take my word for it. We are about to become *joint owners* of a huge Nevada sheep ranch."

Wonderful, I thought. But meanwhile we were leaving the scene of a very conspicuous wreck that was sure to be noticed by morning, and the whole front of my car was gummed up with wool and sheep's blood. There was no way I could leave it parked on the street in Elko, where I'd planned to stop for the night (maybe two or three nights, for that matter) to visit with some old friends who were attending a kind of Appalachian Conference for sex-film distributors at the legendary Commercial Hotel. . . .

Never mind that, I thought. Things have changed. I was suddenly a Victim of Tragedy—injured and on the run, far out in the middle of sheep country—1,000 miles from home with a car full of obviously criminal hitchhikers who were spattered with blood and cursing angrily at one another as we zoomed through the blinding monsoon.

Jesus, I thought: Who *are* these people?

Who indeed? They seemed not to notice me. The two women fighting in the backseat were hookers. No doubt about that. I had seen them in my headlights as they struggled in the wreckage of the Cadillac, which had killed about sixty sheep. They were desperate with Fear and Confusion, crawling wildly across the sheep. . . . One was a tall

black girl in a white minidress . . . and now she was screaming at the
other one, a young blond white woman. They were both drunk.
Sounds of struggle came from the backseat. "Get your hands off me,
*Bitch*!" Then a voice cried out, "Help me, Judge! Help! She's *killing*
me!"

What? I thought. *Judge?* Then she said it again, and a horrible chill
went through me. . . . *Judge?* No. That would be over the line. Unacceptable.

He lunged over the seat and whacked their heads together. "Shut
up!" he screamed. "Where are your fucking *manners?*"

He went over the seat again. He grabbed one of them by the hair.
"God *damn* you," he screamed. "Don't embarrass this man. He saved
our lives. We owe him respect—not this goddamned squalling around
like whores."

A shudder ran through me, but I gripped the wheel and stared
straight ahead, ignoring this sudden horrible freak show in my car. I lit
a cigarette, but I was not calm. Sounds of sobbing and the ripping of
cloth came from the backseat. The man they called Judge had straightened himself out and was now resting easily in the front seat, letting out
long breaths of air. . . . The silence was terrifying: I quickly turned up
the music. It was Los Lobos again—something about "One Time One
Night in America," a profoundly morbid tune about Death and Disappointment:

> *A lady dressed in white*
> *With the man she loved*
> *Standing along the side of their pickup truck*
> *A shot rang out in the night*
> *Just when everything seemed right . . .*

Right. A shot. A shot rang out in the night. Just another headline written down in America. . . . Yes. There was a loaded .454 Magnum
revolver in a clearly marked oak box on the front seat, about halfway
between me and the Judge. He could grab it in a split second and blow
my head off.

"Good work, Boss," he said suddenly. "I owe you a big one, for this.
I was *done for,* if you hadn't come along." He chuckled. "Sure as hell,

Boss, sure as hell. I was Dead Meat—killed a lot worse than what happened to those goddamn stupid sheep!"

Jesus! I thought. Get ready to hit the brake. This man is a Judge on the lam with two hookers. He has *no choice* but to kill me, and those floozies in the backseat too. We were the only witnesses. . . .

This eerie perspective made me uneasy. . . . Fuck this, I thought. These people are going to get me locked up. I'd be better off just pulling over right here and killing all three of them. *Bang, Bang, Bang!* Terminate the scum.

"How far is town?" the Judge asked.

I jumped, and the car veered again. "Town?" I said. "*What* town?" My arms were rigid and my voice was strange and reedy.

He whacked me on the knee and laughed. "Calm down, Boss," he said. "I have everything under control. We're almost home." He pointed into the rain, where I was beginning to see the dim lights of what I knew to be Elko.

"Okay," he snapped. "Take a left, straight ahead." He pointed again and I slipped the car into low. There was a red and blue neon sign glowing about a half-mile ahead of us, barely visible in the storm. The only words I could make out were NO and VACANCY.

"Slow down!" the Judge screamed. "This is *it*! Turn! Goddamnit, turn!" His voice had the sound of a whip cracking. I recognized the tone and did as he said, curling into the mouth of the curve with all four wheels locked and the big engine snarling wildly in Compound Low and the blue flames coming out of the tailpipe. . . . It was one of those long perfect moments in the human driving experience that makes *everybody* quiet. Where is P.J.? I thought. This would bring him to his knees.

We were sliding sideways very fast and utterly out of control and coming up on a white steel guardrail at seventy miles an hour in a thunderstorm on a deserted highway in the middle of the night. Why not? On some nights Fate will pick you up like a chicken and slam you around on the walls until your body feels like a beanbag. . . . BOOM! BLOOD! DEATH! So long, Bubba—You knew it would End like this. . . .

We stabilized and shot down the loop. The Judge seemed oddly calm as he pointed again. "This is it," he said. "This is my place. I keep a few suites here." He nodded eagerly. "We're finally safe, Boss. We can do anything we want in this place."

The sign at the gate said:

ENDICOTT'S MOTEL
DELUXE SUITES AND WATERBEDS
ADULTS ONLY / NO ANIMALS

Thank God, I thought. It was almost too good to be true. A place to *dump* these bastards. They were quiet now, but not for long. And I knew I couldn't handle it when these women woke up.

The Endicott was a string of cheap-looking bungalows, laid out in a horseshoe pattern around a rutted gravel driveway. There were cars parked in front of most of the units, but the slots in front of the brightly lit places at the darker end of the horseshoe were empty.

"Okay," said the Judge. "We'll drop the ladies down there at our suite, then I'll get you checked in." He nodded. "We both need some *sleep*, Boss—or at least *rest*, if you know what I mean. Shit, it's been a long night."

I laughed, but it sounded like the bleating of a dead man. The adrenaline rush of the sheep crash was gone, and now I was sliding into pure Fatigue Hysteria.

The Endicott "Office" was a darkened hut in the middle of the horseshoe. We parked in front of it and then the Judge began hammering on the wooden front door, but there was no immediate response. . . . "Wake up, goddamnit! It's me—the *Judge*! Open up! This is Life and Death! I need *help*!"

He stepped back and delivered a powerful kick at the door, which rattled the glass panels and shook the whole building. "I know you're in there!" he screamed. "You can't hide! I'll kick your ass till your nose bleeds!"

There was still no sign of life, and I quickly abandoned all hope. Get out of here, I thought. This is wrong. I was still in the car, half in and half out. . . . The Judge put another fine snap kick at a point just over the doorknob and uttered a sharp scream in some language I didn't recognize. Then I heard the sound of breaking glass.

I leapt back into the car and started the engine. Get away! I thought. Never mind sleep. It's flee or die, now. People get killed for doing this kind of shit in Nevada. It was far over the line. Unacceptable behavior. This is why God made shotguns. . . .

I saw lights come on in the Office. Then the door swung open and I saw the Judge leap quickly through the entrance and grapple briefly with a small bearded man in a bathrobe, who collapsed to the floor after the Judge gave him a few blows to the head. . . . Then he called back to me. "Come on in, Boss," he yelled. "Meet Mister Henry."

I shut off the engine and staggered up the gravel path. I felt sick and woozy, and my legs were like rubberbands.

The Judge reached out to help me. I shook hands with Mr. Henry, who gave me a key and a form to fill out. "Bullshit," said the Judge. "This man is my *guest*. He can have anything he wants. Just put it on my bill."

"Of course," said Mr. Henry. "Your *bill*. Yes. I have it right here." He reached under his desk and came up with a nasty-looking bundle of adding-machine tapes and scrawled Cash/Payment memos. . . . "You got here just in time," he said. "We were about to notify the Police."

"*What?*" said the Judge. "Are you *nuts*? I have a goddamn *platinum* American Express card! My credit is *impeccable*."

"Yes," said Mr. Henry. "We *know* that. We have total respect for you. Your signature is better than gold bullion."

The Judge smiled and whacked the flat of his hand on the counter. "You bet it is!" he snapped. "So get out of my goddamn *face*! You must be crazy to fuck with Me like this! You *fool*! Are you ready to go to *court?*"

Mr. Henry sagged. "*Please*, Judge," he said. "Don't do this to me. All I need is your card. Just let me run an *imprint*. That's all." He moaned and stared more or less at the Judge, but I could see that his eyes were not focused. . . . "They're going to *fire* me," he whispered. "They want to put me in *jail*."

"Nonsense!" the Judge snapped. "I would *never* let that happen. You can always *plead*." He reached out and gently gripped Mr. Henry's wrist. "Believe me, Bro," he hissed. "You have *nothing to worry about*. You are *cool*. They will *never* lock you up! They will *Never* take you away! Not out of *my* courtroom!"

"Thank you," Mr. Henry replied. "But all I need is your card and your signature. That's the problem: I forgot to run it when you checked in."

"So what?" the Judge barked. "I'm good for it. How much do you need?"

"About twenty-two thousand," said Mr. Henry. "Probably twenty-three thousand by now. You've had those suites for nineteen days with total room service."

"What?" the Judge yelled. "You thieving bastards! I'll have you crucified by American Express. You are *finished* in this business. You will *never work again*! *Not anywhere in the world!*" Then he whipped Mr. Henry across the front of his face so fast that I barely saw it. "Stop crying!" he said. "Get a grip on yourself! This is embarrassing!"

Then he slapped the man again. "Is that all you want?" he said. "Only a *card*? A stupid little card? A piece of plastic *shit*?"

Mr. Henry nodded. "Yes, Judge," he whispered. "That's all. Just a stupid little card."

The Judge laughed and reached into his raincoat, as if to jerk out a gun or at least a huge wallet. "You want a *card*, whoreface? Is that *it*? Is that all you want? You filthy little scumbag! Here it is!"

Mr. Henry cringed and whimpered. Then he reached out to accept the Card, the thing that would set him free . . . The Judge was still grasping around in the lining of his raincoat. "What the fuck?" he muttered. "This thing has *too many pockets*! I can *feel* it, but I can't find the slit!"

Mr. Henry seemed to believe him, and so did I, for a minute. . . . Why not? He was a Judge with a platinum credit card—a very high roller. You don't find many Judges, these days, who can handle a full caseload in the morning and run wild like a goat in the afternoon. That is a very hard dollar, and very few can handle it . . . but the Judge was a Special Case.

Suddenly he screamed and fell sideways, ripping and clawing at the lining of his raincoat. "Oh, Jesus!" he wailed. "I've lost my wallet! It's *gone*. I left it out there in the Limo, when we hit the fucking sheep."

"So what?" I said. "We don't need it for this. I have *many* plastic cards."

He smiled and seemed to relax. "How many?" he said. "We might need more than one."

. . .

I woke up in the bathtub—who knows how much later—to the sound of the hookers shrieking next door. *The New York Times* had fallen in and blackened the water. For many hours I tossed and turned like a crack baby in a cold hallway. I heard thumping Rhythm & Blues—serious rock & roll, and I knew that something wild was going on in the Judge's suites. The smell of amyl nitrate came from under the door. It was no use. It was impossible to sleep through this orgy of ugliness. I was getting worried. I was already a marginally legal person, and now I was stuck with some crazy Judge who had my credit card and owed me $23,000.

I had some whiskey in the car, so I went out into the rain to get some ice. I had to get out. As I walked past the other rooms, I looked in people's windows and feverishly tried to figure out how to get my credit card back. Then from behind me I heard the sound of a tow-truck winch. The Judge's white Cadillac was being dragged to the ground. The Judge was whooping it up with the tow-truck driver, slapping him on the back.

"What the hell? It was only property damage," he laughed.

"Hey, Judge," I called out. "I never got my card back."

"Don't worry," he said. "It's in my room—come on."

I was right behind him when he opened the door to his room, and I caught a glimpse of a naked woman dancing. As soon as the door opened, the woman lunged for the Judge's throat. She pushed him back outside and slammed the door in his face.

"Forget that credit card—we'll get some cash," the Judge said. "Let's go down to the Commercial Hotel. My friends are there and they have *plenty* of money."

We stopped for a six-pack on the way. The Judge went into a sleazy liquor store that turned out to be a front for kinky marital aids. I offered him money for the beer, but he grabbed my whole wallet.

Ten minutes later, the Judge came out with $400 worth of booze and a bagful of Triple-X-Rated movies. "My buddies will like this stuff," he said. "And don't worry about the money, I told you I'm good for it. These guys carry serious cash."

The marquee above the front door of the Commercial Hotel said:

WELCOME: ADULT FILM PRESIDENTS
STUDEBAKER SOCIETY
FULL ACTION CASINO / KENO IN LOUNGE

"Park right here in front," said the Judge. "Don't worry. I'm well known in this place."

Me too, but I said nothing. I have been well known at the Commercial for many years, from the time when I was doing a lot of driving back and forth between Denver and San Francisco—usually for Business reasons, or for Art, and on this particular weekend I was there to meet quietly with a few old friends and business associates from the Board of Directors of the Adult Film Association of America. I had been, after all, the Night Manager of the famous O'Farrell Theatre, in San Francisco—"Carnegie Hall of Sex in America."

I was the Guest of Honor, in fact—but I saw no point in confiding these things to the Judge, a total stranger with no Personal Identification, no money, and a very aggressive lifestyle. We were on our way to the Commercial Hotel to borrow money from some of his friends in the Adult Film business.

What the hell? I thought. It's only Rock & Roll. And he was, after all, a Judge of some kind. . . . Or maybe not. For all I knew, he was a criminal pimp with no fingerprints, or a wealthy black shepherd from Spain. But it hardly mattered. He was good company. (If you had a taste for the edge work—and I did, in those days. And so, I felt, did the Judge.) He had a bent sense of fun, a quick mind, and no Fear of anything.

The front door of the Commercial looked strangely busy at this hour of night in a bad rainstorm, so I veered off and drove slowly around the block in low gear.

"There's a side entrance on Queer Street," I said to the Judge, as we hammered into a flood of black water. He seemed agitated, which worried me a bit.

"Calm down," I said. "We don't want to make a scene in this place. All we want is money."

"Don't worry," he said. "I know these people. They are friends. Money is nothing. They will be happy to see me."

We entered the hotel through the Casino entrance. The Judge seemed calm and focused until we rounded the corner and came face to face with an eleven-foot polar bear standing on its hind legs, ready to pounce. The Judge turned to jelly at the sight of it. "I've had enough of this goddamn beast!" he shouted. "It doesn't belong here. We should blow its head off."

I took him by the arm. "Calm down, Judge," I told him. "That's White King. He's been dead for thirty-three years."

The Judge had no use for animals. He composed himself and we swung into the lobby, approaching the desk from behind. I hung back—it was getting late, and the lobby was full of suspicious-looking stragglers from the Adult Film crowd. Private cowboy cops wearing six-shooters in open holsters were standing around. Our entrance did not go unnoticed.

The Judge looked competent, but there was something menacing in the way he swaggered up to the desk clerk and whacked the marble countertop with both hands. The lobby was suddenly filled with tension, and I quickly moved away as the Judge began yelling and pointing at the ceiling.

"Don't give me that crap," he barked. "These people are my friends. They're expecting me. Just ring the goddamn room again." The desk clerk muttered something about his explicit instructions not to. . . .

Suddenly the Judge reached across the desk for the house phone. "What's the number?" he snapped. "I'll ring it myself." The clerk moved quickly. He shoved the phone out of the Judge's grasp and simultaneously drew his index finger across his throat. The Judge took one look at the muscle converging on him and changed his stance.

"I want to cash a check," he said calmly.

"A *check*?" the clerk said. "Sure thing, buster. I'll cash your god-damned check." He seized the Judge by his collar and laughed. "Let's get this bozo out of here. And put him in jail."

I was moving toward the door, and suddenly the Judge was right behind me. "Let's go," he said. We sprinted for the car, but then the Judge stopped in his tracks. He turned and raised his fist in the direction of the hotel. "Fuck you!" he shouted. "I'm the Judge. I'll be back, and I'll bust every one of you bastards. The next time you see me coming, you'd better run."

We jumped into the car and zoomed away into the darkness. The Judge was acting manic. "Never mind those pimps," he said. "I'll have them all on a chain gang in forty-eight hours." He laughed and slapped me on the back. "Don't worry, Boss," he said. "I know where we're going." He squinted into the rain and opened a bottle of Royal Salute. "Straight ahead," he snapped. "Take a right at the next corner. We'll go see Leach. He owes me twenty-four thousand dollars."

I slowed down and reached for the whiskey. What the hell, I thought. Some days are weirder than others.

"Leach is my secret weapon," the Judge said, "but I have to watch him. He could be violent. The cops are always after him. He lives in a balance of terror. But he has a genius for gambling. We win eight out of ten every week." He nodded solemnly. "That is *four out of five,* Doc. That is Big. *Very* big. That is eighty percent of everything." He shook his head sadly and reached for the whiskey. "It's a *horrible* habit. But I can't give it up. It's like having a money machine."

"That's wonderful," I said. "What are you bitching about?"

"I'm *afraid,* Doc. Leach is a *monster,* a criminal hermit who understands nothing in life except point spreads. He should be locked up and castrated."

"So what?" I said. "Where does he live? We are desperate. We have no cash and no plastic. This freak is our only hope."

The Judge slumped into himself, and neither one of us spoke for a minute. . . . "Well," he said finally. "Why not? I can handle almost anything for twenty-four big ones in a brown bag. What the fuck? Let's *do* it. If the bastard gets ugly, we'll kill him."

"Come on, Judge," I said. "Get a grip on yourself. This is only a gambling debt."

"Sure," he replied. "That's what they *all* say."

### DEAD MEAT IN THE FAST LANE: THE JUDGE RUNS AMOK . . . DEATH OF A POET, BLOOD CLOTS IN THE REVENUE STREAM . . . THE MAN WHO LOVED SEX DOLLS

We pulled into a seedy trailer court behind the stockyards. Leach met us at the door with red eyes and trembling hands, wearing a soiled bathrobe and carrying a half-gallon of Wild Turkey.

"Thank God you're home," the Judge said. "I can't *tell* you what kind of horrible shit has happened to me tonight. . . . But now the worm has turned. Now that we have *cash,* we will crush them all."

Leach just stared. Then he took a swig of Wild Turkey. "We are doomed," he muttered. "I was about to slit my wrists."

"Nonsense," the Judge said. "We won Big. I bet the same way you did. You gave me the *numbers.* You even predicted the Raiders would stomp Denver. Hell, it was obvious. The Raiders are unbeatable on Monday night."

Leach tensed, then he threw his head back and uttered a high-pitched quavering shriek. The Judge seized him. "Get a grip on yourself," he snapped. "What's wrong?"

"I went sideways on the bet," Leach sobbed. "I went to that goddamn sports bar up in Jackpot with some of the guys from the shop. We were all drinking Mescal and screaming, and I lost my head."

Leach was clearly a bad drinker and a junkie for mass hysteria. "I got drunk and bet on the Broncos," he moaned, "then I doubled up. We lost everything."

A terrible silence fell on the room. Leach was weeping helplessly. The Judge seized him by the sash of his greasy leather robe and started jerking him around by the stomach. They ignored me, and I tried to pretend it wasn't happening. . . . It was too ugly.

There was an ashtray on the table in front of the couch. As I reached out for it, I noticed a legal pad of what appeared to be Leach's poems, scrawled with a red Magic Marker in some kind of primitive verse form. There was one that caught my eye. There was something particularly ugly about it. There was something *repugnant* in the harsh slant of the handwriting. It was about pigs.


### I TOLD HIM IT WAS WRONG

—F. X. Leach
Omaha, 1968

*A filthy young pig*
*got tired of his gig*
*and begged for a transfer*
*to Texas.*

*Police ran him down*
*on the Outskirts of town*
*and ripped off his Nuts*
*with a coat hanger.*
*Everything after that was like*
*coming home*
*in a cage on the*
*back of a train from*
*New Orleans on a Saturday night*
*with no money and cancer and*
*a dead girlfriend.*
*In the end it was no use*
*He died on his knees in a barnyard*
*with all the others watching.*
*Res Ipsa Loquitur.*


"They're going to kill me," Leach said. "They'll be here by midnight. I'm doomed." He uttered another low cry and reached for the Wild Turkey bottle, which had fallen over and spilled.

   "Hang on," I said. "I'll get more."

(Paul Chesley)

On my way to the kitchen I was jolted by the sight of a naked woman slumped awkwardly in the corner with a desperate look on her face, as if she'd been shot. Her eyes bulged and her mouth was wide open and she appeared to be reaching out for me.

I leapt back and heard laughter behind me. My first thought was that Leach, unhinged by his gambling disaster, had finally gone over the line with his wife-beating habit and shot her in the mouth just before we knocked. She appeared to be crying out for help, but there was no voice.

I ran into the kitchen to look for a knife, thinking that if Leach had gone crazy enough to kill his wife, now he would have to kill me, too, since I was the only witness. Except for the Judge, who had locked himself in the bathroom.

Leach appeared in the doorway, holding the naked woman by the neck, and hurled her across the room at me. . . .

Time stood still for an instant. The woman seemed to hover in the air, coming at me in the darkness like a body in slow motion. I went into a stance with the bread knife and braced for a fight to the death.

Then the thing hit me and bounced softly down to the floor. It was a rubber blow-up doll: one of those things with five orifices that young stockbrokers buy in adult bookstores after the singles bars close.

"Meet Jennifer," he said. "She's my punching bag." He picked it up by the hair and slammed it across the room.

"Ho, ho," he chuckled, "no more wife beating. I'm cured, thanks to Jennifer." He smiled sheepishly. "It's almost like a miracle. *These dolls saved my marriage.* They're a lot smarter than you think." He nodded gravely. "Sometimes I have to beat *two at once.* But it always calms me down, you know what I mean?"

*Whoops,* I thought. Welcome to the night train. "Oh, *hell yes,*" I said quickly. "How do the neighbors handle it?"

"No problem," he said. "They love me."

Sure, I thought. I tried to imagine the horror of living in a muddy industrial slum full of tin-walled trailers and trying to protect your family against brain damage from knowing that every night when you look out your kitchen window there will be a man in a leather bathrobe flogging two naked women around the room with a quart bottle of Wild Turkey. Sometimes for two or three hours . . . It was horrible.

"Where is your wife?" I asked. "Is she still here?"

"Oh, yes," he said quickly. "She just went out for some cigarettes She'll be back *any minute.*" He nodded eagerly. "Oh, yes, she's very *proud* of me. We're almost reconciled. She really loves these dolls."

I smiled, but something about his story made me nervous. "How many do you have?" I asked him.

"Don't worry," he said. "I have all we need." He reached into a nearby broom closet and pulled out another one—a half-inflated Chinese-looking woman with rings in her nipples and two electric cords attached to her head. "This is Ling-Ling," he said. "She screams when I hit her." He whacked the doll's head and it squawked stupidly.

Just then I heard car doors slamming outside the trailer, then loud knocking on the front door and a gruff voice shouting, "Open up! Police!"

Leach grabbed a .44 Magnum out of a shoulder holster inside his bathrobe and fired two shots through the front door. "You *bitch,*" he screamed. "I should have killed you a long time ago."

He fired two more shots, laughing calmly. Then he turned to face me and put the barrel of the gun in his mouth. He hesitated for a moment, staring directly into my eyes. Then he pulled the trigger and blew off the back of his head.

The dead man seemed to lunge at me, slumping headfirst against my legs as he fell to the floor—just as a volley of shotgun blasts came through the front door, followed by harsh shouts on a police bullhorn from outside. Then another volley of buckshot blasts that exploded the TV set and set the living room on fire, filling the trailer with dense brown smoke that I recognized instantly as the smell of Cyanide gas being released by the burning plastic couch.

Voices were screaming through the smoke, "*Surrender!* HANDS UP *behind your goddamn head!* DEAD MEAT!" Then more shooting. Another deafening fireball exploded out of the living room, I kicked the corpse off my feet and leapt for the back door, which I'd noticed earlier when I scanned the trailer for "alternative exits," as they say in the business—in case one might become necessary. I was halfway out the door when I remembered *the Judge.* He was still locked in the bathroom, maybe helpless in some kind of accidental drug coma, unable to get to his feet as flames roared through the trailer. . . .

Ye Fucking Gods! I thought. I can't let him burn.

Kick the door off its hinges. Yes. Whack! The door splintered and I saw him sitting calmly on the filthy aluminum toilet stool, pretending to read a newspaper and squinting vacantly at me as I crashed in and grabbed him by one arm. "Fool!" I screamed. "Get up! Run! They'll *murder* us!"

He followed me through the smoke and burning debris, holding his pants up with one hand. . . . The Chinese sex doll called Ling-Ling hovered crazily in front of the door, her body swollen from heat and her hair on fire. I slapped her aside and bashed the door open, dragging the Judge outside with me. Another volley of shotgun blasts and bullhorn yells erupted somewhere behind us. The Judge lost his footing and fell heavily into the mud behind the doomed Airstream.

"Oh, God!" he screamed. "Who *is* it?"

"The *Pigs,*" I said. "They've gone *crazy.* Leach is dead! They're trying to *kill* us. We have to get to the car!"

He stood up quickly. "Pigs?" he said. "*Pigs?* Trying to *kill* me?"

He seemed to stiffen, and the dumbness went out of his eyes. He raised both fists and screamed in the direction of the shooting. "You *bastards*! You *scum*! You will *die* for this. You stupid white-trash pigs!

"Are they *nuts?*" he muttered. He jerked out of my grasp and reached angrily into his left armpit, then down to his belt and around behind his back like a gunfighter trying to slap leather. . . . But there was no leather there. Not even a sleeve holster.

"*Goddamnit!*" he snarled. "Where's my goddamn *weapon?* Oh, Jesus! I left it in the car!" He dropped into a running crouch and sprinted into the darkness, around the corner of the flaming Airstream. "Let's *go!*" he hissed. "I'll *kill* these bastards! I'll blow their fucking heads off!"

*Right,* I thought, as we took off in a kind of low-speed desperate crawl through the mud and the noise and the gunfire, terrified neighbors screaming frantically to each other in the darkness. The red convertible was parked in the shadows, near the front of the trailer right next to the State Police car, with its chase lights blinking crazily and voices burping out of its radio.

The Pigs were nowhere to be seen. They had apparently *rushed* the place, guns blazing—hoping to kill Leach before he got away. I jumped into the car and started the engine. The Judge came through the passenger door and reached for the loaded .454 Magnum. . . . I watched in horror as he jerked it out of its holster and ran around to the front of the cop car and fired two shots into the grille.

*"Fuck you!"* he screamed. "Take *this*, you Scum! Eat shit and die!" He jumped back as the radiator exploded in a blast of steam and scalding water. Then he fired three more times through the windshield and into the squawking radio, which also exploded.

"Hot damn!" he said as he slid back into the front seat. "Now we have them trapped!" I jammed the car into reverse and lost control in the mud, hitting a structure of some kind and careening sideways at top speed until I got a grip on the thing and aimed it up the ramp to the highway. . . . The Judge was trying desperately to reload the .454, yelling at me to slow down, so he could finish the bastards off! His eyes were wild and his voice was unnaturally savage.

I swerved hard left to Elko and hurled him sideways, but he quickly recovered his balance and somehow got off five more thundering shots in the general direction of the burning trailer behind us.

"Good work, Judge," I said. "They'll never catch us now." He smiled and drank deeply from our Whiskey Jug, which he had somehow picked up as we fled. . . . Then he passed it over to me, and I too drank deeply as I whipped the big V-8 into passing gear, and we went from forty-five to ninety in four seconds and left the ugliness far behind us in the rain.

I glanced over at the Judge as he loaded five huge bullets into the Magnum. He was very calm and focused, showing no signs of the drug coma that had crippled him just moments before. . . . I was impressed. The man was clearly a Warrior. I slapped him on the back and grinned. "Calm down, Judge," I said. "We're almost home."

I knew better, of course. I was *1,000 miles* from home, and we were almost certainly doomed. There was no hope of escaping the dragnet that would be out for us, once those poor fools discovered Leach in a puddle of burning blood with the top of his head blown off. The squad car was destroyed—thanks to the shrewd instincts of the Judge—but I knew it would not take them long to send out an all-points alarm. Soon there would be angry police roadblocks at every exit between Reno and Salt Lake City. . . .

So what? I thought. There were many side roads, and we had a *very* fast car. All I had to do was get the Judge out of his killing frenzy and find a truck stop where we could buy a few cans of Flat Black spray paint. Then we could slither out of the state before dawn and find a place to hide.

But it would not be an easy run. In the quick space of four hours we had destroyed two automobiles and somehow participated in at least one killing—in addition to all the other random, standard-brand crimes like speeding and arson and fraud and attempted murder of State Police officers while fleeing the scene of a homicide. . . . No. We had a Serious problem on our hands. We were trapped in the middle of Nevada like crazy rats, and the cops would shoot to Kill when they saw us. No doubt about that. We were Criminally Insane. . . . I laughed and shifted up into Drive. The car stabilized at 115 or so. . . .

The Judge was eager to get back to his women. He was still fiddling with the Magnum, spinning the cylinder nervously and looking at his watch. "Can't you go any faster?" he muttered. "How far is Elko?"

Too far, I thought, which was true. Elko was fifty miles away and there would be roadblocks. Impossible. They would trap us and probably butcher us.

Elko was out, but I was loath to break this news to the Judge. He had no stomach for bad news. He had a tendency to flip out and flog anything in sight when things weren't going his way.

It was wiser, I thought, to humor him. Soon he would go to sleep.

I slowed down and considered. Our options were limited. There would be roadblocks on every paved road out of Wells. It was a main crossroads, a gigantic full-on truck stop where you could get anything you wanted twenty-four hours a day, within reason of course. And what we needed was not in that category. We needed to disappear. That was one option.

We could go south on 93 to Ely, but that was about it. That would be like driving into a steel net. A flock of pigs would be waiting for us, and after that it would be Nevada State Prison. To the north on 93 was Jackpot, but we would never make that either. Running east into Utah was hopeless. We were trapped. They would run us down like dogs.

There were other options, but not all of them were mutual. The Judge had his priorities, but they were not mine. I understood that me and the Judge were coming up on a parting of the ways. This made me nervous. There were other options, of course, but they were all High

Risk. I pulled over and studied the map again. The Judge appeared to be sleeping, but I couldn't be sure. He still had the Magnum in his lap.

The Judge was getting to be a problem. There was no way to get him out of the car without violence. He would not go willingly into the dark and stormy night. The only other way was to kill him, but that was out of the question as long as he had the gun. He was very quick in emergencies. I couldn't get the gun away from him, and I was not about to get into an argument with him about who should have the weapon. If I lost, he would shoot me in the spine and leave me in the road.

I was getting too nervous to continue without chemical assistance. I reached under the seat for my kit bag, which contained five or six Spansules of Black Acid. Wonderful, I thought. This is just what I need. I ate one and went back to pondering the map. There was a place called Deeth, just ahead, where a faintly marked side road appeared to wander uphill through the mountains and down along a jagged ridge into Jackpot from behind. Good, I thought, this is it. We could sneak into Jackpot by dawn.

Just then I felt a blow on the side of my head as the Judge came awake with a screech, flailing his arms around him like he was coming out of a nightmare. "What's happening, goddamnit?" he said. "Where are we? They're after us." He was jabbering in a foreign language that quickly lapsed into English as he tried to aim the gun. "Oh, God!" he screamed. "They're right on top of us. Get moving, goddamnit. I'll kill every bastard I see."

He was coming out of a nightmare. I grabbed him by the neck and put him in a headlock until he went limp. I pulled him back up in the seat and handed him a Spansule of acid. "Here, Judge, take this," I said. "It'll calm you down."

He swallowed the pill and said nothing as I turned onto the highway and stood heavily on the accelerator. We were up to 115 when a green exit sign that said DEETH NO SERVICES loomed suddenly out of the rain just in front of us. I swerved hard to the right and tried to hang on. But it was no use. I remember the sound of the Judge screaming as we lost control and went into a full 360-degree curl and then backwards at seventy-five or eighty through a fence and into a pasture.

For some reason the near-fatal accident had a calming effect on the Judge. Or maybe it was the acid. I didn't care one way or the other after

I took the gun from his hand. He gave it up without a fight. He seemed to be more interested in reading the road signs and listening to the radio. I knew that if we could slip into Jackpot the back way, I could get the car painted any color I wanted in thirty-three minutes and put the Judge on a plane. I knew a small private airstrip there, where nobody asks too many questions and they'll take a personal check.

At dawn we drove across the tarmac and pulled up to a seedy-looking office marked AIR JACKPOT EXPRESS CHARTER COMPANY. "This is it Judge," I said and slapped him on the back. "This is where you get off." He seemed resigned to his fate until the woman behind the front desk told him there wouldn't be a flight to Elko until lunchtime.

"Where is the pilot?" he demanded.

"I am the pilot," the woman said, "but I can't leave until Debby gets here to relieve me."

"Fuck this!" the Judge shouted. "Fuck lunchtime. I have to leave *now*, you bitch."

The woman seemed truly frightened by his mood swing, and when the Judge leaned in and gave her a taste of the long knuckle, she collapsed and began weeping uncontrollably. "There's more where that came from," he told her. "Get up! I have to get out of here now."

He jerked her out from behind the desk and was dragging her toward the plane when I slipped out the back door. It was daylight now. The car was nearly out of gas, but that wasn't my primary concern. The police would be here in minutes, I thought. I'm doomed. But then, as I pulled onto the highway, I saw a sign that said, WE PAINT ALL NIGHT.

As I pulled into the parking lot, the Jackpot Express plane passed overhead. So long, Judge, I thought to myself. You're a brutal hustler and a Warrior and a great copilot, but you know how to get your way. You will go far in the world.

## EPILOGUE: CHRISTMAS DREAMS AND CRUEL MEMORIES . . . NATION OF JAILERS . . . STAND BACK! THE JUDGE WILL SEE YOU NOW

That's about it for now, Jann. This story is too depressing to have to confront professionally in these morbid weeks before Christmas. . . . I have only vague memories of what it's like there in New York, but sometimes I have flashbacks about how it was to glide in perfect speedy silence around the ice rink in front of NBC while junkies and federal informants in white beards and sleazy red jumpsuits worked the crowd mercilessly for nickels and dollars and dimes covered with Crack residue.

I remember one Christmas morning in Manhattan when we got into the Empire State Building and went up to the Executive Suite of some famous underwear company and shoved a 600-pound red tufted-leather Imperial English couch out of a corner window on something like the eighty-fifth floor. . . .

The wind caught it, as I recall, and it sort of drifted around the corner onto Thirty-fourth Street, picking up speed on its way down, and hit the striped awning of a Korean market, you know, the kind that sells everything from kimchi to Christmas trees. The impact blasted watermelons and oranges and tomatoes all over the sidewalk. We could barely see the impact from where we were, but I remember a lot of activity on the street when we came out of the elevator. . . . It looked like a war zone. A few gawkers were standing around in a blizzard, muttering to each other and looking dazed. They thought it was an underground explosion—maybe a subway or a gas main.

Just as we arrived on the scene, a speeding cab skidded on some watermelons and slammed into a Fifth Avenue bus and burst into flames. There was a lot of screaming and wailing of police sirens. Two cops began fighting with a gang of looters who had emerged like ghosts out of the snow and were running off with hams and turkeys and big jars of caviar. . . . Nobody seemed to think it was strange. *What the hell? Shit happens. Welcome to the Big Apple. Keep alert. Never ride in open cars or walk too close to a tall building when it snows.* . . . There were Christmas trees scattered all over the street and cars were stopping to grab them and speeding away. We stole one and took it to Missy's place on the Bowery, because we knew she didn't have one. But she wasn't home, so we put the tree out on the fire escape and set it on fire with kerosene.

That's how I remember Xmas in New York, Jann. It was always a time of angst and failure and turmoil. Nobody ever seemed to have any money on Christmas. Even rich people were broke and jabbering frantically on their telephones about Santa Claus and suicide or joining a church with no rules. . . . The snow was clean and pretty for the first twenty or thirty minutes around dawn, but after that it was churned into filthy mush by drunken cabbies and garbage compactors and shitting dogs.

Anybody who acted happy on Christmas was lying—even the ones who were getting paid $500 an hour. . . . The Jews were especially sulky, and who could blame them? The birthday of Baby Jesus is always a nervous time for people who know that ninety days later they will be accused of murdering him.

So what? We have our *own* problems, eh? Jesus! I don't know how you can ride all those motorcycles around in the snow, Jann. Shit, we can *all* handle the back wheel coming loose in a skid. But the *front* wheel is something else—and that's what happens when it snows. WHACKO. One minute you feel as light and safe as a snowflake, and the next minute you're sliding sideways under the wheels of a Bekins van. . . . Nasty traffic jams, horns honking, white limos full of naked Jesus freaks going up on the sidewalk in low gear to get around you and the mess you made on the street . . . *Goddamn this scum. They are more and more in the way. And why aren't they home with their families on Xmas? Why do they need to come out here and die on the street like iron hamburgers?*

I hate these bastards, Jann. And I suspect you feel the same. . . . They might call us bigots, but at least we are *Universal* bigots. Right? Shit on those people. Everybody you see these days might have the power to get you locked up. . . . Who knows why? They will have reasons straight out of some horrible Kafka story, but in the end it won't matter any more than a full moon behind clouds. Fuck them.

Christmas hasn't changed much in twenty-two years, Jann—not even 2,000 miles west and 8,000 feet up in the Rockies. It is still a day that only amateurs can love. It is all well and good for children and acid freaks to believe in Santa Claus—but it is still a profoundly morbid day for us working professionals. It is unsettling to know that one out of every twenty people you meet on Xmas will be dead this time next year. . . . Some people can accept this, and some can't. That is why God made whiskey, and also why Wild Turkey comes in $300 shaped canisters during most of the Christmas season, and also why criminal shitheads all over New York City will hit you up for $100 tips or they'll twist your windshield wipers into spaghetti and urinate on your door handles.

People all around me are going to pieces, Jann. My whole support system has crumbled like wet sugar cubes. That is why I try never to employ anyone over the age of twenty. Every Xmas after that is like another notch down on the ratchet, or maybe a few more teeth off the flywheel. . . . I remember on Xmas in New York when I was trying to sell a Mark VII Jaguar with so many teeth off the flywheel that the whole drivetrain would lock up and whine every time I tried to start the engine for a buyer. . . . I had to hire gangs of street children to muscle the car back and forth until the throw-out gear on the starter was lined up very precisely to engage the few remaining teeth on the flywheel. On some days I would leave the car idling in a fireplug zone for three or four hours at a time and pay the greedy little bastards a dollar an hour to keep it running and wet-shined with fireplug water until a buyer came along.

We got to know each other pretty well after nine or ten weeks, and they were finally able to unload it on a rich artist who drove as far as the toll plaza at the far end of the George Washington Bridge, where the engine seized up and exploded like a steam bomb. "They had to tow it away with a firetruck," he said. "Even the leather seats were on fire. They laughed at me."

There is more and more Predatory bullshit in the air these days. Yesterday I got a call from somebody who said I owed money to Harris Wofford, my old friend from the Peace Corps. We were in Sierra Leone together.

He came out of nowhere like a heat-seeking missile and destroyed the U.S. Attorney General in Pennsylvania. It was

Wonderful. Harris is a Senator now, and the White House creature is not. Thornburgh blew a forty-four–point lead in three weeks, like Humpty Dumpty. . . . WHOOPS! Off the wall like a big Lizard egg. The White House had seen no need for a safety net.

It was a major disaster for the Bush brain trust and every GOP political pro in America, from the White House all the way down to City Hall in places like Denver and Tupelo. The whole Republican party was left stunned and shuddering like a hound dog passing a peach pit. . . . At least that's what they said in Tupelo, where one of the local GOP chairmen flipped out and ran off to Biloxi with a fat young boy from one of the rich local families . . . then he tried to blame it on Harris Wofford when they arrested him in Mobile for aggravated Sodomy and kidnapping. He was ruined, and his Bail was only $5,000, but none of his friends would sign for it. They were mainly professional Republicans and bankers who had once been in the Savings and Loan business, along with Neil Bush the *manqué,* son of the President.

Neil had just walked in on the infamous Silverado Savings & Loan scandal in Colorado. But only by the skin of his teeth, after his father said he would have to abandon him to a terrible fate in the Federal Prison System if his son was really a crook. The evidence was overwhelming, but Neil had a giddy kind of talent *negotiating*—like Colonel North and the Admiral, who also walked. . . . It was shameless and many people bitched. But what the fuck do they expect from a Party of high-riding Darwinian rich boys who've been running around in the White House like pampered animal for twelve straight years? They can do whatever they want, and why not. "These are Good Boys," John Sununu once said of his staff. "They only shit in the pressroom."

Well . . . Sununu is gone now, and so is Dick Thornburgh, who is currently seeking night work in the bank business somewhere on the outskirts of Pittsburgh. It is an ugly story. He decided to go out on his own—like Lucifer, who plunged into Hell—and he got beaten like a redheaded stepchild by my old Peace Corps buddy Harris Wofford, who caught him from behind like a bull wolverine so fast that Thornburgh couldn't even get out of the way. . . . He was mangled and humiliated. It was the worst public disaster since Watergate.

The GOP was plunged into national fear. How could it happen? Dick Thornburgh had sat on the right hand of God. As AG, he had stepped out like some arrogant Knight from the Round Table and declared that *his* boys—4,000 or so Justice Department prosecutors—were no longer subject to the rules of the Federal Court System.

But he was wrong. And now Wofford is using Thornburgh's corpse as a launching pad for a run on the White House and hiring experts to collect bogus debts from old buddies like me. Hell, I *like* the idea of Harris being President. He always seemed honest and I knew he was smart, but I am leery of giving him money.

That is politics in the 1990s. Democratic presidential candidates have not been a satisfying investment recently. Camelot was thirty years ago, and we still don't know who killed Jack Kennedy. That lone bullet on the stretcher in Dallas sure as hell didn't pass through two human bodies, but it was the one that pierced the heart of the American Dream in our century, maybe forever.

Camelot is on Court TV now, limping into Rehab clinics and forced to deny low-rent Rape accusations in the same sweaty West Palm Beach courthouse where Roxanne Pulitzer went on trial for fucking a trumpet and lost.

It has been a long way down—not just for the Kennedys and the Democrats, but for all the rest of us. Even the rich and the powerful, who are coming to understand that change can be quick in the Nineties and one of these days it will be them in the dock on TV, fighting desperately to stay out of prison.

Take my word for it. I have been there, and it gave me an eerie feeling. . . . Indeed. There are many cells in the mansion, and more are being added every day. We are becoming a nation of jailers.

And that's about it for now, Jann. Christmas is on us and it's all downhill from here on. . . . At least until Groundhog Day, which is soon. . . . So, until then, at least, take my advice, as your family doctor, and don't do *anything* that might cause either one of us to have to appear before the Supreme Court of the United States. If you know what I'm saying. . . .

Yes. He is Up There, Jann. The Judge. And he will be there for a long time, waiting to gnaw on our skulls. . . . Right. Put *that* in your leather pocket the next time you feel like jumping on your new motorcycle and screwing it all the way over thru traffic and passing cop cars at 140.

Remember F. X. Leach. He crossed the Judge, and he paid a terrible price. . . . And so will you, if you don't slow down and quit harassing those girls in your office. The Judge is in charge now, and He won't tolerate it. Beware.

# Heeere's Johnny!

## <u>FEAR AND LOATHING AT JACK'S HOUSE . . .</u><br><u>THE LONELIEST PLACE IN THE WORLD</u>

It was a dark and stormy night when I set out from my house to Jack Nicholson's place far away in a valley on the other side of town. It was his birthday, and I had a huge raw elk heart for him. I have known Jack for many years, and we share a certain sense of humor among other things, and in truth there was nothing inherently strange in the notion of bringing a freshly taken elk heart out to his home on the night of his birthday.

It was lightly frozen and beginning to leak from the chambers, so I put it in a Ziploc bag and tossed it in the back of the Jeep. Hot damn, I thought, Jack's children will love this. I knew they had just arrived that day from Los Angeles, and I wanted to have a surprise for them. "You won't be late, will you?" Jack had asked. "You know the kids go to bed early."

"Don't worry," I said. "I'm leaving in ten minutes."

And it was just about then that the night began to go wrong. Time withered away. Some kind of episode occurred, and before I knew it I was running two hours late—two hours, keep that in mind because it will make a difference later on.

Okay. So I set out to see Jack and his children with all kinds of jokes and gimcracks in my car. In addition to the bleeding elk heart, there was a massive outdoor amplifier, a tape recording of a pig being eaten alive by bears, a 1,000,000-watt spotlight, and a 9-mm Smith & Wesson semiautomatic pistol with teakwood handles and a box of high-powered ammunition. There was also a 40-million-candlepower parachute flare that would light up the valley for 40 miles for 40 seconds that would seem to anyone lucky enough to be awake at the time like the first blinding flash of a midrange nuclear device that might signal the end of the world. It was a handheld mortar, in fact, with a plastic lanyard on one end and the black snout of a firing tube on the other. I had found it on sale a few weeks earlier at West Marine Hardware in Sausalito for $115, down from $210. It was irresistible—even cheap, I felt, for such a spectacular display—and I was looking forward to using it. The directions were vague, and mainly in foreign languages, but the diagrams made it clear that The USER should wear suitable eye protection, hold projectile vertically as far from body as possible, then JERK FIRING RING STRAIGHT DOWN and DO NOT ALLOW PROJECTILE TO TILT.

Okay, I thought, I can do this. I know flares. I have fired those huge gray military things, where you pull off one end and put it on the other, then bash your palm against the bottom and feel both your arms go numb all the way up to your skull from an explosion equal to a 105-mm howitzer blast. So I wasn't worried about this cheap red load from Sausalito. Once you get a feeling for handling nitroglycerine fuses, you never lose it.

(HST archives)

. . .

I was thinking about these things as I wound my way up the long winding road to Jack's house. It was ten miles of darkness, and by the time I got there I was feeling a little jumpy, so I pulled over and parked on a bluff overlooking the Nicholson home.

There were no other cars on the road. I unloaded the huge amplifier and mounted it firmly on top of the Jeep. The horn pointed out across the valley, then I placed the flare neatly beside it and leaned back against the hood to smoke a cigarette. Far down through the pines I could see the queer-looking lights of Jack's house. The night was extremely quiet and the LED in my Jeep said it was nine degrees above zero and the time was no later than 2:30 A.M., or maybe 2:45. I remember hearing a gospel tune on the radio, then I plugged the horn into the amplifier and beamed up the pig-screaming tape to about 119 decibels.

The noise was intolerable, at first. I had to cover my head and crouch behind the Jeep to get away from it. I wanted to turn it off, but just then I saw headlights coming up the road and I had to get out of sight . . . The car never even slowed down as it passed me, despite the hideous screams of what sounded like a whole herd of pigs being slaughtered.

My first thought, for some reason, was that it was not Bill Clinton, because he would have at least honked. Ho ho, good joke, eh? It's odd how Bill Clinton jokes seem to pop up at unnatural moments like these—when you're doing something that feels deeply right and normal and you feel in a high sense of humor as you set about your task, which then somehow goes wrong for reasons beyond your control and sows the seeds of tragedy.

Nobody needs this—but some people seem to want it, and on that giddy winter night in the Rockies, I was one of them. No power of reason or nature could have persuaded me that the small, friendly, and finely organized chain of events already in motion would not be received by the family down below with anything but joy, surprise, and gratitude.

. . .

I kept the amplifier going with the pig screams every twenty or thirty seconds, bracketed around bursts of rapid gunfire—and then I put the million-watt strobe down on the house, dragging it back and forth across the deck and the living room windows.

I did this for ten minutes or so, but nothing happened. The only response from below was a silent spasm of lights being turned off, as if they were all going to bed.

Well, I thought, that is a rude way to act when guests come with presents, even if they are a bit late. So what? There is no excuse for rudeness.

My next move was potentially fatal. I attempted to launch the rocket, but the firing ring broke and the thing started hissing, so I quickly hurled it away and heard it tumbling down the hill toward the house. O God, I thought, those are magnum phosphorous flares, and this place is going to be like the bridge in *Apocalypse Now* when that goddamn thing explodes.

I hastily packed the amp into the Jeep and picked up as many of my empty brass cartridges as I could find in the snow—and it was then, as I fled, that I remembered my birthday gift, which had somehow popped out of its bag and was bleeding all over the backseat.

I was beginning to have mixed feelings about this visit. There was something out of whack, and I figured the best thing to do was get out of this valley immediately. There was only one road out. (If some worrywart had called 911 to report an outburst of screaming and shooting at the Nicholson place, that could pose a problem, given that I was far down at the end of a dead-end canyon with no other way to escape but the river, and that was not an option.)

But *why*? I thought. Why am I drifting into negativity? Never mind this talk about "escape." I am here on a mission of joy. And there are no neighbors, anyway. It was a dark and peaceful place—yet extremely desolate in many ways, and not a good place to be trapped in.

I dismissed these negative thoughts as I hooked a hard left into Jack's driveway, intent on delivering my birthday present. The iron jackals on the gateposts no longer disturbed me, and I knew I could do this thing quickly.

. . .

I drove the Jeep all the way up to the front door and left the motor running as I fetched the bleeding elk heart out of the backseat and carried it up to the house. I rang the doorbell a few times before I gave up and left the heart—about ten inches tall and seven inches wide—propped against the door in a way that would cause it to tumble into the house whenever the door was opened. It seemed like the right thing to do, in light of the rudeness I'd experienced, and panic was setting in. On my way back to the truck I made sure the gun was clear by cranking off the rest of the clip straight up in the air and flinging my bloody hands distractedly toward the house because I was sure I'd seen somebody watching me from inside the darkened kitchen window, which angered me even further, because I felt I was being snubbed.

But I left quickly, with no other noise or weirdness except the shooting, which sounded unnaturally loud and caused pain in both of my eardrums. I jerked the Jeep into low and whiplashed out to the road. It was time to go home and sleep heavily—and there were no signs of police or any other disturbance as I drove carefully down the icy road. I locked in on Venus, the Morning Star, and pulled safely into my garage before sunrise.

. . .

The rest of the morning was spent in a work frenzy. My fax machine beeped constantly. There were the usual messages from the White House, two dangerously bogus offers from Hollywood, and a 60-page, single-spaced transcript of General Douglas MacArthur's final address to The Long Gray Line of steely-eyed cadets on The Plain at West Point in the spring of 1962, and another 39 pages of his "Old Soldiers Never Die" speech to Congress after he'd been fired.

These things spew into my house day after day, and I do my best to analyze them. Different people want different things in this world, and you have to be careful about taking risks. Hungry people have the cunning of wild beasts. A thing that seemed strange and wrong yesterday can seem perfectly reasonable tomorrow, or vice versa.

. . .

It did not seem strange, for instance, to learn that Bill Clinton's main concern these days is with his place in history, his legacy, his permanent image in high-school textbooks 100 years from now. He has done his work, he feels, and now is the time to secure his place on a pedestal in the pantheon of Great American Presidents, along with Lincoln and Coolidge and Kennedy.

And why not? George Bush had that problem, and so did Richard Nixon. Nobody needs to go down in history like that. Only a criminal freak would want to be remembered as a Crook or a Dupe or a Creature of some treacherous monster like J. Edgar Hoover . . . But those risks come with the territory when you finally move into the White House. You bet. They *will* write something—many things, in fact: books, movies, legends, and maybe even filthy jokes about back-stabbing and sodomy that will follow you all the way to the grave. Look at Nixon, look at Reagan, or even JFK. History has never been gentle in its judgments on bedrock degenerates—but it is also true that some degenerates are treated more gently than others, and that is what worries Bill Clinton. He is liked, but not well liked, and that is a very fragile base to maintain for another two and a half years. Voters *like* him now because they believe he has made them richer—and they will probably vote for Al Gore in 2000. (Jesus. That has an eerie ring to it, eh? *Vote Gore in 2000.* Prepare yourself for that. It will happen. Beware.)

I was brooding on these things on that bright winter morning when the phone machine rang and I heard a female voice screeching hysterically: "Watch out, the police are coming" and "Blood Everywhere" and "Terrible tragedy at Jack's house last night."

Ye gods, I thought. What is she talking about? What tragedy? Hell, I was there at about three and the place looked peaceful to me. What could have happened?

The answer was not long in coming. Both phones rang at once, but I suddenly felt queasy and couldn't answer. Then I heard the voice of the sheriff on one phone and some angry raving on the other from Paul Pascarella, the famous artist, who said he was on his way to Jack's house at top speed with a shotgun and a .44 Magnum. The house was under siege, he said. Cops were everywhere. Some maniac stalker tried to kill Jack and the kids last night, but he got away and the cops think he's still loose in the woods. He's a killer, just got out of prison, I think Jack's okay, O God this is horrible. Then he went into the canyon and lost contact.

The sheriff's message told much the same tale. "This is going to be a very big story," he said. "I'm already setting up a command post to deal with the national media. They're calling it an assassination attempt. We've closed off the road and sent a posse with dogs to search the area. It's a manhunt. We'll be on CNN by noon—and, by the way, do you happen to know anything about this? If you do, please call me before it's too late."

Too late? I thought. Nonsense. Too late for what? Are we dealing with lunatics here? Why would I want to kill Jack? It was madness.

Indeed, and it was just about then that it hit me. Of course. That's *me* that they're chasing with dogs out there in the woods. *I* am the crazed bushy-haired assassin who tried to get into the house last night and murder the whole family. What the hell? It was only a joke.

A joke? Ho ho. Nobody else was laughing. They had already found an unexploded rocket bomb in the trees above the house. . . . Every cop in the county was cranked up and working double-overtime to capture this monster before he could butcher the whole Nicholson family and bring eternal shame on Aspen's already sleazy name. Hideous scandals involving rich perverts, depraved children, and degenerate Hollywood whores looking for publicity are so common here as to be politically tolerable and even stylish. . . . Indeed, *that* is why this shit-rain of "second-home pimps" has invaded this valley like a plague of rich lice in recent years. . . . And we are not talking about small-time lice here, not at all.

Ah, but I digress. We were talking about my failed attempt to deliver some birthday presents to my old friend Jack and his kids on a frozen snowy night in the winter of 1997.

The *real* problem on that night turned out to be something that did not occur to me, at the time—if only because it was so queer and unlikely as to beam new light on words like *incredible, bizarre,* and *impossible.* . . .

But it happened, for good or ill—and now that I mention it, 4,000–1 tragedies like this one are the main reason I decided to renounce conventional crime as a way of life so many, many years ago—and turn to the writing life.

. . .

Jack had been menaced in public by a murderous certified *stalker* who had made several previous attempts on his life in Los Angeles—and

the reason he had come to the Rockies was to be completely anonymous and solitary with Raymond and Lorraine, safe from the perils of
Hollywood. He was, in a word, on the *lam*—just another jittery parent
whose children had arrived to join him at his utterly isolated cabin
home in the Rockies.

. . .

Who could have known, for instance, that *all* telephone service to
Jack's bleak valley would be cut off by the blizzard that night? . . .
"Yeah, it was right about then that the phones went dead," the sheriff
told me. "They tried to call 911, but the phone lines had apparently
been cut. That's when he flipped out and barricaded the family in the
basement behind a heap of antique furniture with nothing at all for a
weapon except a common fireplace poker." He chuckled. "The fool
didn't even have a gun in the house. Thank God for that, eh? He could
have killed the children by accident."

Which was true. As a *rule* it is better *not* to keep loaded weapons
lying around the house when children are visiting. Even with a criminally insane stalker creeping around outside with a chainsaw. It is a far
far better thing to have good locks and screechers on the doors, and a
fulltime phone to the police station. . . . This turned out to be no comfort at all to Jack and his family that night. The freak outside had a
grudge, and he had come a long way to settle it. The setting was made
to order (just like in *The Shining*).

The phones kept ringing and the news kept getting worse. Some people begged me to confess and others urged me to hurry out to Jack's with
a 12-gauge riot gun and join the search party. Everybody who called
seemed genuinely alarmed and afraid. Even Heidi was acting weird. She
knew I had gone out to Jack's the previous night, and for all I knew she
thought I'd tried to kill him for some reason. Why not? I might have had
a seizure and flipped out. Who knows what a dope fiend might do? Especially with children around. I might not even remember it.

The phone rang again, and this time it was Jack. He had just got the
phone working again. *Oh God*, I thought. *What am I going to say? Get
a grip on yourself. Omerta.*

"Uh, Doc, how you doing?" he said calmly. It may have been a Saturday, because he said something like "Who's playing this afternoon?"

"Never mind those fucking football games," I said. "What's this nightmare about the police out there at your house? I'm hearing weird things about it."

There was a silence, a pause. I could hear him taking a breath. He said, "Well, yeah, let me ask you a thing or two." He paused. "You know, that elk heart. . . ."

That's what really freaked him out, all that blood. He said, "When I looked at it—we were looking at it for clues"—I guessed he was talking about the cops—"when I took a close look at it, I saw that there were icicles in the middle of the heart, the part that still hadn't thawed. I didn't say anything to the cops, of course, but it seems like I remember you keeping a frozen elk heart in your refrigerator. Didn't you show me something like that, along with a bird and a ferret? Don't I remember you throwing a frozen elk heart at me last winter?"

*That fucker,* I thought. *The creepy little bastard.* That was good, putting that together—just a *sliver* inside, frozen. All the rest had turned to mush and blood—it's actually pretty good to eat, elk heart . . . this one wasn't going to be eaten anytime soon; it looked like a gizzard of some human being. Bigger than a human heart. "Yeah, maybe . . ." I said.

"I thought so, I thought it was you, when I saw that ice," he said. "I haven't told them yet; you know, they're still out here, the police task force, digging for new evidence, people sleeping in the woods . . . Goddamn, Doc, I'm glad you told me. We have had a hell of a night here. It's been horrible."

The joke was over. I was never formally accused of it; Jack told the sheriff it was just a false alarm. "I know this guy," he said, "and he is not the killer."

## Epilogue

That is what I mean about personal security in this town. You can buy a lot of protection, if you are filthy rich, and it obviously makes those people feel better about themselves—surrounded at all times by hundreds of greedy freelance cops with a license to kill anytime, anywhere, for any reason blessed by God. They are volatile people, at best, and always dangerous.

We get more black-truck security caravans in this valley than any-place in the world that comes quickly to mind except Washington, D.C., and Vatican City. There is a lot of available cash in these places, a lot of quasi-secret money changing hands . . . of governments being toppled on the other side of the world, of kingdoms being under-mined, and whole families of U.S. presidents and movie stars like Julia Roberts and Harry Dean Stanton being bought and sold and coddled like concubines, by criminal scum like Neil Bush, convicted crook and brother of our sitting president George W. . . . Not to mention the cur-rent Secretary of the (U.S.) Army and gilded clutch of criminally fugi-tive executives from ENRON, including the monstrous chairman Kenneth Lay. . . . These people roam free and unmolested in Aspen, cloistered by off-duty cops and Hollywood yo-yos and bimbos and suckfish. . . . I know these people. They are more and more my neigh-bors in these first horrible years of our new Century. . . .

. . .

There is never any shortage of applicants for *paid*-police jobs in the Roaring Fork Valley. All ambitious young cops want to be hired in places like Palm Beach and Sausalito and Aspen. They crave their 15 minutes of fame, and their police research has told them that Aspen is the most likely place to get it. . . .

. . .

Which is normal enough in this town. It has long been a haven for sybaritic outlaws and other social criminals as long as they had a good story and didn't hurt the neighbors—not quite a *sanctuary*, but at least a sort of retro-legal gray area, where real-life words like Crime and Guilt mean different things to different people, even in the same household.

## Kiss, Kiss

"Hey baby, you want to come over here and swim naked with me?"

"Say *what*?"

"You know what I mean, sweetie. I want to dance on the head of your pin. How about it?"

"Oh my God, you crazy bitch! I should have killed you a long time ago."

"You're lying," she said. "Come here and smoke a marijuana cigarette with me." She dropped her thin little robe and raised her perfect arms above her shoulders, whipping her hair down and behind her until it touched the top of her thighs. "I am Xania," she said, "Goddess of Wind and Pussy."

I was stunned. It was hard to believe that this girl was only eight years old. She appeared to be twice that age.

"I find you extremely beautiful," I said to her. "I must be going crazy."

She laughed and danced out of my reach. I was drinking heavily that night and my thumb had been recently broken in a car accident. The pain was relentless. It flashed up my arm like a bolt of hot lightning, from my lifeline to my armpit, so I couldn't touch the girl or even kiss her without pain.

Who *was* this wild little floozy? And why *me*? I may be a teenage girl trapped in the body of an elderly dope fiend. . . . But that doesn't make me a pervert. "Don't worry," I told her. "I don't want to penetrate you, my dear—I just want to suck on your back."

She shuddered, seeming to glisten in the thin light of this California dawn. . . .

. . .

People are talking about O. J. Simpson on TV today. They want to see reruns of his Trial on daytime TV. Yes. Eighty-eight percent of adults who responded to this Poll were strongly in favor of CBS broadcasting uncut tapes of the Trial of O. J. Simpson on worldwide TV.

Eighty-eight percent is also the number of Americans who allegedly favor the continued presence of U.S. troops in Afghanistan and the Death Penalty for all foreigners accused of "terrorism." They are Patriotic Americans who like to kill. Just like yourself, Doc. So what? They love their country.

Sure they do, Bubba. We'll see how much they love their goddamn country when they get busted for smoking a joint in Public—or even in Private, if Bush has his way. They will find themselves cuffed in a Federal courtroom on felony charges of *Conspiracy to Kill a Judge*. Ho ho. How do you like your Security blanket *now*, dude? We will kill the ones who eat us, and eat the ones we kill. Onward Christian Soldiers. Mahalo.

I was brooding on these things while I struggled to understand what horrible god would put me face to face with this naked child in my own home, with no warning, on this peaceful Saturday morning when all I wanted to do was watch a basketball game. It was wrong, deeply wrong.

Fuck those people. I've had a bellyful of those vengeful Christian bastards and their Rules for righteous punishment. What would the Pope have me do with this human sex doll that I have on my hands?

Fuck the Pope. He is a Pervert like all the others. Those fruit-bags have had their way for 2,000 years, and look what we have to show for it. Boom boom. Sorry honey, but that money you had in the bank just went bye-bye. Our horse *failed to finish.* Earnings were insufficient. You will suffer huge tax penalties, on top of everything else. Didn't I tell you that the End of the World (as we know it) will happen in the summer of 2012? That is what my people tell me, and I have no reason to doubt it.

Get a grip on yourself, Doc. Do you really want to suck on that little girl's back?

Why not? I thought. I have loved and admired the female spine for many years, beginning with Sally down in Mobile. The Spine is far and away the most beautiful bone in the human body. Does The Church have a problem with me wanting to suck on a human back? Nonsense. Get over it, Father—just tell me how much it will cost. . . . I am a gentle man, but some things make me weird, and this is one of them.

Ah, but no more of that mushy stuff, eh? We are soldiers and we don't need it. A love of this nature is dangerous, but only if it gets out of control. That would be Wrong, as they say in the Vatican—perhaps borderline *evil.* Would the Pope have me killed for sucking on a beautiful human spine, a creature born of God?

Well . . . Yes, in a word, he would. We live in kinky times, but maybe not quite *that* kinky. There is some shit those perverts won't eat.

(Mike McAllister)

# The War on Fat

Hot damn! It is summer again in America, and the goofy Child President has declared his long-overdue *War on Fat*. The nation is plunged, once again, into another life-or-death WAR against the forces of Evil. Wonderful. Let's get it over with. We are Patriotic people, but there *is* some shit we won't eat. . . . It is *one* thing to be trampled like scum by our own Military Police, and quite a goddamn *other* to be wallowed and stomped on by Fat People.

I have seen a lot of horrible wars in my time, folks, but I tell you this desperate War on Fat is going to be like a terminal Sewer fire in Miami. It is unthinkable. These greasy, blubbery bastards will be huge favorites to conquer and dominate us. The summer book odds are hovering around 9–1 & climbing. The spectre of doom by Fat is right in front of our eyes.

My weird neighbor, Omar, has about 4 percent fat on his body—extremely lean meat, in a word, and more & more likely to activate the body-screecher at any self-respecting International Airport—*Hey man, you're not Fat enough to be boarded on this airplane. I'll kill you with an axe if you come any further.* . . .

Mark Twain would love this story: "Let me get this straight, Boss—are you telling me to Okay fat people and *arrest* the skinny ones? Jesus. Please, Boss, don't make me do this. Fat people are *horrible* to touch. I can't stand it."

And meanwhile the President is poking us day and night to "shrug off yr. sorrows and come out to *run* with me." Run, run, run like a bastard and never look back. . . . Wow. That is very strange thinking, eh? Forget thinking, just JOG and get over it.

I'll bet Tonya Harding said that. She is a sassy little creature, for sure. . . . There is talk that the monumentally lewd O'Farrell Theatre in San Francisco will make her the headliner in their new outdoor *Erotic Boxing* spectacles this summer. Jim Mitchell knows Talent when he sees it. I will be at ringside when Tonya opens against Charlotte Rampling in July. Call Jeff Armstrong for media certification. Mahalo.

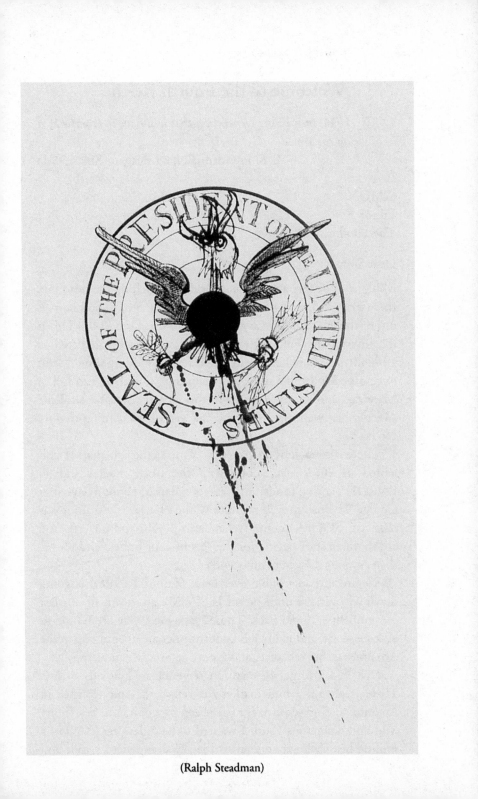

(Ralph Steadman)

# Welcome to the Fourth Reich

*This may be the Generation that will have to face the End
of the World.*
  —U.S. President Ronald Reagan, Xmas, 1985

SIMON
Editor
The London *Independent*

Dear Simon,

Millions of people around the world are watching the headlines
these days, and most of them are getting the Fear. Good news is
out of the question in this brutal year of our Lord 2002. This is
the time of the Final Shit Rain, as Nostradamus predicted in
1444 A.D., and anybody who thinks he was kidding should strut
out purposefully, like some all-American girl with a head full of
Mandrax, and try to get a *job* in this country. . . . Yes sir, little
sweetie, just walk right up here and get what's coming to you.
Ho ho ho.

There *are* no jobs in America, Simon; the job market collapsed in 2001 A.D., along with the stock market and all
ENRON pension funds. *All* markets collapsed about 3 days after
George W. Bush moved into the White House. . . . Yeah, it was
*that* fast. BOOM, presto, welcome to bombs and poverty. You
are about to start paying for the sins of your fathers and forefathers, even if they were innocent.

We are in bad trouble over here, Simon. The deal is going
down all over the once-proud U.S.A. We are down to our last
cannonball(s). Stand back! Those Pentagon swine are frantic to
kick some ass, and many job opportunities are opening up in the
Armaments, Surveillance, and New Age Security industries.

Hell, did I forget to mention *those* jobs? How silly of me.
There is always a bull market for vengeance and violence in
America, and on some days I have been part of it. You bet. In my
wild and dangerous youth I wanted to be a dashing jet pilot, a
smiling beast who zooms across the sky doing victory rolls and

monster sonic booms just over the beach in Laguna. Hot damn, Simon, I could walk on water in those days. I had a license to kill.

I have been a news addict all my life, and I feel pretty comfortable with my addiction. It has been good to me, although not necessarily *for* me, or my overall comfort level. Being a news junkie has taken me down some very queer roads, and into the valley of death a few times—not always for strictly professional reasons, alas—but those things *do* come with the territory, and you want to understand this: It is the key to survival in my business, as it is in many others.

And you definitely want to have a shockproof sense of humor, which is hard to learn in school and even harder to teach. (It is also an irritating phrase to keep putting on paper over and over—so from now on we will use the ancient and honorable word "WA," instead of "Sense of humor." It will smooth out our word-rhythms, and we can move along more briskly.)

Okay. We were talking about the *news*—information or intelligence gleaned from afar, etc., etc.

The news is *bad* today, in America and *for* America. There is *nothing* good or hopeful about it—except for Nazis, warmongers, and rich greedheads—and it is getting worse and worse in logarithmic progressions since the fateful bombing of the World Trade Towers in New York. That will always be a festering lowwatermark in this nation's violent history, but it was not the official birthday of the end of the American Century.

No. That occurred on the night of the presidential election in the year 2000, when the nexus of power in this country shifted from Washington, D.C., to "the ranch" in Crawford, Texas. The most disastrous day in American history was November 7, 2000. That was when the *takeover* happened, when the generals and cops and right-wing Jesus freaks seized control of the White House, the U.S. Treasury, and our Law Enforcement machinery.

So long to all that, eh? "Nothing will ever be the same again," the whorish new President said at the time. "As of now we are in the grip of a National Security Emergency that will last for the rest of our lives."

Fuck you, I quit. Mahalo.

I would never claim to speak for my whole nation, Simon; I am not the Voice of America—but neither am I a vicious machine-gun Nazi warmonger with blood on my hands and hate in my heart for every human being in the world who is not entirely *white*—and, if you wonder why I mention this thuggish characterization, understand that I am only responding to it in this way because my old friend, the weird artist Ralph Steadman, is saying these horrible things about me in England, Wales, and Kent—and directly *to* me, in fact, when we speak on the trans-Atlantic telephone.

"That is bullshit, Ralph," I tell him. "Are you getting senile? Do you know who you are talking to?"

"Of course I do," he replies. "You are the same brutal redneck I've known all my life—except that now you are turning into what you always were from the start—just another murderous American. . . ."

So that is how this thing got jump-started, Simon. And ever since (I think) I talked to you on yr. birthday I have been feverishly writing down my various fears and worries and profoundly angst-ridden visions about our immediate future.

So good luck, Simon. Pls advise me at once in re: yr. space & rates. How about $20,000, eh? I can ramble on for many hours about my recent experience as an American in these days at the end of *our* Century. Or maybe just 1,000 words, or 2,000. Think about it, and R.S.V.P. soonest. Thanx,

                                        HUNTER
                                   *May 10, 2002*

# Amor Vincit Omnia

*He not busy being born is busy dying.*
                              —Bob Dylan

## The White Helicopter

She flew low over central Paris—the Dream of the Princess in the White Helicopter.

Took lessons for months—*very* difficult; you can't *hire* many people who could fly a chopper in low over downtown Paris and park it in midair above a prison long enough to send a man down a line with an Uzi and come back up . . .

Then put it down on the roof of the prison and carry her lover off on the skid—and then to put the thing down in a nearby parking lot and have everything organized so finely that they disappeared instantly in the waiting car.

Perfect. Nadine, you can have a job with me anytime. This may be a love story. . . .

                              . . .

There were other things happening in the news last week—mainly politics, but we need a break from that now.

There was, in fact, this truly elegant little tale that came out of Paris, and it was about The Girl in the White Helicopter who rescued her lover from prison. It was one of those fine little love stories that can make you smile in your sleep at night.

The real action last week was in Romance & full-on madness . . .

The wife of French bank robber Michel Vaujour flew low over central Paris in a white helicopter and hovered over the roof of La Santé prison. A man armed with a submachine gun slid down a line to the roof . . . Vaujour, wearing a blue and red warm-up suit, was hidden from guards behind a chimney. He grabbed one of the chopper's landing skids and climbed aboard. The gunman leaped in after him, and the copter whisked them to a nearby soccer field, where all three disappeared . . . Nadine Vaujour, the robber's wife, had been taking copter-flying lessons for many months, French authorities learned later.

Even a dumb brute could fall in love with a story like that. It has the purity of a myth and the power of being simple flat-out true, and it spoke to our highest instincts. It was a perfect crime, done for love, and it was carried out with awesome precision and a truly crazy kind of fearlessness by a beautiful girl in a white helicopter.

There is more to the story, of course. That perfect escape was last May, and the honeymoon lasted all summer. But in the autumn Michel went back to work, and a *New York Times* dispatch out of Paris in late September said he'd been "seriously wounded and captured in a shootout while trying to rob a bank." He had been shot in the head and was lying in a coma at the Pitie-Salpetriere Hospital.

"Officials said Mr. Vaujour's wife, who masterminded the May escape, was arrested Saturday morning at a hideout in southwestern France."

When I read it I felt a chill. All the real love stories end wrong, and I was just about to close the file on this one . . .

"Mrs. Vaujour was already well known to police," said an earlier *Times* item. "She and Mr. Vaujour were married in 1979 while he was in a different jail serving a previous sentence. (He was moved frequently to prevent an escape.) They had a daughter, who was born in jail in September 1981, while Mrs. Vaujour was being held in preventive detention."

I was struck by the almost unholy power and purity of the Vaujours' love for each other, which ran through their lives like a red thread. Above all else, they were lovers, and they honored the word by the terrible intensity they brought to it.

With Juan at Owl Farm, 1997

(Deborah Fuller)

# Hey Rube, I Love You

It is Sunday morning now and I am writing a love letter. Outside my kitchen window the sky is bright and planets are colliding. My head is hot and I feel a little edgy. My brain is beginning to act like a V-8 engine with the sparkplug wires crossed. Things are no longer what they seem to be. My telephones are haunted, and animals whisper at me from unseen places.

Last night a huge black cat tried to jump me in the swimming pool, then it suddenly disappeared. I did another lap and noticed three men in green trench coats watching me from behind a faraway door. Whoops, I thought, something weird is happening in this room. Lay low in the water and creep toward the middle of the pool. Stay away from the edges. Don't be strangled from behind. Keep alert. The work of the Devil is never fully revealed until after midnight.

It was right about then that I started thinking about my love letter. The skylights above the pool were steamed up, strange plants were moving in the thick and utter darkness. It was impossible to see from one end of the pool to the other.

I tried to stay quiet and let the water calm down. For a moment I thought I heard another person coming into the pool, but I couldn't be sure. A ripple of terror caused me to drop deeper in the water and assume a karate position. There are only two or three things in the world more terrifying than the sudden realization that you are naked and alone and something large and aggressive is coming close to you in dark water.

It is moments like this that make you want to believe in hallucinations—because if three large men in trench coats actually *were* waiting for me in the shadows behind that door and something else was slithering toward me in the darkness, I was doomed.

Alone? No, I was *not* alone. I understood that. I had already seen three men and a huge black cat, and now I thought I could make out the shape of another person approaching me. She was lower in the water than I was, but I could definitely see it was a woman.

Of course, I thought. It must be my sweetheart, sneaking up to give me a nice surprise in the pool. Yessir, this is just like that twisted little bitch. She is a hopeless romantic and she knows this pool well. We once swam here every night and played in the water like otters.

. . .

Jesus Christ! I thought, what a paranoid fool I've been. I must have been going crazy. A surge of love went through me as I stood up and moved quickly to embrace her. I could already feel her naked body in my arms. . . . Yes, I thought, love does conquer all.

. . .

But not for long. No, it took me a minute or two of thrashing around in the water before I understood that I was, in fact, completely alone in the pool. *She* was not here and neither were those freaks in the corner. And there *was* no cat. I was a fool and a dupe. My brain was seizing up and I felt so weak that I could barely climb out of the pool.

Fuck this, I thought. I can't handle this place anymore. It's destroying my life with its weirdness. Get away and never come back. It had mocked my love and shattered my sense of romance. This horrible experience would get me nominated for *Rube of the Year* in any high school class.

Dawn was coming up as I drove back down the road. There were no comets colliding, no tracks in the snow except mine, and no sounds for 10 miles in any direction except Lyle Lovett on my radio and the howl of a few coyotes. I drove with my knees while I lit up a glass pipe full of hashish.

When I got home I loaded my Smith & Wesson .45 and fired a few bursts at a beer keg in the yard, then I went back inside and started scrawling feverishly in a notebook. . . . What the hell? I thought. Everybody writes love letters on Sunday morning. It is a natural form of worship, a very high art. And on some days I am very good at it.

Today, I felt, was definitely one of those days. You bet. Do it *now*. Just then my phone rang and I jerked it off the hook, but there was nobody on the line. I sagged against the fireplace and moaned, and then it rang again. I grabbed it, but again there was no voice. O God! I thought. Somebody is fucking with me. . . . I needed music, I needed rhythm. I was determined to be calm, so I cranked up the speakers and played "Spirit in the Sky," by Norman Greenbaum.

I played it over and over for the next three or four hours while I hammered out my letter. My heart was Racing and the music was making the peacocks scream. It was Sunday, and I was worshiping in my own way. Nobody needs to be crazy on the Lord's Day.

. . .

My grandmother was never crazy when we went to visit her on Sundays. She always had cookies and tea, and her face was always smiling. That was down in the West End of Louisville, near the Ohio River locks. I remember a narrow concrete driveway and a big gray car in a garage behind the house. The driveway was two concrete strips with clumps of grass growing between them. It led back through the vicious wild rosebushes to what looked like an abandoned shed. Which was true. It *was* abandoned. Nobody walked in that yard, and nobody drove that big gray car. It never moved. There were no tracks in the grass.

It was a LaSalle sedan, as I recall, a slick-looking brute with a powerful straight-eight engine and a floor-mounted gearshift, maybe a 1939 model. We never got it started, because the battery was dead and gasoline was scarce. There was a war on. You had to have special coupons to buy five gallons of gas, and the coupons were tightly rationed. People hoarded and coveted them, but nobody complained, because we were fighting the Nazis and our tanks needed all the gasoline for when they hit the beaches of Normandy.

Looking back on it now, I see clearly that the reason we drove down to the West End to visit my grandmother every other Sunday was to con her out of her gas coupons for the LaSalle. She was an old lady and she didn't need any gasoline. But her car was still registered and she still got her coupons every month.

So what? I would do the same thing myself, if my mother had gasoline and I didn't. We *all* would. It is the Law of Supply and Demand— and this is, after all, the final messy year of the American Century, and people are getting nervous. Hoarders are coming out of the closet, muttering darkly about Y2K and buying cases of Dinty Moore's Beef Stew. Dried figs are popular, along with rice and canned hams. I, personally, am hoarding bullets, many thousands of them. Bullets will always be valuable, especially when yr. lights go out and your phone goes dead and your neighbors start running out of food. That is when you will find out who your friends are. Even close family members will turn on you. After the year 2000, the only people who'll be safe to have as friends will be dead people.

*HST, March 1998*

. . .

I used to respect William Burroughs because he was the first white man ever busted for marijuana in my time. William was the Man. He was the victim of an illegal police raid at his home at 509 Wagner Street in Old Algiers, a low-rent suburb across the river from New Orleans, where he was settling in for a while to do some shooting and smoke marijuana.

William didn't fuck around. He was serious about everything. When the Deal went down William was There, with a gun. Whacko! *BOOM.* Stand back. I *am* the Law. He was my hero a long time before I ever heard of him.

But he was *Not* the first white man to be busted for weed in my time. No. That was Robert Mitchum, the actor, who was arrested three months earlier in Malibu at the front door of his hideaway beach house for possession of marijuana and suspicion of molesting a teenage girl in 1948. I remember the photos: Mitchum wearing an undershirt & snarling at the cops with the sea rolling up and palm trees blowing.

Yessir, that was my boy. Between Mitchum and Burroughs & Marlon Brando & James Dean & Jack Kerouac, I got myself a serious running start before I was 20 years old, and there was no turning back. Buy the ticket, take the ride.

So welcome to *Thunder Road,* Bubba. It was one of those movies that got a grip on me when I was too young to resist. It convinced me that the only way to drive was at top speed with a car full of whiskey, and I have been driving that way ever since, for good or ill.

The girl in the photos with Mitchum looked about 15 years old & she was also wearing an undershirt, with an elegant little nipple jutting out. The cops were trying to cover her chest with a raincoat as they rushed through the door. Mitchum was also charged with Sodomy and Contributing to the Delinquency of a Minor.

I was having my own troubles with police in those years. We stole cars and drank gin and did a lot of fast driving at night to places like Nashville & Atlanta & Chicago. We needed music on those nights, and it usually came on the radio—on the 50,000-watt clear-channel stations like WWL in New Orleans and WLAC in Nashville.

That is where I went wrong, I guess—listening to WLAC & driving all night across Tennessee in a stolen car that wouldn't be reported for three days. That is how I got introduced to the Howlin' Wolf. We didn't know him, but we liked him & we knew what he was talking about. "I Smell a Rat" is a pure rock & roll monument to the axiom that says "There is no such thing as Paranoia." The Wolf could kick out the jams, but he had a melancholy side to him. He could tear your heart out like the worst kind of honky-tonk. If history judges a man by his heroes, like they say, then let the record show that Howlin' Wolf was one of mine. He was a monster.

Music has always been a matter of energy to me, a question of Fuel. Sentimental people call it Inspiration, but what they really mean is Fuel.

I have always needed fuel. I am a serious consumer. On some nights I still believe that a car with the gas needle on empty can run about fifty more miles if you have the right music very loud on the radio. A new high-end Cadillac will go ten or fifteen miles faster if you give it a full dose of "Carmelita." This has been proven many times. That is why you see so many Cadillacs parked in front of truck stops on Highway 66 around midnight. These are Speed Pimps, and they are loading up on more than gasoline. You watch one of these places for a while & you see a pattern: A big fast car pulls up in front of the doors and a wild-looking girl gets out, stark naked except for a fur coat or a ski parka, and she runs into the place with a handful of money, half-crazy to buy some flat-out guaranteed driving music.

It happens over & over, and sooner or later you get hooked on it, you get addicted. Every time I hear "White Rabbit" I am back on the greasy midnight streets of San Francisco, looking for music, riding a fast red motorcycle downhill into The Presidio, leaning desperately into the curves through the eucalyptus trees, trying to get to the Matrix in time to hear Grace Slick play the flute.

There was no piped-in music on those nights, no headphones or Walkmans or even a plastic windscreen to keep off the rain. But I could hear the music anyway, even when it was five miles away. Once you heard the music done right, you could pack it into yr. brain & take it anywhere, forever.

Yessir. That is my wisdom and that is my song. It is Sunday and I am making new rules for myself. I will open my heart to spirits and pay more attention to animals. I will take some harp music and drive down to the Texaco station, where I can get a pork taco and read a

*New York Times.* After that, I will walk across the street to the Post Office and slip my letter into her mailbox.

. . .

*KNOW YOUR DOPE FIEND. YOUR LIFE MAY DEPEND ON IT!*
*You will not be able to see his eyes because of Tea-Shades, but his knuckles will be white from inner tension and his pants will be crusted with semen from constantly jacking off when he can't find a rape victim. He will stagger and babble when questioned. He will not respect your badge. The Dope Fiend fears nothing. He will attack, for no reason, with every weapon at his command—including yours. BEWARE. Any officer apprehending a suspected marijuana addict should use all necessary force immediately. One stitch in time (on him) will usually save nine on you. Good luck.*

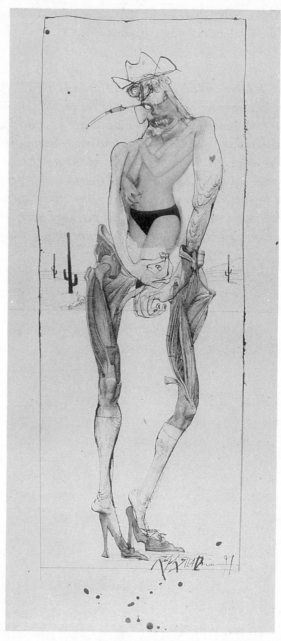

(Ralph Steadman)

# Fear and Loathing at the Taco Stand

Going to Hollywood is a dangerous high-pressure gig for most people, under any circumstances. It is like pumping hot steam into thousands of different-size boilers. The laws of physics mandate that some will explode before others—although all of them will explode sooner or later unless somebody cuts off the steam.

I love steam myself, and I have learned to survive under savage and unnatural pressures. I am a steam freak. Hollywood is chicken feed to me. I can take it or leave it. I have been here before, many times. On some days it seems like I have lived at the Château Marmont for half my life. There is blood on these walls, and some of it is mine. Last night I sliced off the tips of two fingers and bled so profusely in the elevator that they had to take it out of service.

But nobody complained. I am not just liked at the Château, I am well liked. I have important people thrown out or blacklisted on a whim. Nobody from the Schwarzenegger organization, for instance, can even get a drink at the Château. They are verboten. There is a ghastly political factor in doing any business with Hollywood. You can't get by without five or six personal staff people—and at least one personal astrologer.

I have always hated astrologers, and I like to have sport with them. They are harmless quacks in the main, but some of them get ambitious and turn predatory, especially in Hollywood. In Venice Beach I ran into a man who claimed to be Johnny Depp's astrologer. "I consult with him constantly," he told me. "We are never far away. I have many famous clients." He produced a yellow business card and gave it to me. "I can do things for you," he said. "I am a player."

I took his card and examined it carefully for a moment, as if I couldn't quite read the small print. But I knew he was lying, so I leaned toward him and slapped him sharply in the nuts. Not hard, but very quickly, using the back of my hand and my fingers like a bullwhip, yet very discreetly.

He let out a hiss and went limp, unable to speak or breathe. I smiled casually and kept on talking to him as if nothing had happened. "You filthy little creep," I said to him. "I *am* Johnny Depp!"

Outside on the boulevard I saw a half-naked girl on roller skates being mauled by two dogs. They were Great Danes, apparently running loose. Both had their paws on her shoulder, and the gray one had her head in its mouth. But there was no noise, and nobody seemed to notice.

I grabbed a fork off the bar and rushed outside to help her, giving the bogus astrologer another slap in the nuts on my way out. When I got to the street, the dogs were still mauling the girl. I stabbed the big one in the ribs with my fork, which sank deep into the tissue. The beast yelped crazily and ran off with its tail between its legs. The other one quickly released its grip on the girl's head and snarled at me. I slashed at it with the fork, and that was enough for the brute. It backed off and slunk away toward Muscle Beach.

I took the girl back to the Buffalo Club and applied aloe to her wounds. The astrologer was gone, and we had the lounge to ourselves. Her name was Anita, she said, and she had just arrived in L.A. to seek work as a dancer. It was the third time in ten days she'd been attacked by wild dogs on the Venice boardwalk, and she was ready to quit L.A., and so was I. The pace was getting to me. I was not bored, and I still had work to do, but it was definitely time to get out of town. I had to be in Big Sur in three days, and then to a medical conference in Pebble Beach. She was a very pretty girl, with elegant legs and a wicked kind of intelligence about her, but she was also very naïve about Hollywood. I saw at once that she would be extremely helpful on my trip north.

I listened to her for a while, then I offered her a job as my assistant, which I badly needed. She accepted, and we drove back to the Château in Depp's Porsche. As we pulled up the ramp to the underground garage, the attendants backed off and signaled me in. Depp's henchmen had left word that nobody could touch the car except me. I parked it expertly, barely missing a red BMW 840Ci, and we went up the elevator to my suite.

I reached for my checkbook, but it was missing, so I used one of Depp's that I'd found in the glove compartment of his car. I wrote her a healthy advance and signed Depp's name to it. "What the hell?" I said to her. "He's running around out there with my checkbook right now, probably racking up all kinds of bills."

That was the tone of my workdays in Hollywood: violence, joy, and constant Mexican music. At one club I played the bass recorder for several hours with the band. We spent a lot of time drinking gin and lemonade on the balcony, entertaining movie people and the ever-present scribe from *Rolling Stone* magazine . . .

You bet, Bubba, I was taking care of business. It was like the Too Much Fun Club. I had the Cadillac and a green Mustang in the garage, in addition to the Carrera 4 Porsche, but we could only drive one of them up the coast. It was an uptown problem.

Finally it got to be too much, so we loaded up the Northstar Cadillac and fled. Why not? I thought. The girl had proved to be a tremendous help, and besides, I was beginning to like her.

. . .

The sun was going down as we left Malibu and headed north on 101, running smoothly through Oxnard and along the ocean to Santa Barbara. My companion was a little nervous about my speed, so I gave her some gin to calm her down. Soon she relaxed against me, and I put my arm around her. Rosanne Cash was on the radio, singing about the seven-year ache, and the traffic was opening up.

As we approached the Lompoc exit, I mentioned that Lompoc was the site of a federal penitentiary and I once had some friends over there.

"Oh?" she said. "Who were they?"

"Prisoners," I said. "Nothing serious. That's where Ed was."

She stiffened and moved away from me, but I turned up the music and we settled back to drive and watch the moon come up. What the hell? I thought. Just another young couple on the road to the American Dream.

Things started to get weird when I noticed Pismo Beach coming up. I was on the cell phone with Benicio Del Toro, the famous Puerto Rican actor, telling him about the time I was violently jailed in Pismo Beach and how it was making me nervous to even pass a road sign with that name on it. "Yeah," I was saying, "it was horrible. They beat me on the back of my legs. It was a case of mistaken identity." I smiled at my assistant, not wanting to alarm her, but I saw that she was going into a fetal crouch and her fingers were clutching the straps of her seat belt.

Just then we passed two police cars parked on the side of the road, and I saw that we were going a hundred and three.

"Slow down!" Anita was screaming. "Slow down! We'll be arrested. I can't stand it!" She was sobbing and clawing at the air.

"Nonsense," I said. "Those were not police. My radar didn't go off." I reached over to pat her on the arm, but she bit me and I had to pull over. The only exit led to a dangerous-looking section of Pismo Beach, but I took it anyway.

. . .

It was just about midnight when we parked under the streetlight in front of the empty Mexican place on Main Street. Anita was having a nervous breakdown. There was too much talk about jails and police and prisons, she said. She felt like she was already in chains.

I left the car in a crosswalk and hurried inside to get a taco. The girl behind the register warned me to get my car off the street because the police were about to swoop down on the gang of thugs milling around in front of the taco place. "They just had a fight with the cops," she said. "Now I'm afraid somebody is going to get killed."

We were parked right behind the doomed mob, so I hurried out to roust Anita and move the car to safety. Then we went back inside very gently and sat down in a booth at the rear of the room. I put my arm around Anita and tried to calm her down. She wanted gin, and luckily I still had a pint flask full of it in my fleece-lined jacket pocket. She drank greedily, then fell back in the booth and grinned. "Well, so much for that," she chirped. "I guess I really went crazy, didn't I?"

"Yes," I said. "You were out of control. It was like dealing with a vampire."

She smiled and grasped my thigh. "I am a vampire," she said. "We have many a mile to go before we sleep. I am hungry."

"Indeed," I said. "We will have to fill up on tacos before we go any farther. I too am extremely hungry."

Just then the waitress arrived to take our order. The mob of young Chicanos outside had disappeared very suddenly, roaring off into the night in a brace of white pickup trucks. They were a good-natured bunch, mainly teenagers with huge shoulders wearing Dallas Cowboys jerseys and heads like half-shaved coconuts. They were not afraid of the cops, but they left anyway.

The waitress was hugely relieved. "Thank God," she said. "Now

Manuel can live one more night. I was afraid they would kill him. We have only been married three weeks." She began sobbing, and I could see she was about to crack. I introduced myself as Johnny Depp, but I saw the name meant nothing to her. Her name was Maria. She was seventeen years old and had lied about her age to get the job. She was the manager and Manuel was the cook. He was almost twenty-one. Every night strange men hovered around the taco stand and mumbled about killing him.

Maria sat down in the booth between us, and we both put our arms around her. She shuddered and collapsed against Anita, kissing her gently on the cheek. "Don't worry," I said. "Nobody is going to be killed tonight. This is the night of the full moon. Some people will die tonight, but not us. I am protected."

Which was true. I am a Triple Moon Child, and tonight was the Hunter's Moon. I pulled the waitress closer to me and spoke soothingly. "You have nothing to fear, little one," I told her. "No power on Earth can harm me tonight. I walk with the King."

She smiled and kissed me gratefully on the wrist. Manuel stared balefully at us from his perch in the kitchen, saying nothing. "Rest easy," I called out to him. "Nobody is going to kill you tonight."

"Stop saying that!" Anita snapped, as Manuel sank further into himself. "Can't you see he's afraid?" Maria began crying again, but I jerked her to her feet. "Get a grip on yourself," I said sharply. "We need more beer and some pork tacos to go. I have to drive the whole coast tonight."

"That's right," said my companion. "We're on a honeymoon trip. We're in a hurry." She laughed and reached for my wallet. "Come on, big boy," she cooed. "Don't try to cheat. Just give it to me."

"Watch yourself," I snarled, slapping her hand away from my pocket. "You've been acting weird ever since we left L.A. We'll be in serious trouble if you go sideways on me again."

She grinned and stretched her arms lazily above her head, poking her elegant little breasts up in the air at me like some memory from an old Marilyn Monroe calendar and rolling her palms in the air.

"Sideways?" she said. "What difference does it make? Let's get out of here. We're late."

I paid the bill quickly and watched Maria disappear into the kitchen. Manuel was nowhere in sight. Just as I stepped into the street,

I noticed two police cars coming at us from different directions. Then another one slowed down right in front of the taco stand.

"Don't worry," I said to Anita. "They're not looking for us."

I seized her by the leg and rushed her into the Cadillac. There was a lot of yelling as we pulled away through the circling traffic and back out onto Highway 101.

My mind was very much on my work as we sped north along the coast to Big Sur. We were into open country now, running straight up the coast about a mile from the ocean on a two-lane blacktop road across the dunes with no clouds in the sky and a full moon blazing down on the Pacific. It was a perfect night to be driving a fast car on an empty road along the edge of the ocean with a half-mad beautiful woman asleep on the white leather seats and Lyle Lovett crooning dog-gerel about screwheads who go out to sea with shotguns and ponies in small rowboats just to get some kind of warped revenge on a white man with bad habits who was only trying to do them a favor in the first place.

. . .

I lost control of the Cadillac about halfway down the slope. The road was slick with pine needles, and the eucalyptus trees were getting closer together. The girl laughed as I tried to aim the car through the dark-ness with huge tree trunks looming up in the headlights and the bright white moon on the ocean out in front of us. It was like driving on ice, going straight toward the abyss.

We shot past a darkened house and past a parked Jeep, then crashed into a waterfall high above the sea. I got out of the car and sat down on a rock, then lit up the marijuana pipe. "Well," I said to Anita, "this is it. We must have taken a wrong turn."

She laughed and sucked on some moss. Then she sat down across from me on a log. "You're funny," she said. "You're very strange—and you don't know why, do you?"

I shook my head softly and drank some gin.

"No," I said. "I'm stupid."

"It's because you have the soul of a teenage girl in the body of an elderly dope fiend," she whispered. "That is why you have problems." She patted me on the knee. "Yes. That is why people giggle with fear every time you come into a room. That is why you rescued me from those dogs in Venice."

I stared out to sea and said nothing for a while. But somehow I knew she was right. Yes sir, I said slowly to myself, I have the soul of a teenage girl in the body of an elderly dope fiend. No wonder they can't understand me.

This is a hard dollar, on most days, and not many people can stand it.

Indeed. If the greatest mania of all is passion: and if I am a natural slave to passion: and if the balance between my brain and my soul and my body is as wild and delicate as the skin of a Ming vase—

Well, that explains a lot of things, doesn't it? We need look no further. Yes sir, and people wonder why I seem to look at them strangely. Or why my personal etiquette often seems makeshift and contradictory, even clinically insane . . . Hell, I don't miss those whispers, those soft groans of fear when I enter a civilized room. I know what they're thinking, and I know exactly why. They are extremely uncomfortable with the idea that I am a teenage girl trapped in the body of a sixty-five-year-old career criminal who has already died sixteen times. Sixteen, all documented. I have been crushed and beaten and shocked and drowned and poisoned and stabbed and shot and smothered and set on fire by my own bombs. . . .

All these things have happened, and probably they will happen again. I have learned a few tricks along the way, a few random skills and simple avoidance techniques—but mainly it has been luck, I think, and a keen attention to karma, along with my natural girlish charm.

# *Kingdom of Fear*
## Honor Roll

Oscar Acosta
Jeff Armstrong
Lisl Auman
Terri Bartelstein
Ed Bastian
Sean Bell-Thomson
Porter Bibb
Earl Biss
Patricia Blanchet
Bob Bone
Ed Bradley
Bob Braudis
Louisa Joe
Doug Brinkley
Judge Charles Buss
Sue Carolan
Jimmy Carter
Marilyn Chambers
Tim Charles
Bobby Colgan
John Clancey
Dalai Lama
Morris Dees
Benicio Del Toro
Kenny Demmick

Judge J. E. DeVilbiss
Robert Draper
Bob Dylan
Joe Edwards
Jeanette Etheridge
Colonel William S. Evans
Tim Ferris
Jennifer Geiger
Gerald Goldstein
William Greider
Stacey Hadash
Hal Haddon
David Halberstam
Paul Hornung
Abe Hutt
Walter Isaacson
Loren Jenkins
Juan, Jennifer, & Willy
Bill Kennedy
Ken Kesey
Maria Khan
Jerry Lefcourt
Lyle Lovett
Semmes Luckett
Jade Markus

David Matthews-Price
David McCumber
Terry McDonell
Gene McGarr
George McGovern
William McKeen
Michael Mesnick
Nicole Meyer
Jim Mitchell
Tim Mooney
Lou Ann Murphy
Laila Nabulsi
Lynn Nesbit
Jack Nicholson
Paul Oakenfold
Lionel Olay
Heidi Opheim
P.J. O'Rourke
Gail Palmer
Nicola Pecorini
Sean Penn
George Plimpton
Charlotte Rampling
Duke Rice
Keith Richards
Curtis Robinson
David Robinson
Terry Sabonis-Chafee

Shelby Sadler
Paul Semonin
Lauren Simonetti
Kevin Simonson
Madeleine Sloan
Harvey Sloane
Bill Smith
Michael Solheim
Ralph Steadman
Judy Stellings
Michael Stepanian
Geoffrey Stokes
George & Patti Stranahan
Richard Stratton
Jay Stuart
Davison Thompson
Sandy Thompson
Virginia & Jack Thompson
George Tobia
Oliver Treibick
Gerald "Ching" Tyrrell
John Walsh
Floyd Watkins
Curtis Wilkie
Andrew Wylie
Tony Yerkovich
Warren Zevon

## The Too Much Fun Club

Jennifer Stroup, Marysue Rucci, Anita Bejmuk, Hunter S. Thompson,
Deborah Fuller, Wayne Ewing, Tara Parsons, David Rosenthal

# About the Author

HUNTER S. THOMPSON's books include *Fear and Loathing in America,
Screwjack, Hell's Angels, Fear and Loathing in Las Vegas, The Proud
Highway, Better Than Sex,* and *The Rum Diary* and *Kingdom of Fear.* A
contributor to various national and international publications, including a weekly sports column for espn.com, Thompson lives in a fortified compound near Aspen, Colorado.

# Classic books by the late, grea
# HUNTER S. THOMPSON

# "There are only two adjectives writers care about anymore—'brilliant' and 'outrageous'—and Hunter Thompson has a freehold on both of them." —Tom Wolfe

**Fear and Loathing in America**
*The Brutal Odyssey of an*
*Outlaw Journalist*
0-684-87316-8

Spanning the years between 1968 and 1976, these never-before-published letters show Thompson building his legend: running for sheriff in Aspen, Colorado; creating the seminal road book *Fear and Loathing in Las Vegas*; twisting political reporting to new heights for *Rolling Stone*; and making sense of it all in the landmark *Fear and Loathing: On the Campaign Trail '72*.

**The Great Shark Hunt**
*Strange Tales from a Strange Time*
*Gonzo Papers, Volume 1*
0-7432-5045-1

The first volume of Hunter S. Thompson's legendary *Gonzo Papers*. Pieces range from Thompson's *National Observer* days to famous entries from *Rolling Stone*. *Publishers Weekly* hails it as "filled with moral outrage and fiendish humor" and *Cosmopolitan* called it "an indictment of everything shoddy, shifty, and just plain rotten that has afflicted our planet since the 1960s."

**Generation of Swine**
*Tales of Shame and*
*Degradation in the '80s*
*Gonzo Papers, Volume 2*
0-7432-5044-3

The bestselling second volume, this collection of essays from Hunter S. Thompson's days as media critic at *The San Francisco Examiner* chronicles the social and political debauchery and decadence of the 1980s.

**Songs of the Doomed**
*More Notes on the Death of the*
*American Dream*
*Gonzo Papers, Volume 3*
0-7432-4099-5

Spanning four decades, this extraordinary third volume covers high and hideous moments in Thompson's career, with original pieces from *The Rum Diary*, *Prince Jellyfish*, and *The Curse of Lono*, as well as memos to famous friends and coverage of the infamous Roxanne Pulitzer trial. In *Songs of the Doomed*, no one is safe from Thompson's savage wit and astute social commentary.

**Kingdom of Fear**
*Loathsome Secrets of a Star-Crossed Child*
*in the Final Days of the American Century*
0-684-87324-9

Hunter S. Thompson's *New York Times* bestselling memoir: a hilarious, harrowing, historic chronicle of the making of the Gonzo journalist.
"Thompson's voice still jumps right off the page, as wild, vital and gonzo as ever."
—The Washington Post

**The Rum Diary**
*A Novel*
0-684-85647-6

A brilliantly tangled love story of jealousy, treachery, and violent alcoholic lust in the Caribbean boomtown that was San Juan, Puerto Rico, in the late 1950s.
"A great and an unexpected joy...reveals a young Hunter Thompson brimming with talent." —The Philadelphia Inquirer

**Screwjack**
*A Short Story*
0-684-87321-4 (hardcover)

A collection of three wild and outlandish short stories from literary legend Hunter S. Thompson—including rare and elusive lost classics.

**Hey Rube**
*Blood Sport, the Bush Doctrine, and the*
*Downward Spiral of Dumbness. Modern*
*History from the Sports Desk*
0-684-87319-2 (hardcover)

Where do sports, politics, and sex collide? In Hunter S. Thompson's wildly popular ESPN.com columns, collected here for the first time.
"Thompson is a genuinely unique figure in American journalism, a superb comic writer and a ferociously outspoken social and political critic." —The Washington Post

**SIMON & SCHUSTER**
**PAPERBACKS**
A VIACOM COMPANY
www.simonsays.com.